THE WOODS

JAMES **TYNION IV** • MICHAEL **DIALYNAS** • JOSAN **GONZALEZ**

VOL. 5
THE HORDE

BOOM! STUDIOS

THE WOODS Volume Five, November 2016. Published by BOOM! Studios, a division of Boom Entertainment, Inc. The Woods is ™ & © 2016 James Tynion IV. Originally published in single magazine form as THE WOODS No. 17-20. ™ & © 2015, 2016 James Tynion IV. All rights reserved. BOOM! Studios™ and the BOOM! Studios logo are trademarks of Boom Entertainment, Inc., registered in various countries and categories. All characters, events, and institutions depicted herein are fictional. Any similarity between any of the names, characters, persons, events, and/or institutions in this publication to actual names, characters, and persons, whether living or dead, events, and/or institutions is unintended and purely coincidental. BOOM! Studios does not read or accept unsolicited submissions of ideas, stories, or artwork.

A catalog record of this book is available from OCLC and from the BOOM! Studios website, www.boom-studios.com, on the Librarians page.

BOOM! Studios, 5670 Wilshire Boulevard, Suite 450, Los Angeles, CA 90036-5679. Printed in China. First Printing.

ISBN: 978-1-60886-857-5, eISBN: 978-1-61398-528-1

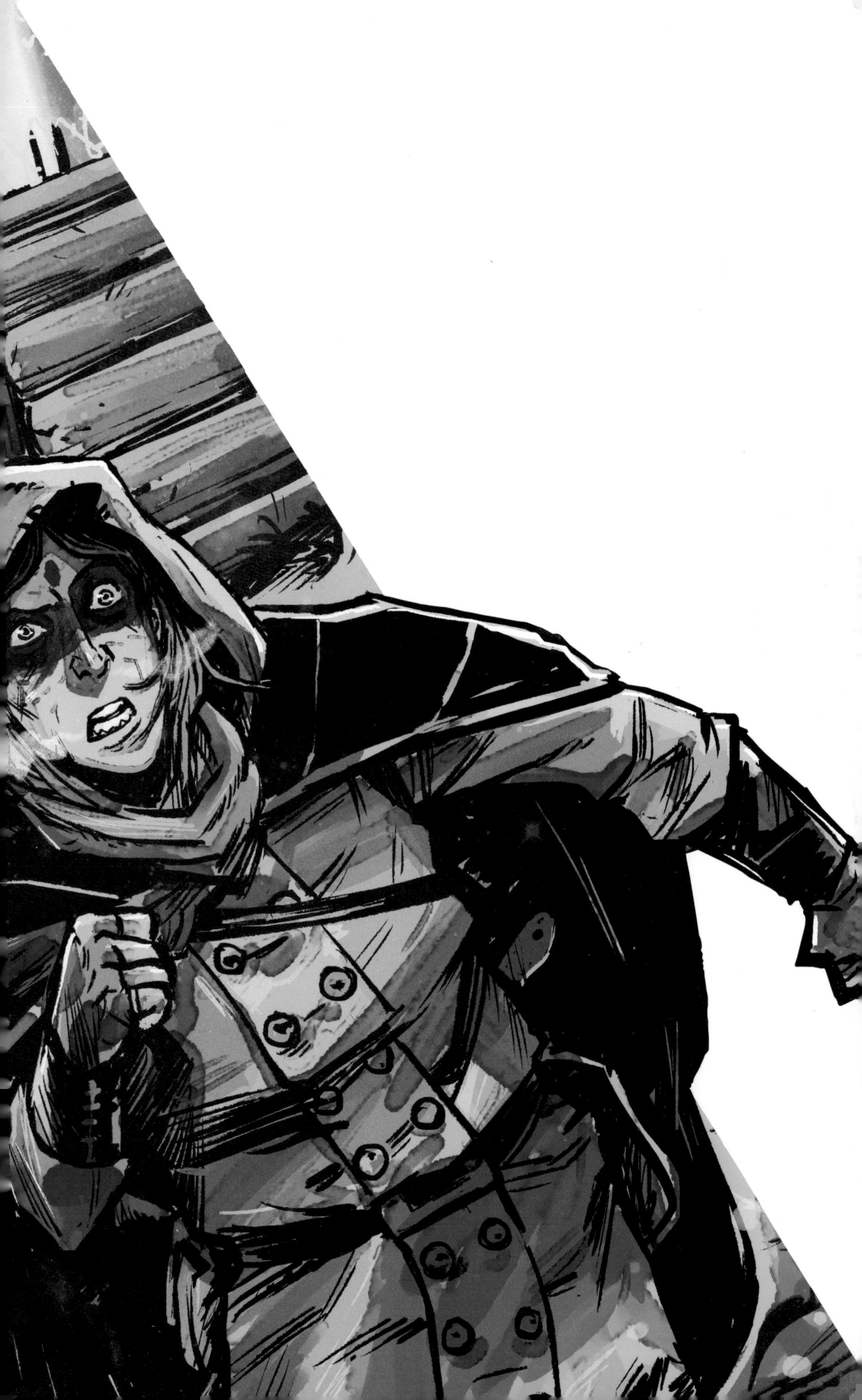

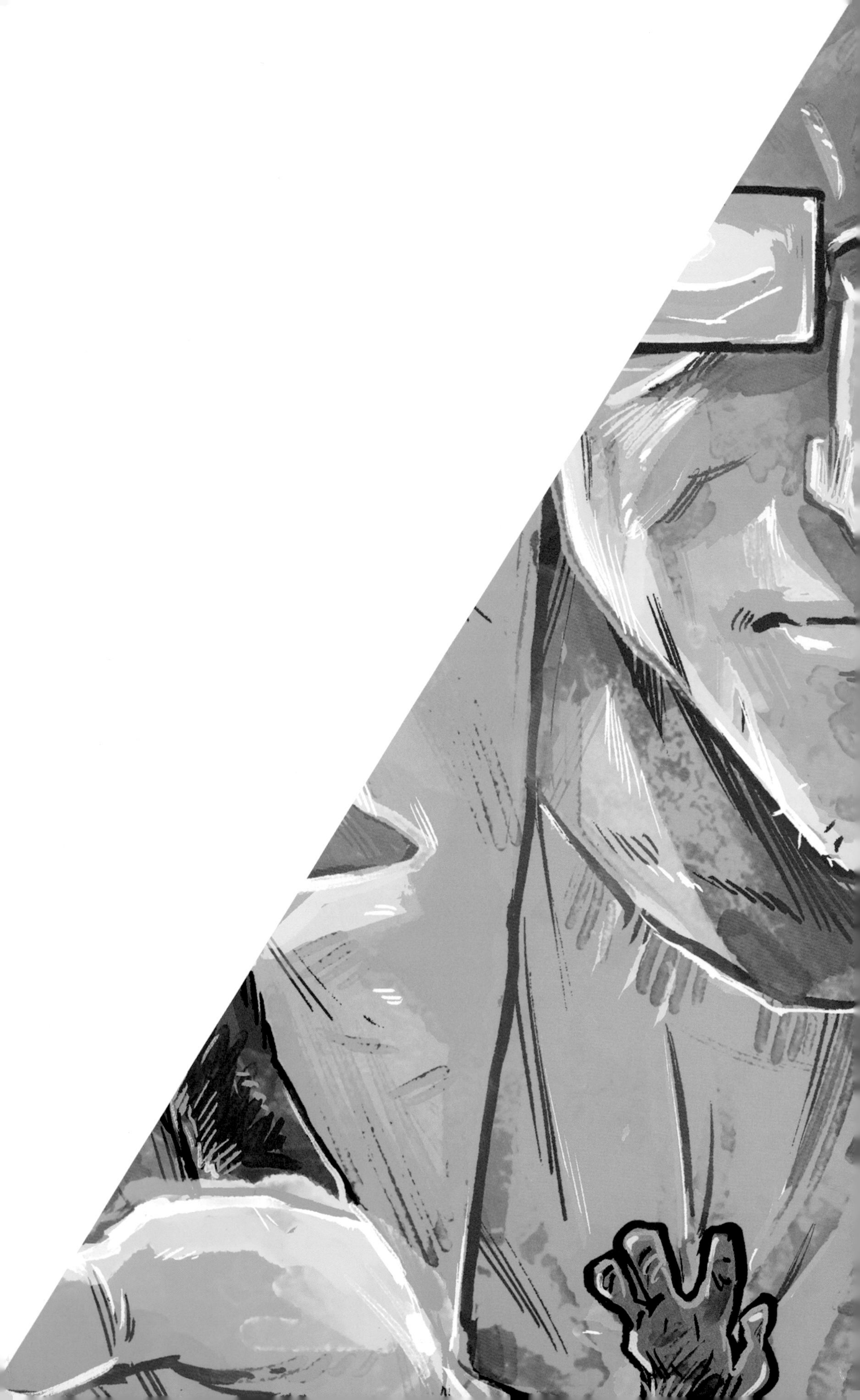

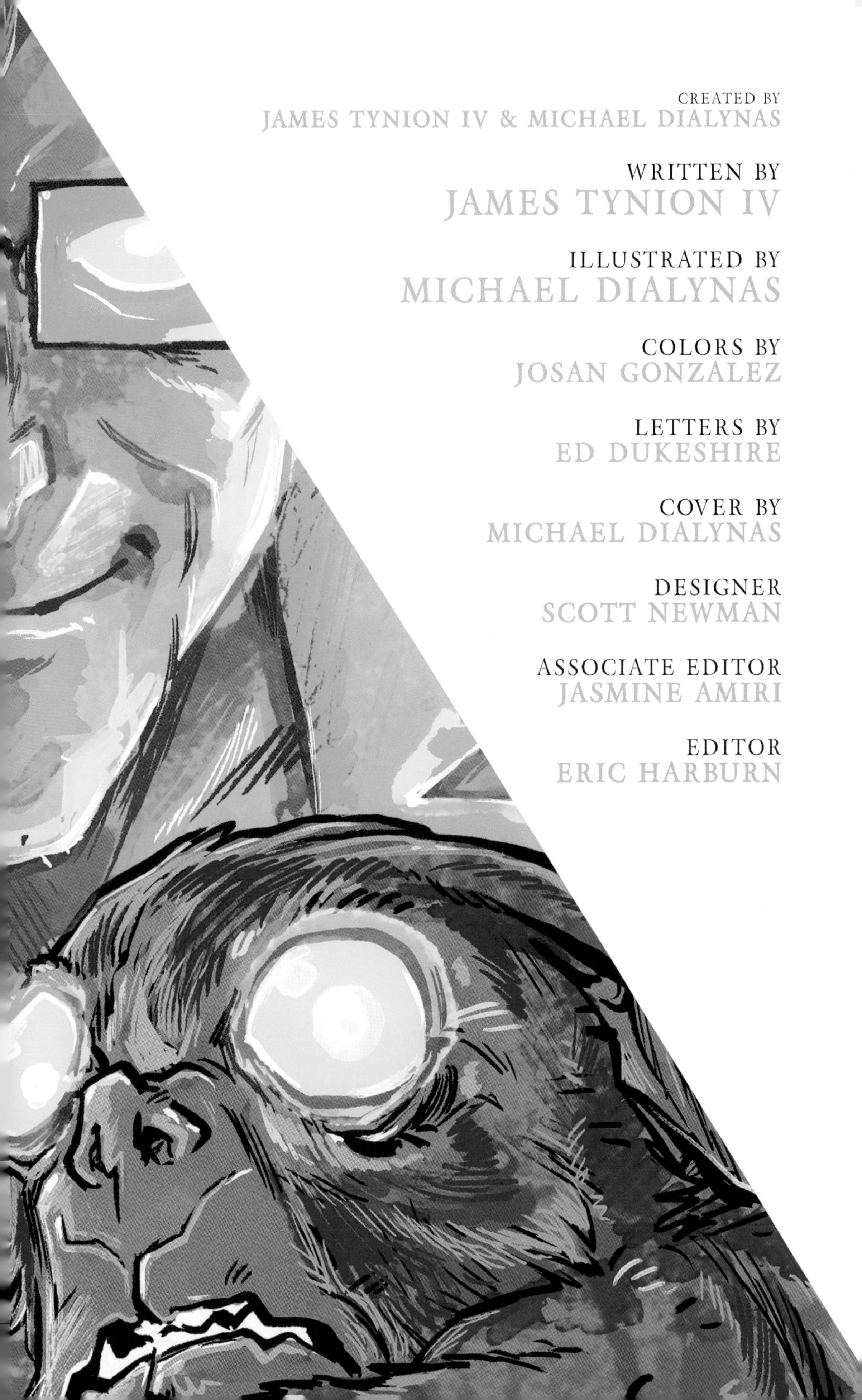

CREATED BY
JAMES TYNION IV & MICHAEL DIALYNAS

WRITTEN BY
JAMES TYNION IV

ILLUSTRATED BY
MICHAEL DIALYNAS

COLORS BY
JOSAN GONZALEZ

LETTERS BY
ED DUKESHIRE

COVER BY
MICHAEL DIALYNAS

DESIGNER
SCOTT NEWMAN

ASSOCIATE EDITOR
JASMINE AMIRI

EDITOR
ERIC HARBURN

CHAPTER SEVENTEEN

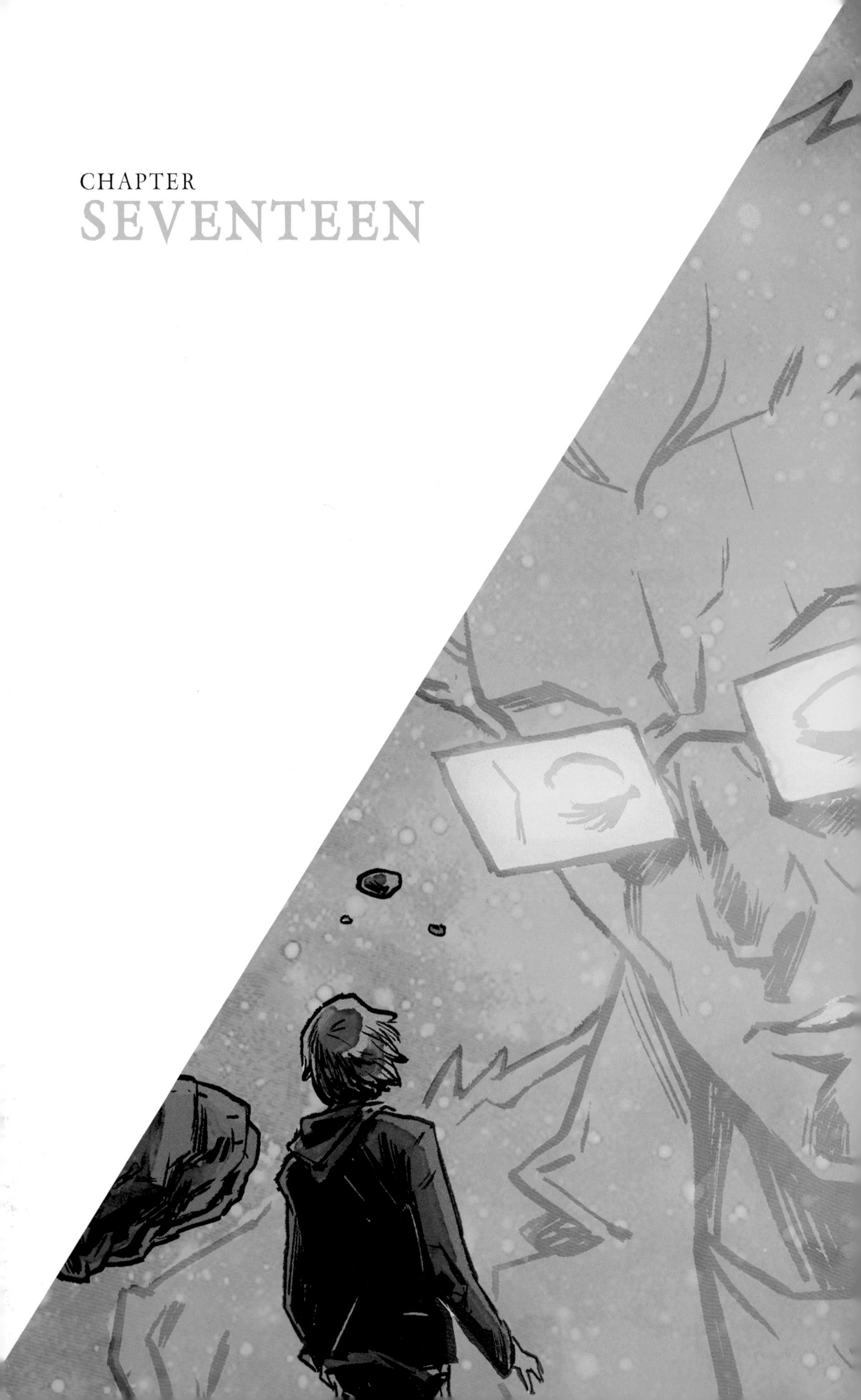

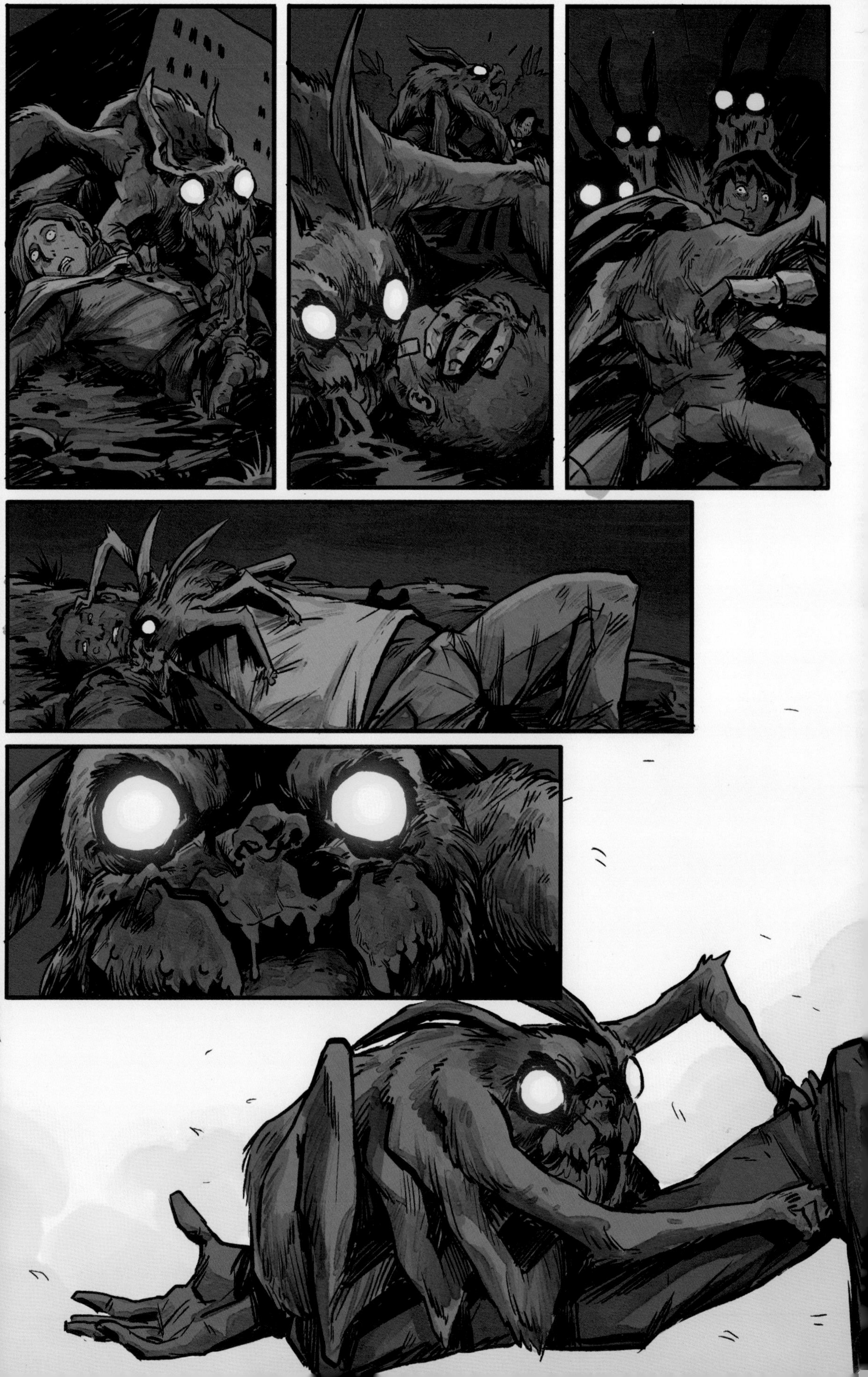

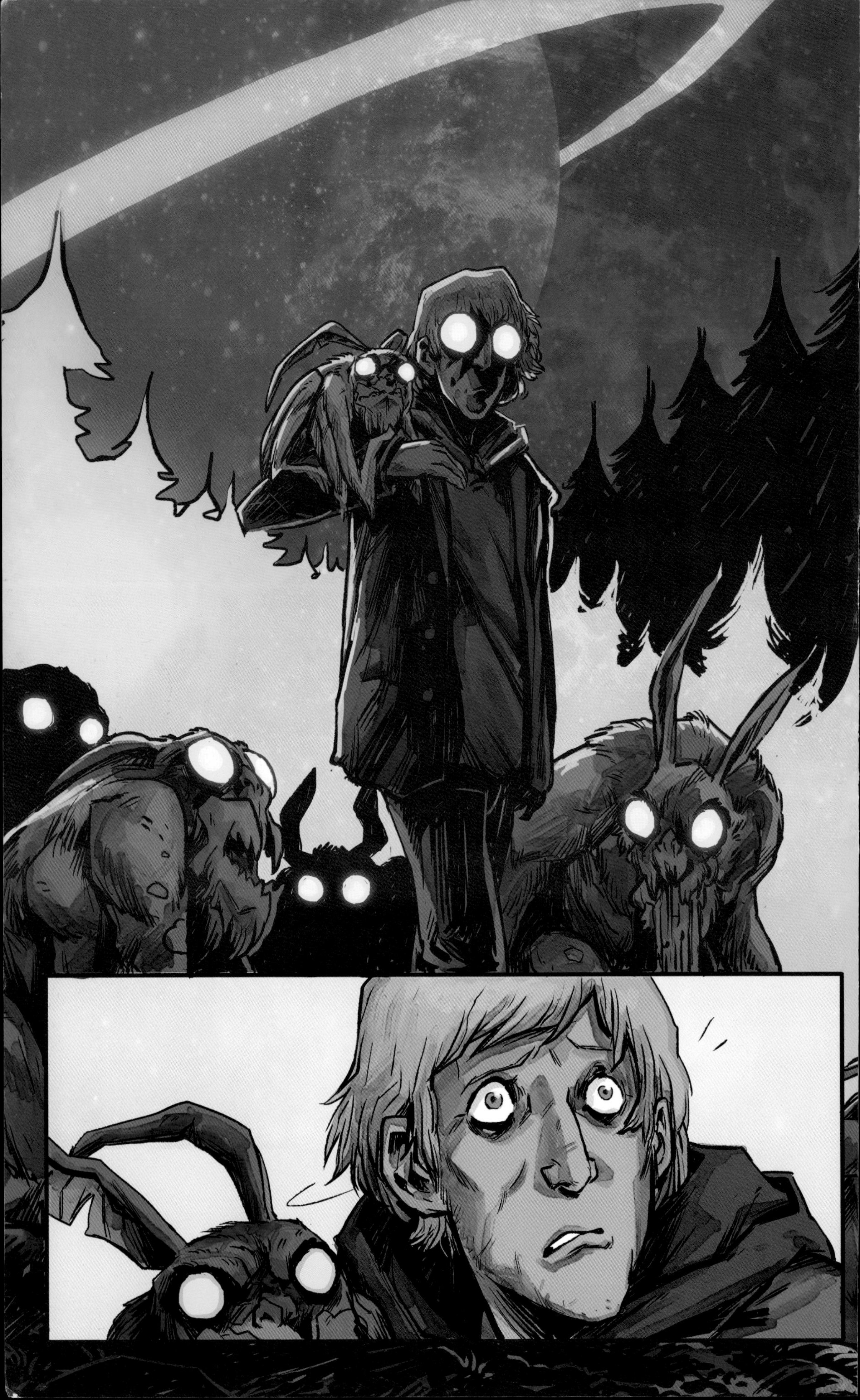

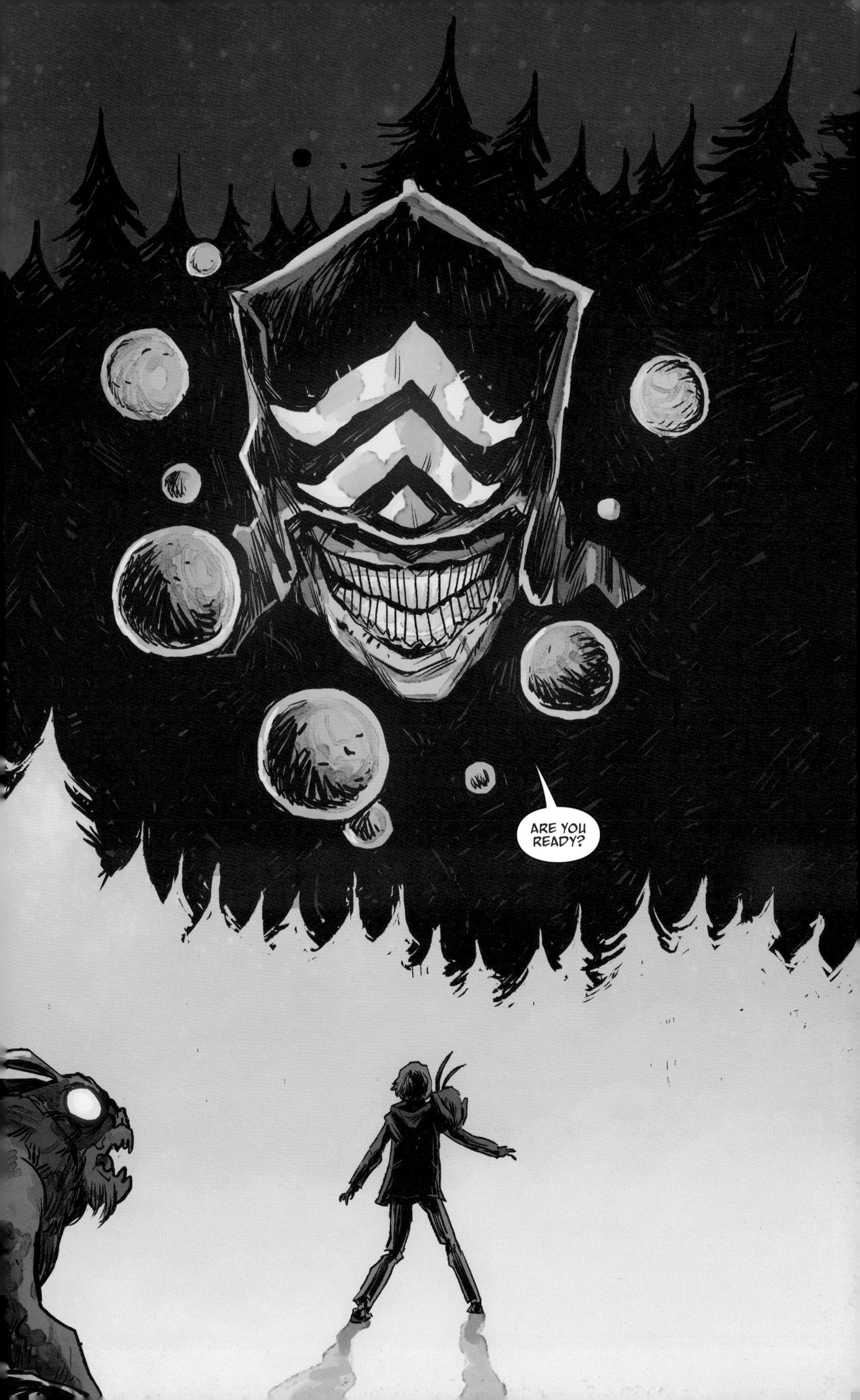
ARE YOU READY?

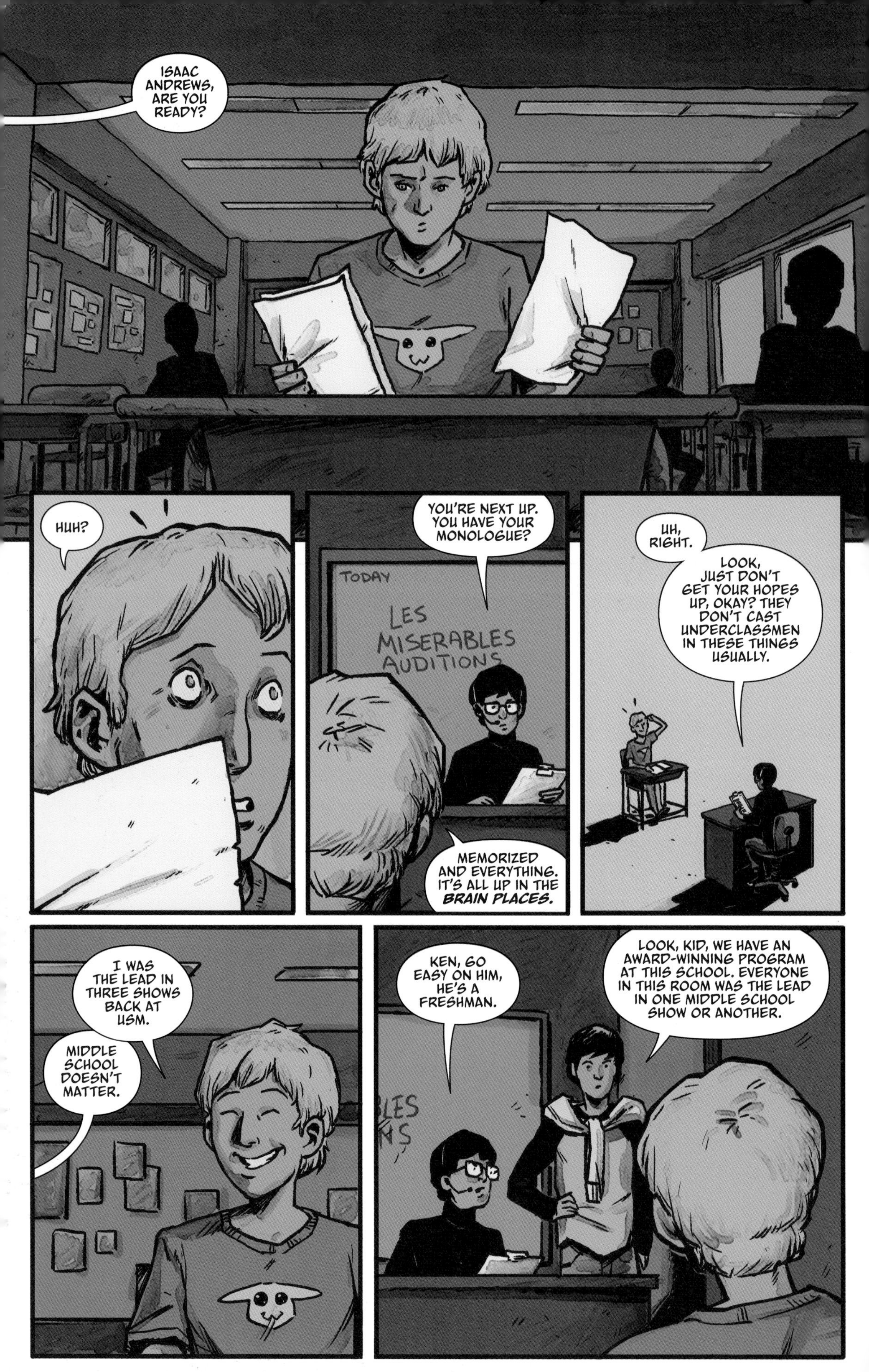
ISAAC ANDREWS, ARE YOU READY?
HUH?
YOU'RE NEXT UP. YOU HAVE YOUR MONOLOGUE?
TODAY
LES MISERABLES AUDITIONS
MEMORIZED AND EVERYTHING. IT'S ALL UP IN THE *BRAIN PLACES.*
UH, RIGHT.
LOOK, JUST DON'T GET YOUR HOPES UP, OKAY? THEY DON'T CAST UNDERCLASSMEN IN THESE THINGS USUALLY.
I WAS THE LEAD IN THREE SHOWS BACK AT USM.
MIDDLE SCHOOL DOESN'T MATTER.
KEN, GO EASY ON HIM, HE'S A FRESHMAN.
LOOK, KID, WE HAVE AN AWARD-WINNING PROGRAM AT THIS SCHOOL. EVERYONE IN THIS ROOM WAS THE LEAD IN ONE MIDDLE SCHOOL SHOW OR ANOTHER.

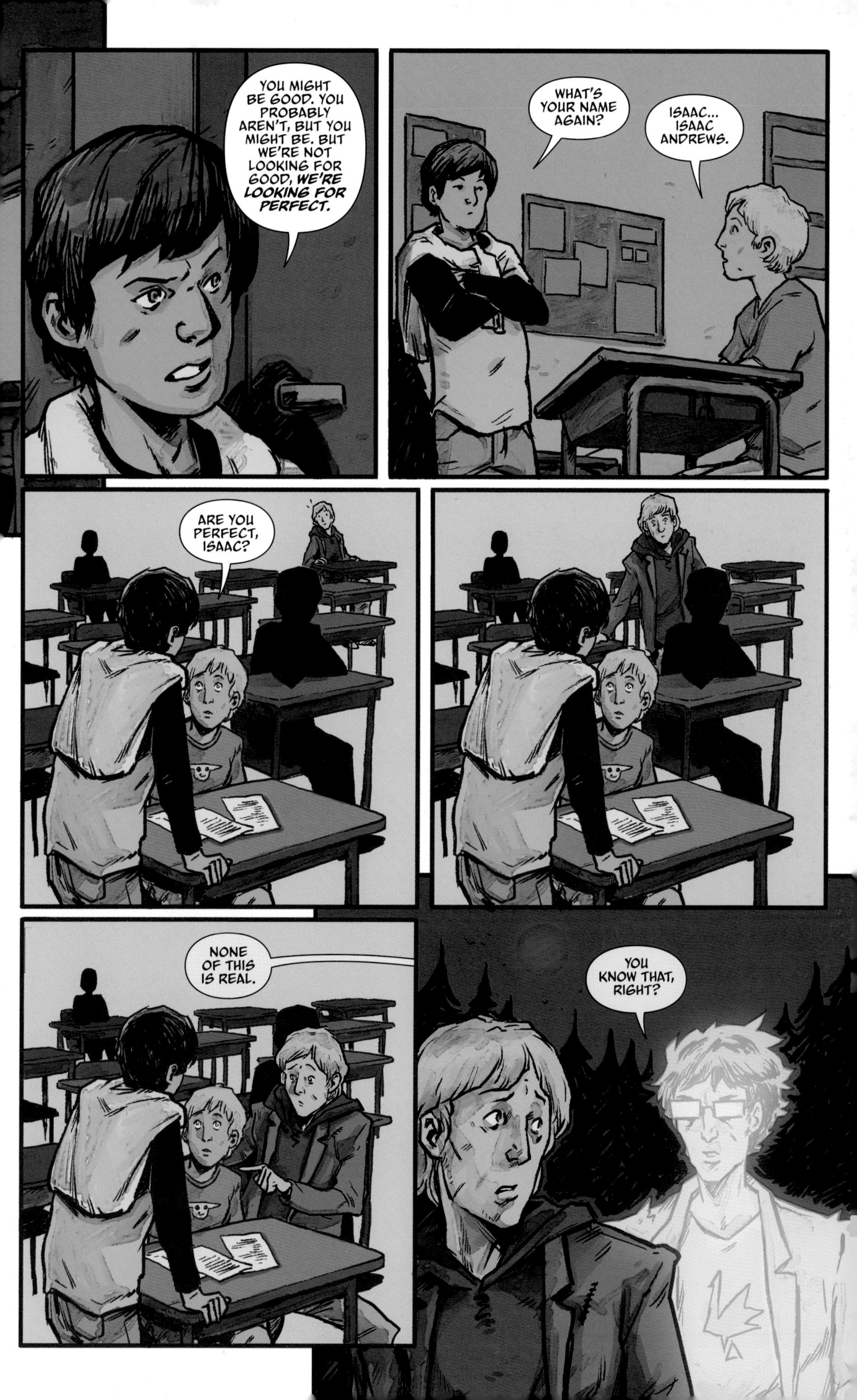
YOU MIGHT BE GOOD. YOU PROBABLY AREN'T, BUT YOU MIGHT BE. BUT WE'RE NOT LOOKING FOR GOOD, WE'RE LOOKING FOR PERFECT.
WHAT'S YOUR NAME AGAIN?
ISAAC... ISAAC ANDREWS.
ARE YOU PERFECT, ISAAC?
NONE OF THIS IS REAL.
YOU KNOW THAT, RIGHT?

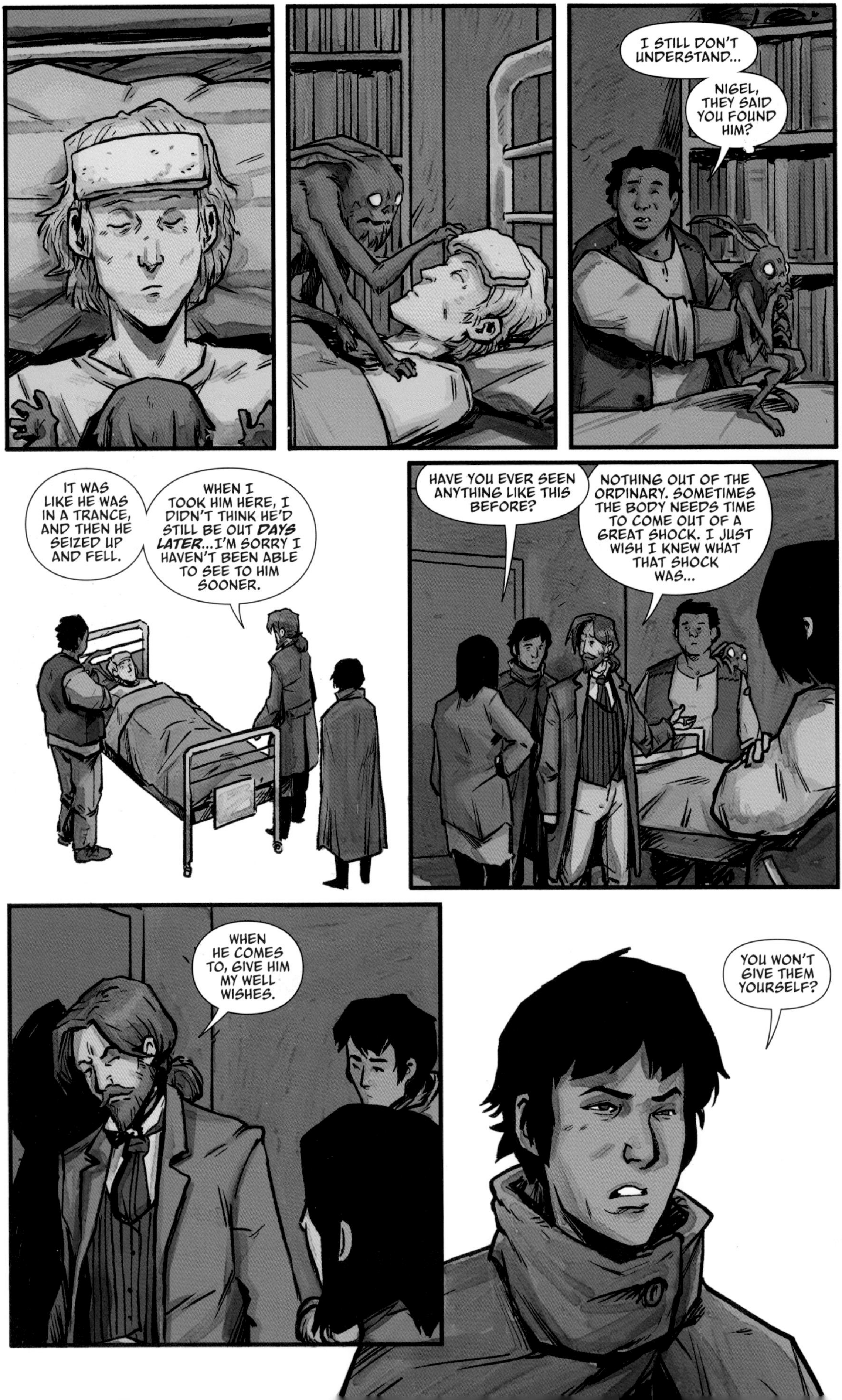
I STILL DON'T UNDERSTAND...
NIGEL, THEY SAID YOU FOUND HIM?
IT WAS LIKE HE WAS IN A TRANCE, AND THEN HE SEIZED UP AND FELL.
WHEN I TOOK HIM HERE, I DIDN'T THINK HE'D STILL BE OUT DAYS LATER...I'M SORRY I HAVEN'T BEEN ABLE TO SEE TO HIM SOONER.
HAVE YOU EVER SEEN ANYTHING LIKE THIS BEFORE?
NOTHING OUT OF THE ORDINARY. SOMETIMES THE BODY NEEDS TIME TO COME OUT OF A GREAT SHOCK. I JUST WISH I KNEW WHAT THAT SHOCK WAS...
WHEN HE COMES TO, GIVE HIM MY WELL WISHES.
YOU WON'T GIVE THEM YOURSELF?

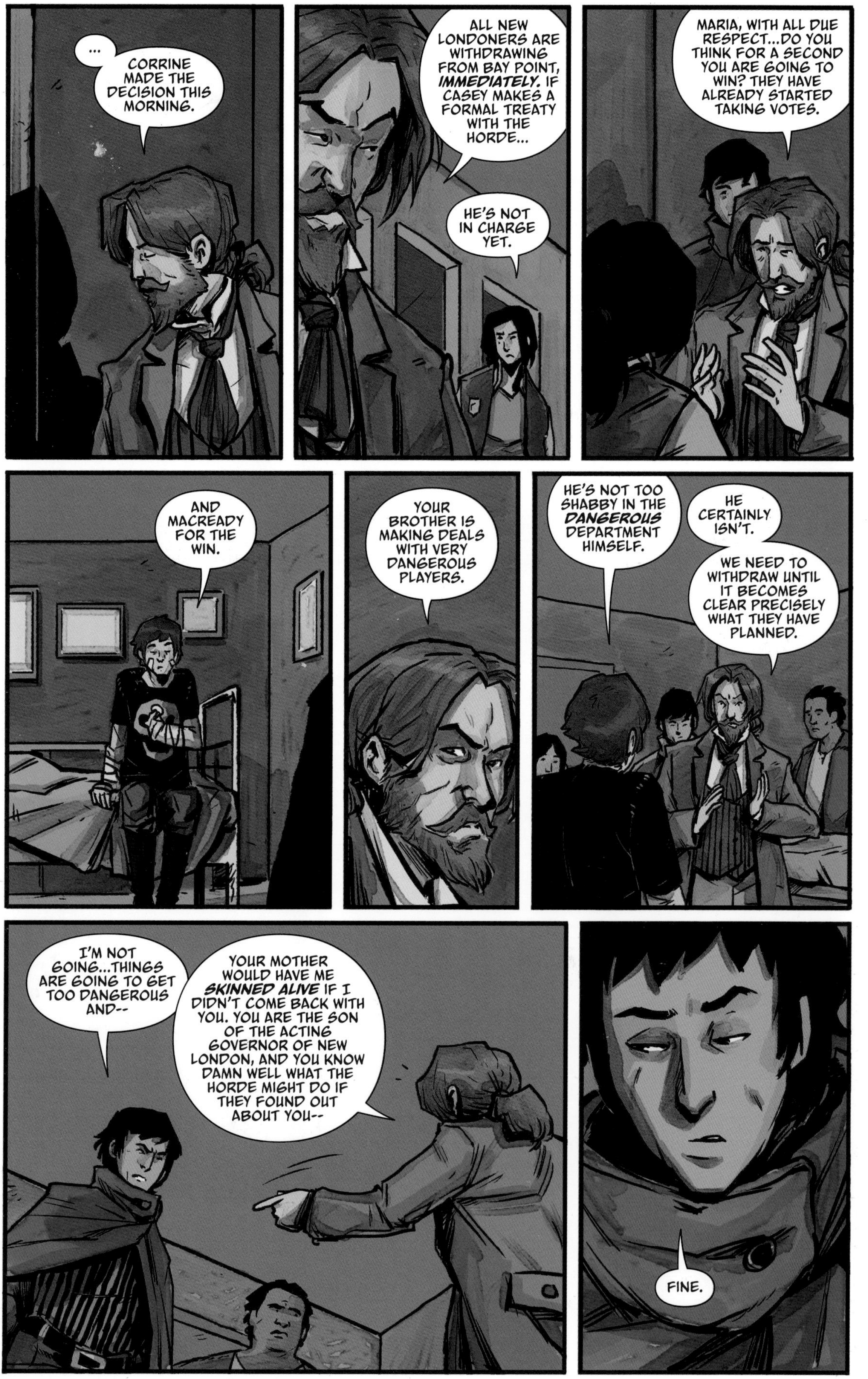
...
CORRINE MADE THE DECISION THIS MORNING.
ALL NEW LONDONERS ARE WITHDRAWING FROM BAY POINT, ***IMMEDIATELY.*** IF CASEY MAKES A FORMAL TREATY WITH THE HORDE...
HE'S NOT IN CHARGE YET.
MARIA, WITH ALL DUE RESPECT...DO YOU THINK FOR A SECOND YOU ARE GOING TO WIN? THEY HAVE ALREADY STARTED TAKING VOTES.
AND MACREADY FOR THE WIN.
YOUR BROTHER IS MAKING DEALS WITH VERY DANGEROUS PLAYERS.
HE'S NOT TOO SHABBY IN THE ***DANGEROUS*** DEPARTMENT HIMSELF.
HE CERTAINLY ISN'T.
WE NEED TO WITHDRAW UNTIL IT BECOMES CLEAR PRECISELY WHAT THEY HAVE PLANNED.
I'M NOT GOING...THINGS ARE GOING TO GET TOO DANGEROUS AND--
YOUR MOTHER WOULD HAVE ME ***SKINNED ALIVE*** IF I DIDN'T COME BACK WITH YOU. YOU ARE THE SON OF THE ACTING GOVERNOR OF NEW LONDON, AND YOU KNOW DAMN WELL WHAT THE HORDE MIGHT DO IF THEY FOUND OUT ABOUT YOU--
FINE.

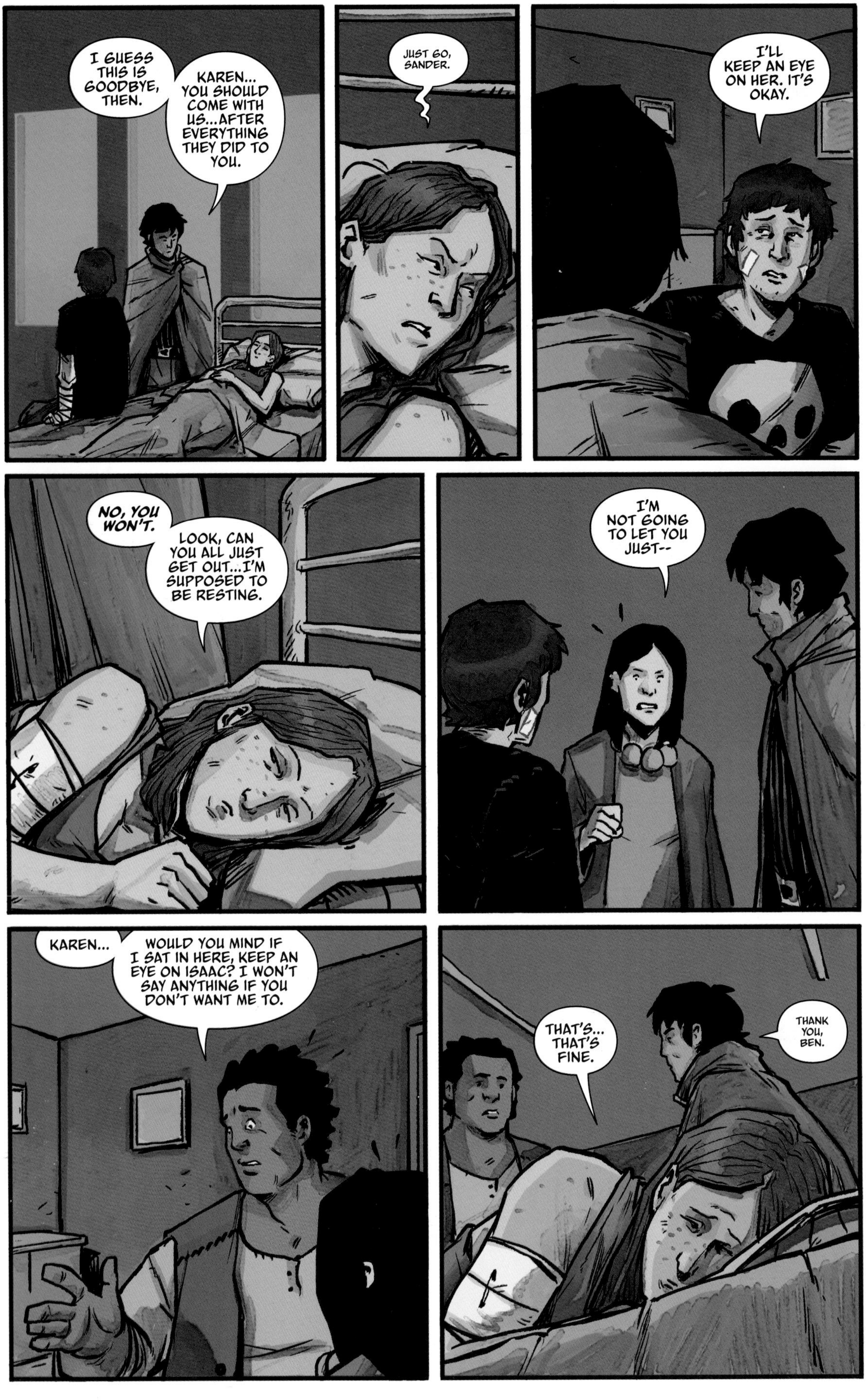
I GUESS THIS IS GOODBYE, THEN.
KAREN... YOU SHOULD COME WITH US...AFTER EVERYTHING THEY DID TO YOU.
JUST GO, SANDER.
I'LL KEEP AN EYE ON HER. IT'S OKAY.
NO, YOU WON'T.
LOOK, CAN YOU ALL JUST GET OUT...I'M SUPPOSED TO BE RESTING.
I'M NOT GOING TO LET YOU JUST--
KAREN...
WOULD YOU MIND IF I SAT IN HERE, KEEP AN EYE ON ISAAC? I WON'T SAY ANYTHING IF YOU DON'T WANT ME TO.
THAT'S... THAT'S FINE.
THANK YOU, BEN.

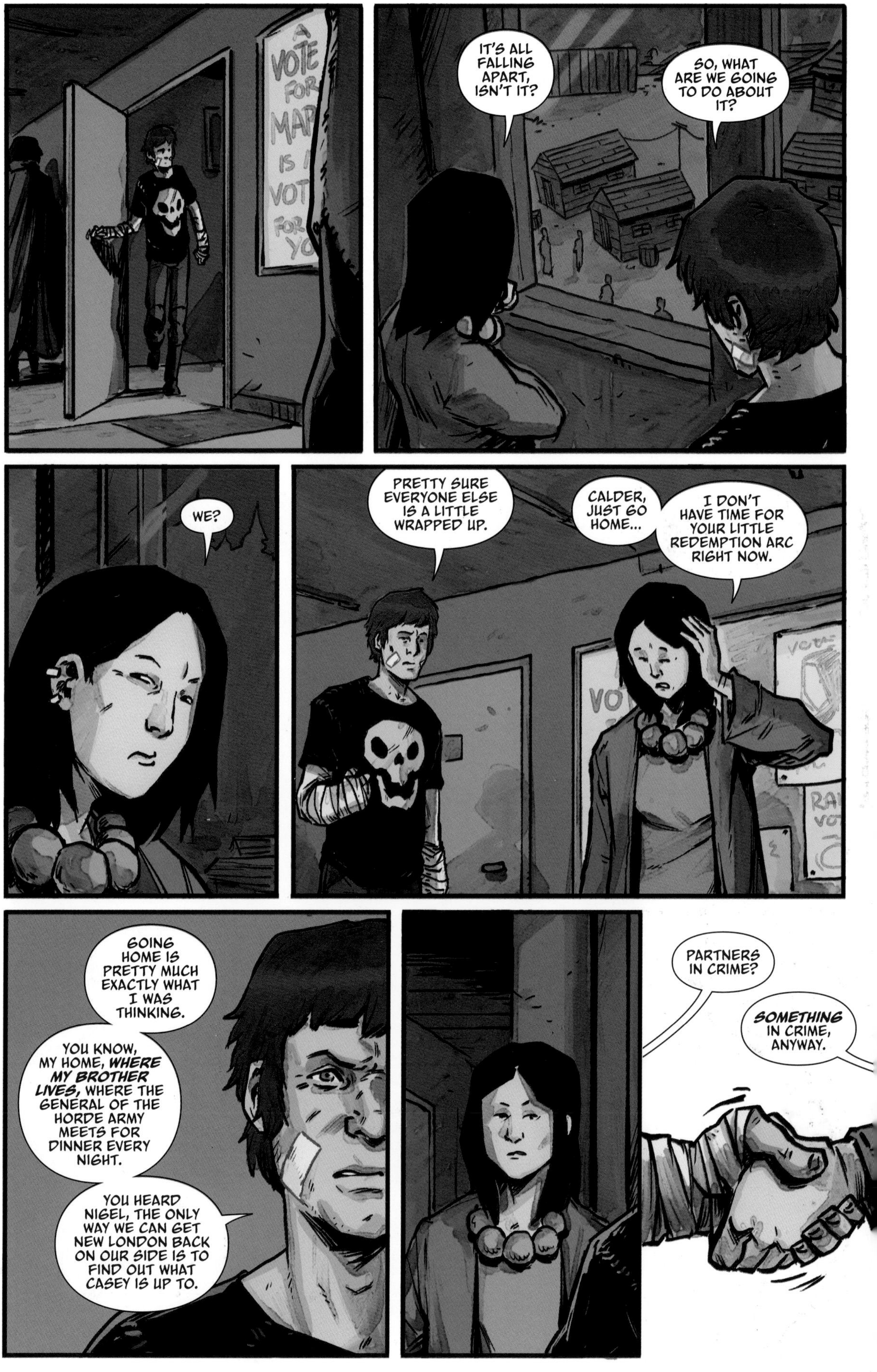
A VOTE FOR MAR
IS A VOTE FOR YO
IT'S ALL FALLING APART, ISN'T IT?
SO, WHAT ARE WE GOING TO DO ABOUT IT?
WE?
PRETTY SURE EVERYONE ELSE IS A LITTLE WRAPPED UP.
CALDER, JUST GO HOME...
I DON'T HAVE TIME FOR YOUR LITTLE REDEMPTION ARC RIGHT NOW.
GOING HOME IS PRETTY MUCH EXACTLY WHAT I WAS THINKING.
YOU KNOW, MY HOME, *WHERE MY BROTHER LIVES,* WHERE THE GENERAL OF THE HORDE ARMY MEETS FOR DINNER EVERY NIGHT.
YOU HEARD NIGEL, THE ONLY WAY WE CAN GET NEW LONDON BACK ON OUR SIDE IS TO FIND OUT WHAT CASEY IS UP TO.
PARTNERS IN CRIME?
SOMETHING IN CRIME, ANYWAY.

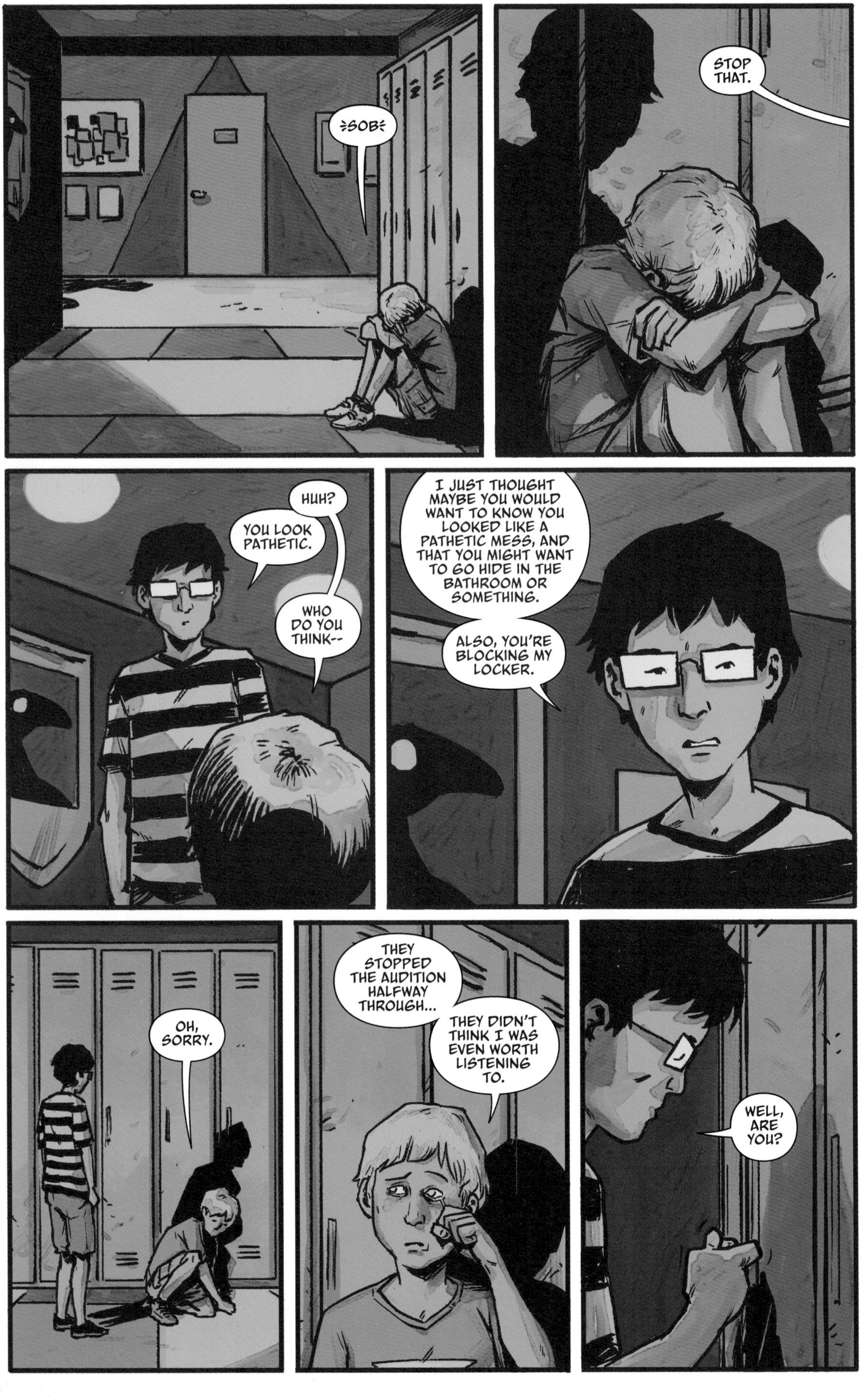
SOB
STOP THAT.
HUH?
YOU LOOK PATHETIC.
WHO DO YOU THINK--
I JUST THOUGHT MAYBE YOU WOULD WANT TO KNOW YOU LOOKED LIKE A PATHETIC MESS, AND THAT YOU MIGHT WANT TO GO HIDE IN THE BATHROOM OR SOMETHING.
ALSO, YOU'RE BLOCKING MY LOCKER.
OH, SORRY.
THEY STOPPED THE AUDITION HALFWAY THROUGH...
THEY DIDN'T THINK I WAS EVEN WORTH LISTENING TO.
WELL, ARE YOU?

WHAT?

WORTH LISTENING TO?

YEAH... YEAH, I AM.

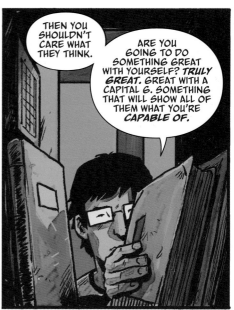

THEN YOU SHOULDN'T CARE WHAT THEY THINK.

ARE YOU GOING TO DO SOMETHING GREAT WITH YOURSELF? *TRULY GREAT.* GREAT WITH A CAPITAL G. SOMETHING THAT WILL SHOW ALL OF THEM WHAT YOU'RE *CAPABLE OF.*

I WANT TO...

THEN SHOW THEM.

ARE YOU READY?

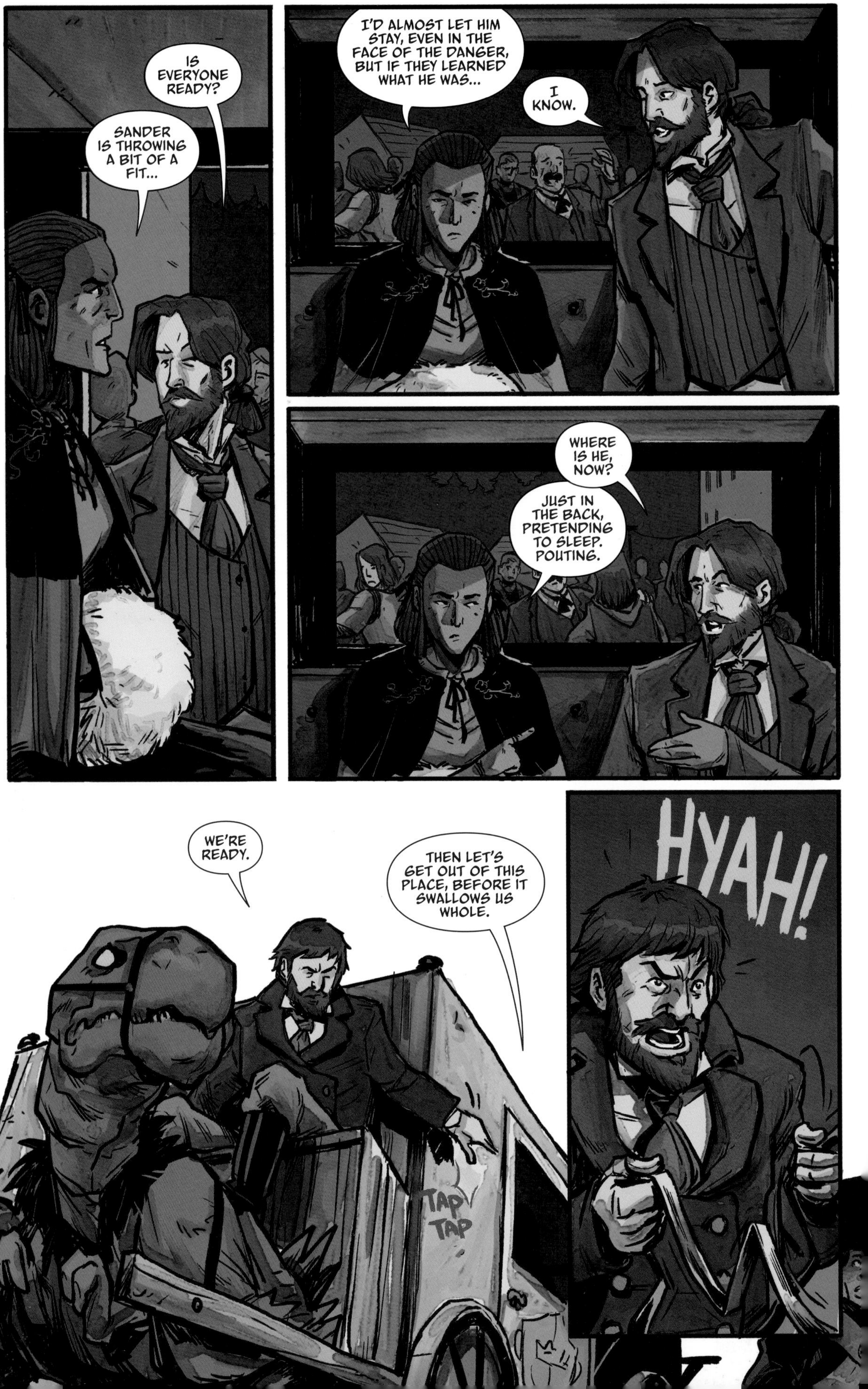
IS EVERYONE READY?
SANDER IS THROWING A BIT OF A FIT...
I'D ALMOST LET HIM STAY, EVEN IN THE FACE OF THE DANGER, BUT IF THEY LEARNED WHAT HE WAS...
I KNOW.
WHERE IS HE, NOW?
JUST IN THE BACK, PRETENDING TO SLEEP. POUTING.
WE'RE READY.
THEN LET'S GET OUT OF THIS PLACE, BEFORE IT SWALLOWS US WHOLE.
TAP TAP
HYAH!

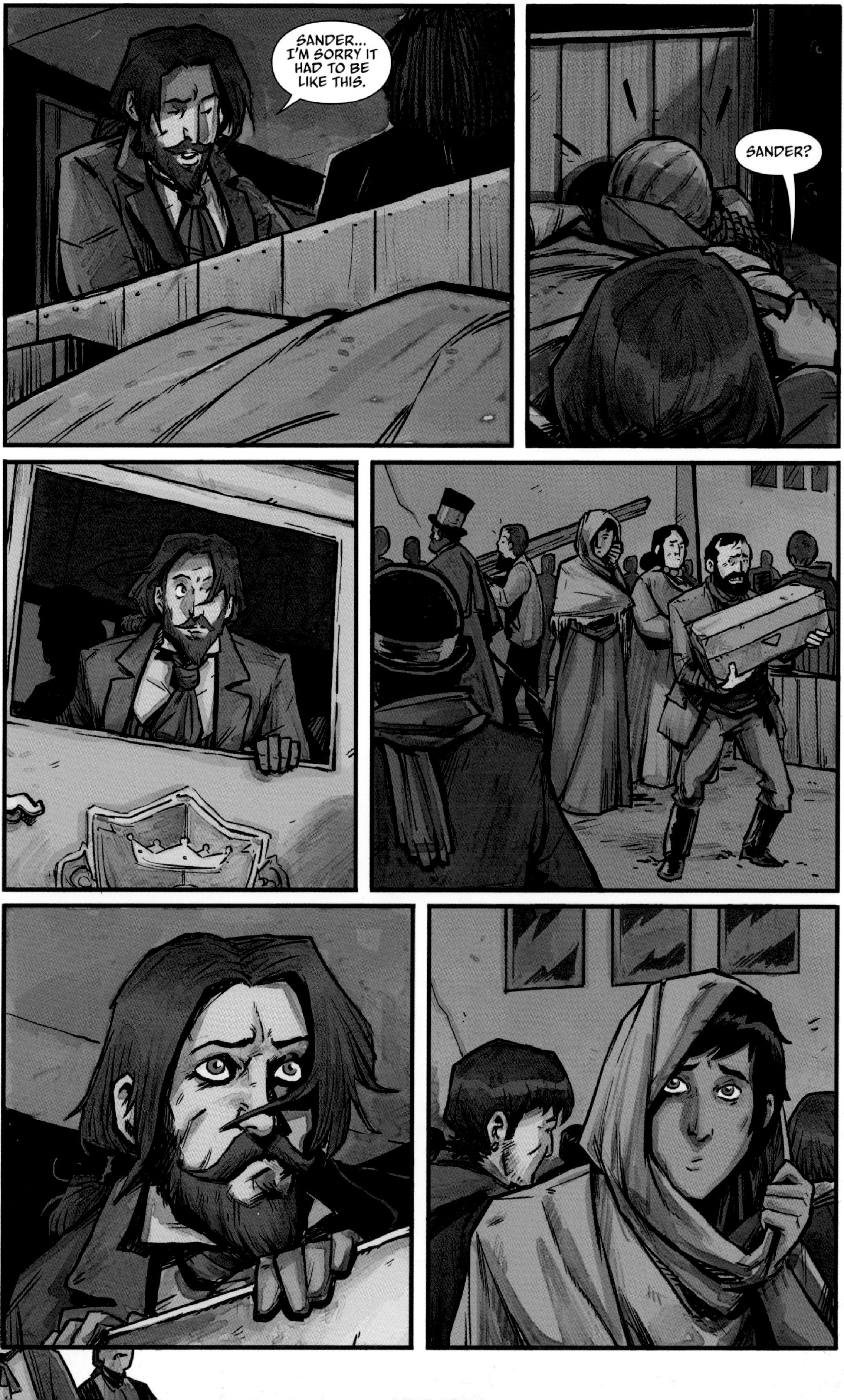
SANDER... I'M SORRY IT HAD TO BE LIKE THIS.
SANDER?

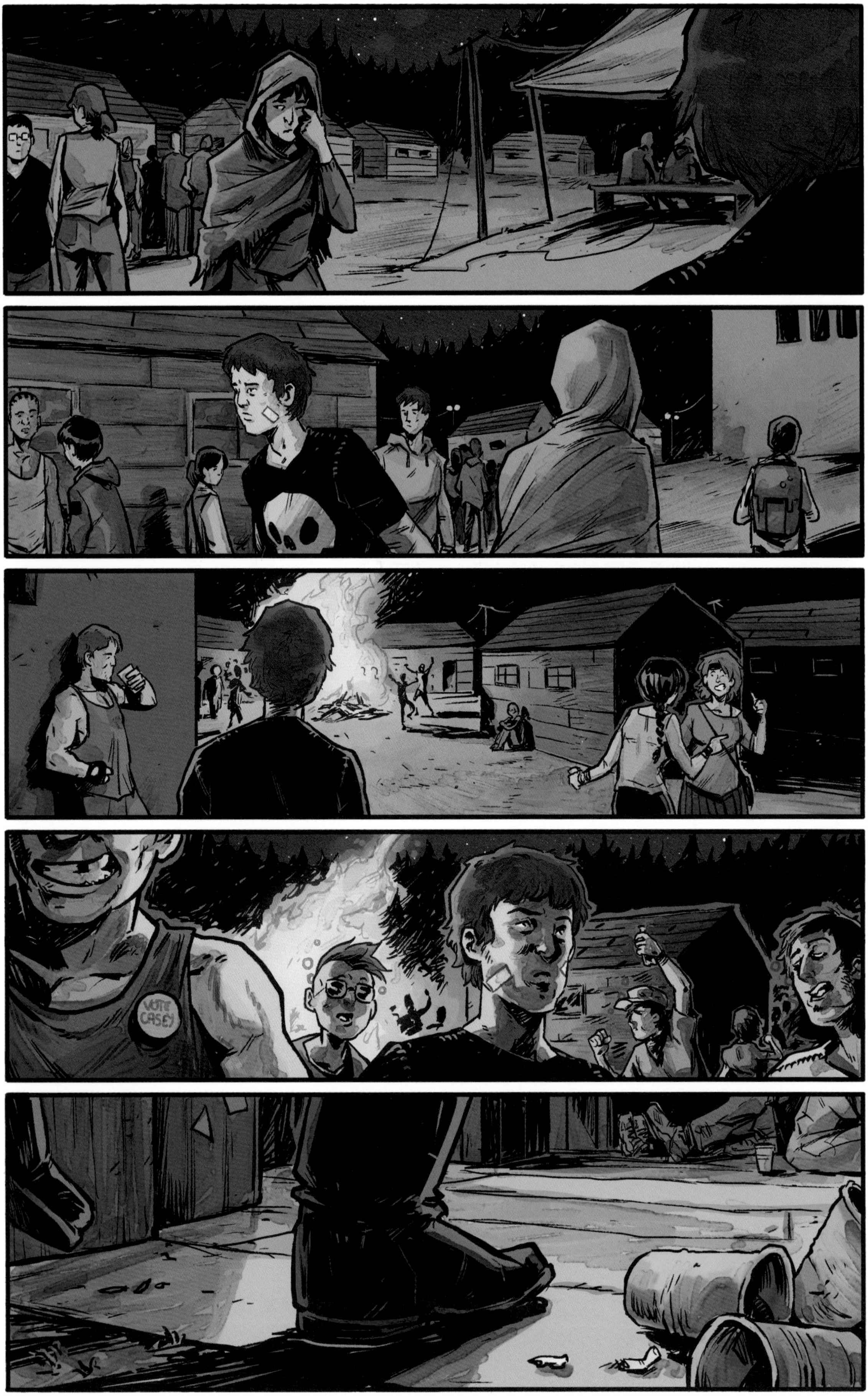
VOTE CASEY

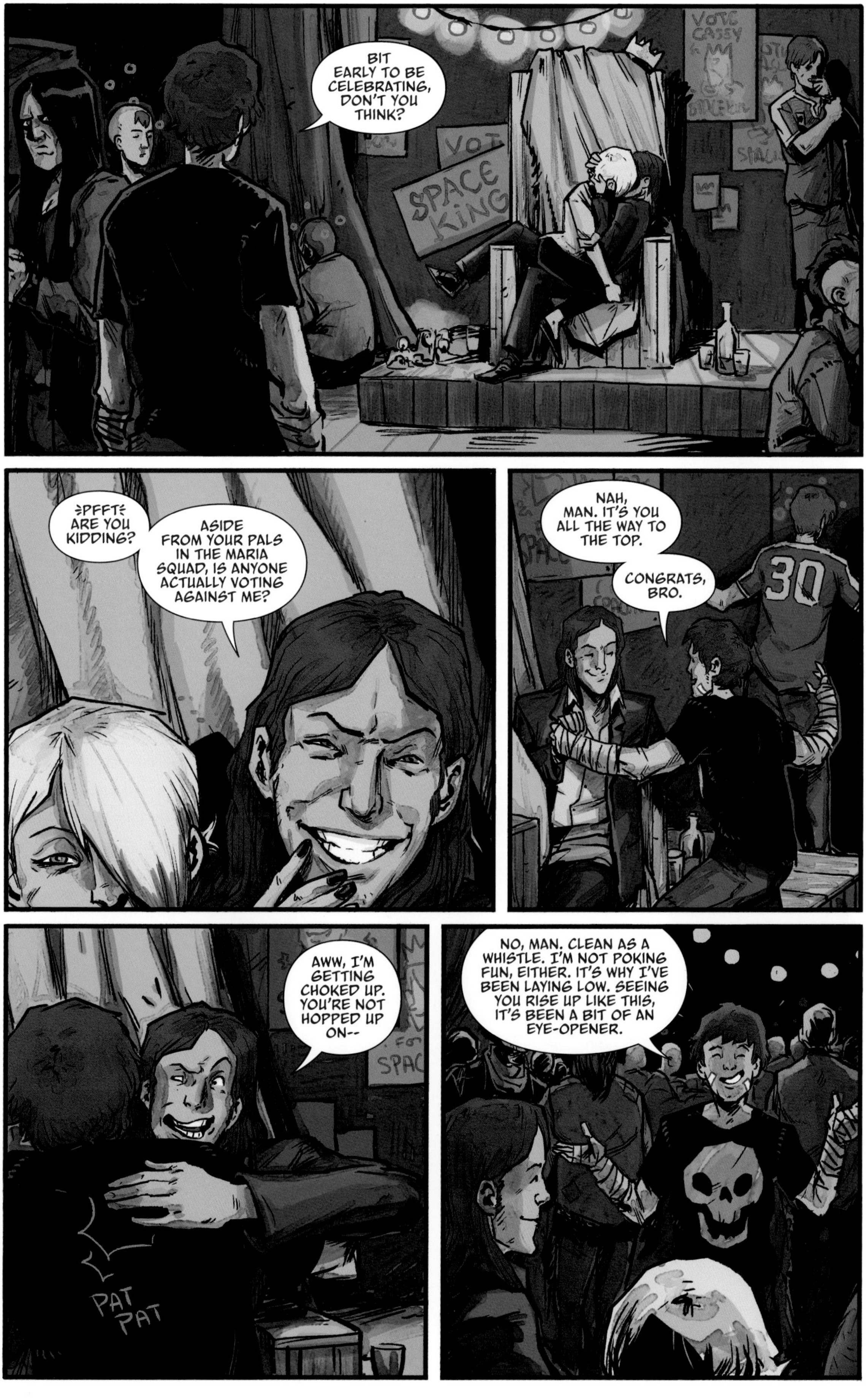
BIT EARLY TO BE CELEBRATING, DON'T YOU THINK?
SPACE KING
ᗒPFFTᗕ ARE YOU KIDDING?
ASIDE FROM YOUR PALS IN THE MARIA SQUAD, IS ANYONE ACTUALLY VOTING AGAINST ME?
NAH, MAN. IT'S YOU ALL THE WAY TO THE TOP.
CONGRATS, BRO.
AWW, I'M GETTING CHOKED UP. YOU'RE NOT HOPPED UP ON--
PAT PAT
NO, MAN. CLEAN AS A WHISTLE. I'M NOT POKING FUN, EITHER. IT'S WHY I'VE BEEN LAYING LOW. SEEING YOU RISE UP LIKE THIS, IT'S BEEN A BIT OF AN EYE-OPENER.

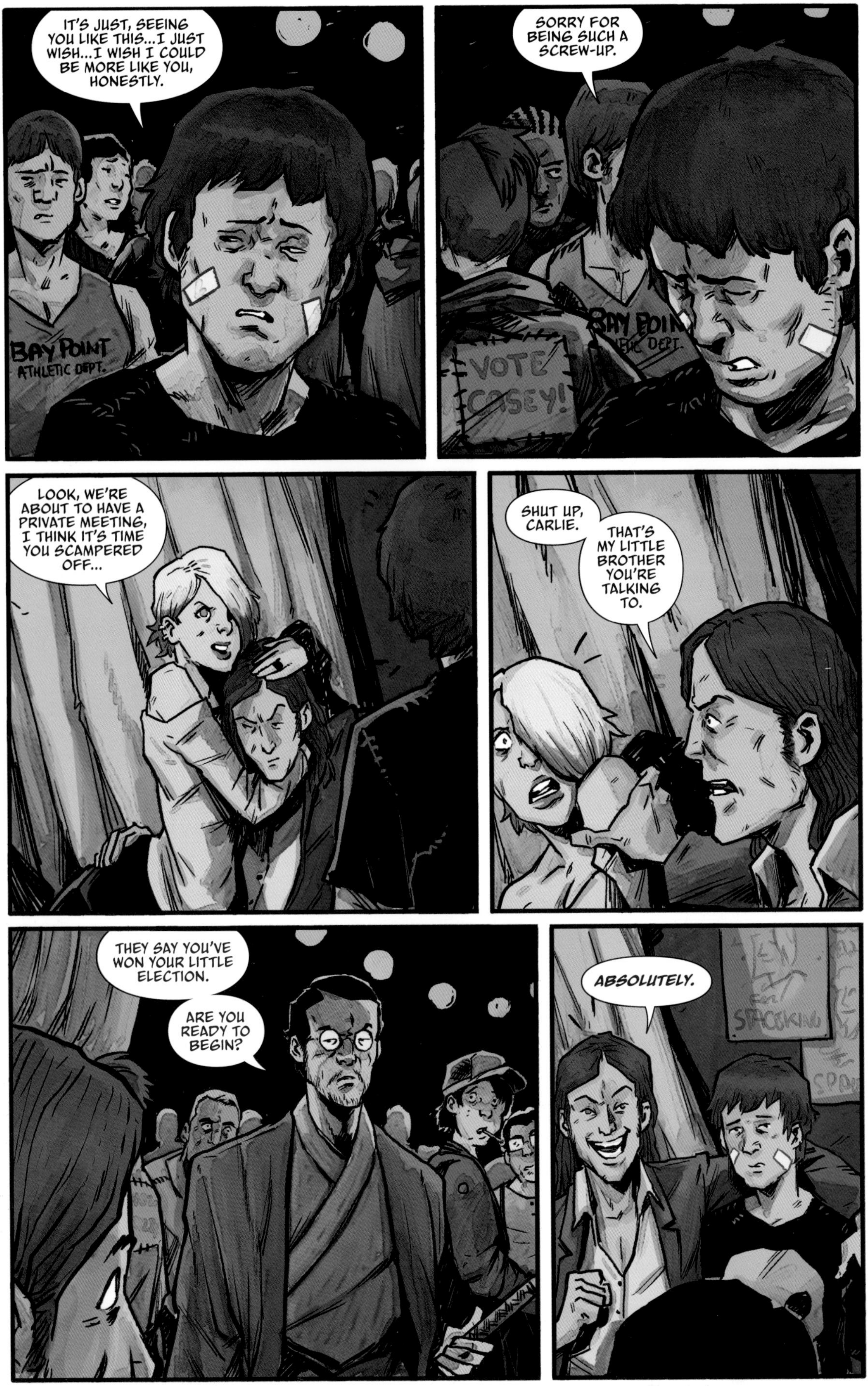
IT'S JUST, SEEING YOU LIKE THIS...I JUST WISH...I WISH I COULD BE MORE LIKE YOU, HONESTLY.
BAY POINT ATHLETIC DEPT.
SORRY FOR BEING SUCH A SCREW-UP.
VOTE CASEY!
LOOK, WE'RE ABOUT TO HAVE A PRIVATE MEETING, I THINK IT'S TIME YOU SCAMPERED OFF...
SHUT UP, CARLIE.
THAT'S MY LITTLE BROTHER YOU'RE TALKING TO.
THEY SAY YOU'VE WON YOUR LITTLE ELECTION.
ARE YOU READY TO BEGIN?
ABSOLUTELY.

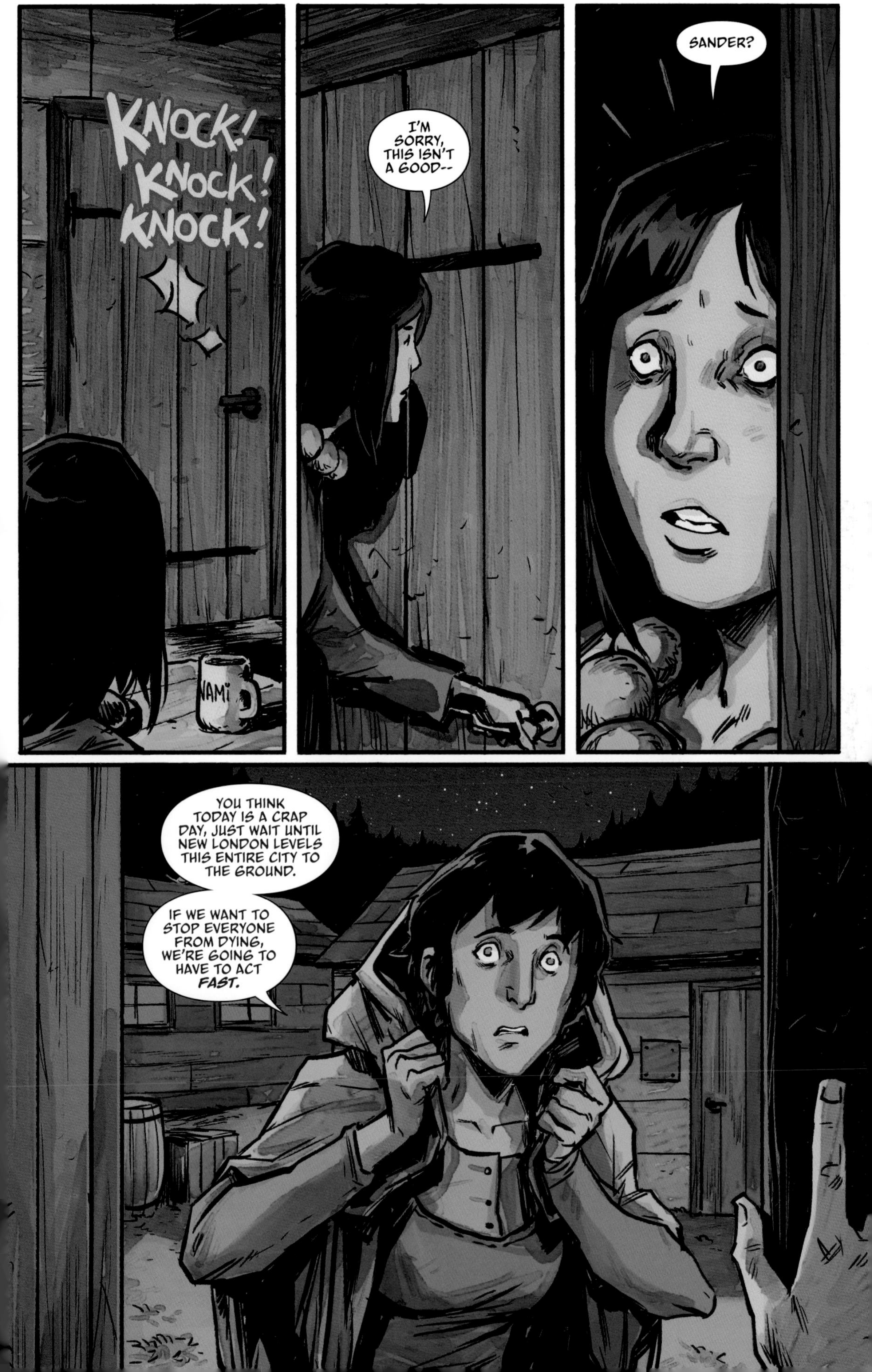
KNOCK! KNOCK! KNOCK!
I'M SORRY, THIS ISN'T A GOOD--
SANDER?
YOU THINK TODAY IS A CRAP DAY, JUST WAIT UNTIL NEW LONDON LEVELS THIS ENTIRE CITY TO THE GROUND.
IF WE WANT TO STOP EVERYONE FROM DYING, WE'RE GOING TO HAVE TO ACT *FAST.*

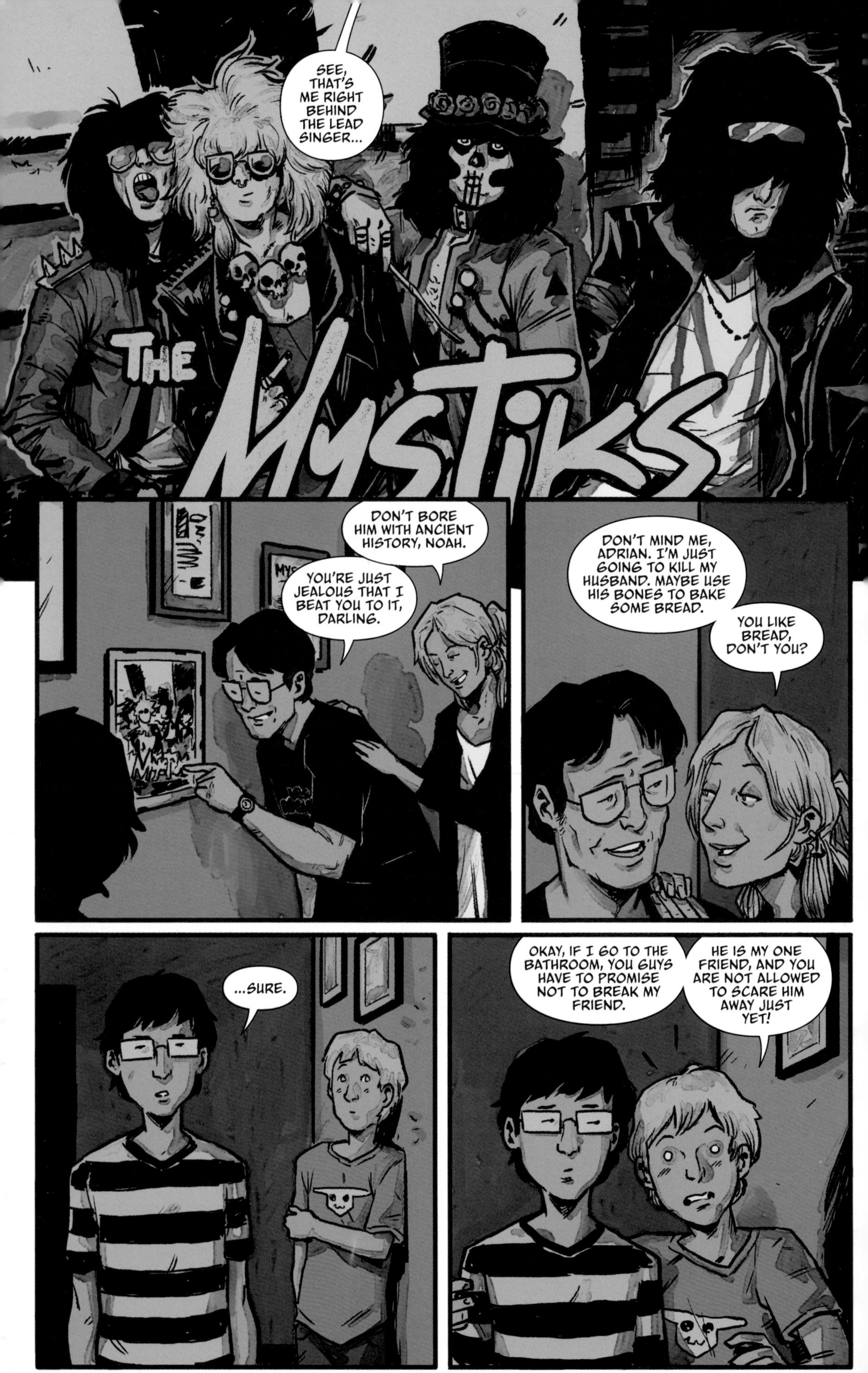
SEE, THAT'S ME RIGHT BEHIND THE LEAD SINGER...
THE MYSTIKS
DON'T BORE HIM WITH ANCIENT HISTORY, NOAH.
YOU'RE JUST JEALOUS THAT I BEAT YOU TO IT, DARLING.
DON'T MIND ME, ADRIAN. I'M JUST GOING TO KILL MY HUSBAND. MAYBE USE HIS BONES TO BAKE SOME BREAD.
YOU LIKE BREAD, DON'T YOU?
...SURE.
OKAY, IF I GO TO THE BATHROOM, YOU GUYS HAVE TO PROMISE NOT TO BREAK MY FRIEND.
HE IS MY ONE FRIEND, AND YOU ARE NOT ALLOWED TO SCARE HIM AWAY JUST YET!

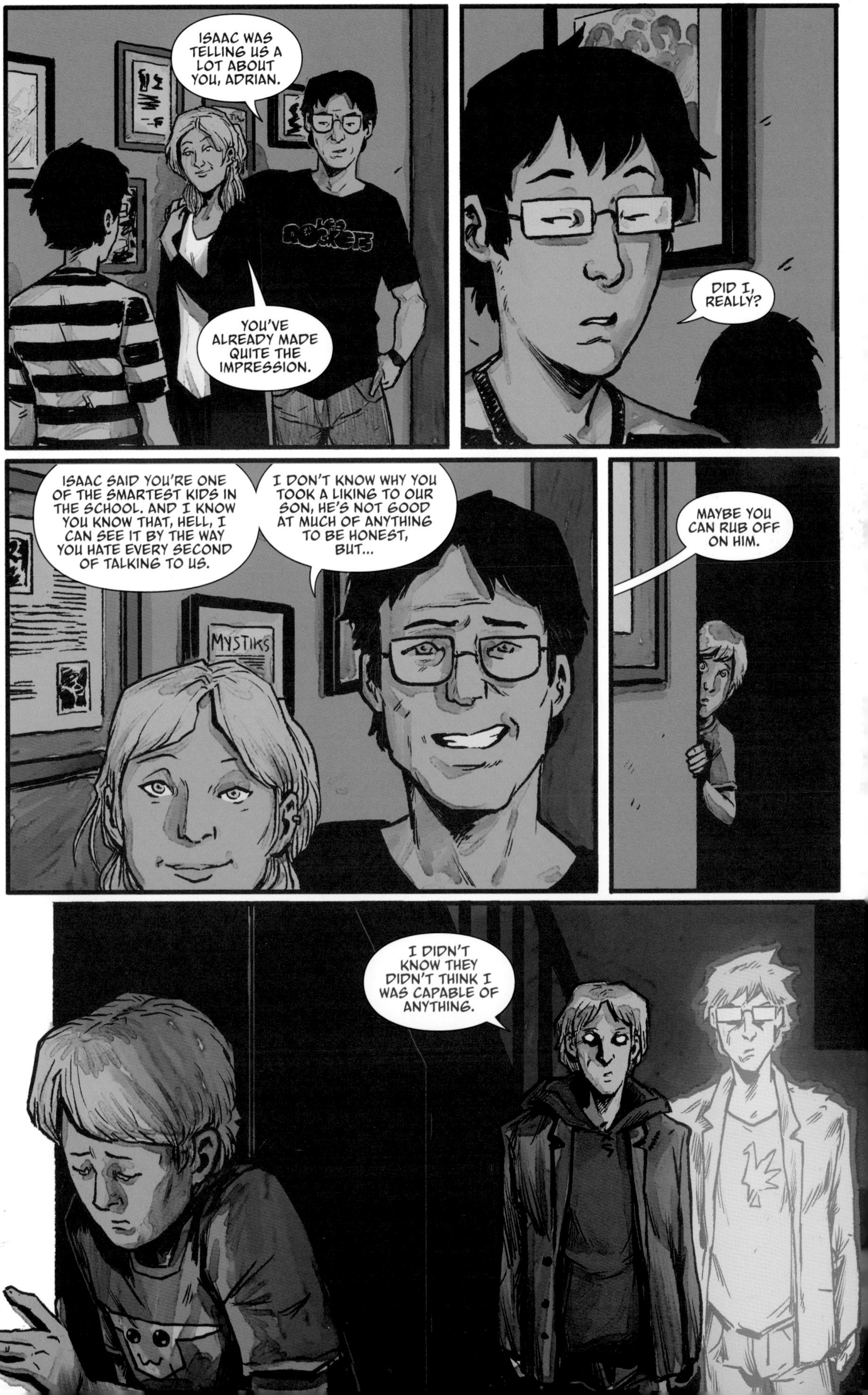
ISAAC WAS TELLING US A LOT ABOUT YOU, ADRIAN.
YOU'VE ALREADY MADE QUITE THE IMPRESSION.
DID I, REALLY?
ISAAC SAID YOU'RE ONE OF THE SMARTEST KIDS IN THE SCHOOL. AND I KNOW YOU KNOW THAT, HELL, I CAN SEE IT BY THE WAY YOU HATE EVERY SECOND OF TALKING TO US.
I DON'T KNOW WHY YOU TOOK A LIKING TO OUR SON, HE'S NOT GOOD AT MUCH OF ANYTHING TO BE HONEST, BUT...
MYSTIKS
MAYBE YOU CAN RUB OFF ON HIM.
I DIDN'T KNOW THEY DIDN'T THINK I WAS CAPABLE OF ANYTHING.

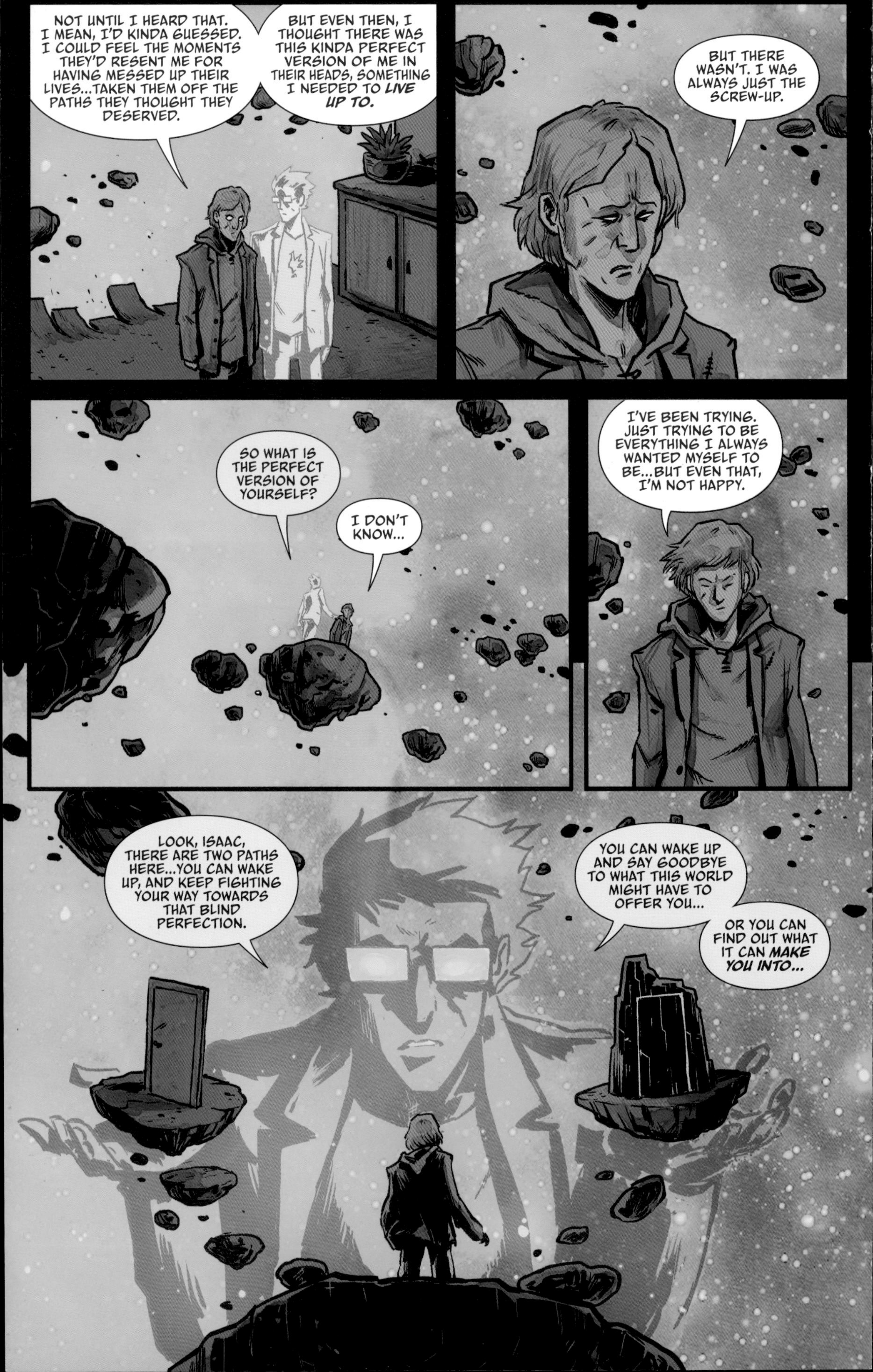
NOT UNTIL I HEARD THAT. I MEAN, I'D KINDA GUESSED. I COULD FEEL THE MOMENTS THEY'D RESENT ME FOR HAVING MESSED UP THEIR LIVES...TAKEN THEM OFF THE PATHS THEY THOUGHT THEY DESERVED.
BUT EVEN THEN, I THOUGHT THERE WAS THIS KINDA PERFECT VERSION OF ME IN THEIR HEADS, SOMETHING I NEEDED TO *LIVE UP TO.*
BUT THERE WASN'T. I WAS ALWAYS JUST THE SCREW-UP.
SO WHAT IS THE PERFECT VERSION OF YOURSELF?
I DON'T KNOW...
I'VE BEEN TRYING. JUST TRYING TO BE EVERYTHING I ALWAYS WANTED MYSELF TO BE...BUT EVEN THAT, I'M NOT HAPPY.
LOOK, ISAAC, THERE ARE TWO PATHS HERE...YOU CAN WAKE UP, AND KEEP FIGHTING YOUR WAY TOWARDS THAT BLIND PERFECTION.
YOU CAN WAKE UP AND SAY GOODBYE TO WHAT THIS WORLD MIGHT HAVE TO OFFER YOU...
OR YOU CAN FIND OUT WHAT IT CAN *MAKE YOU INTO...*

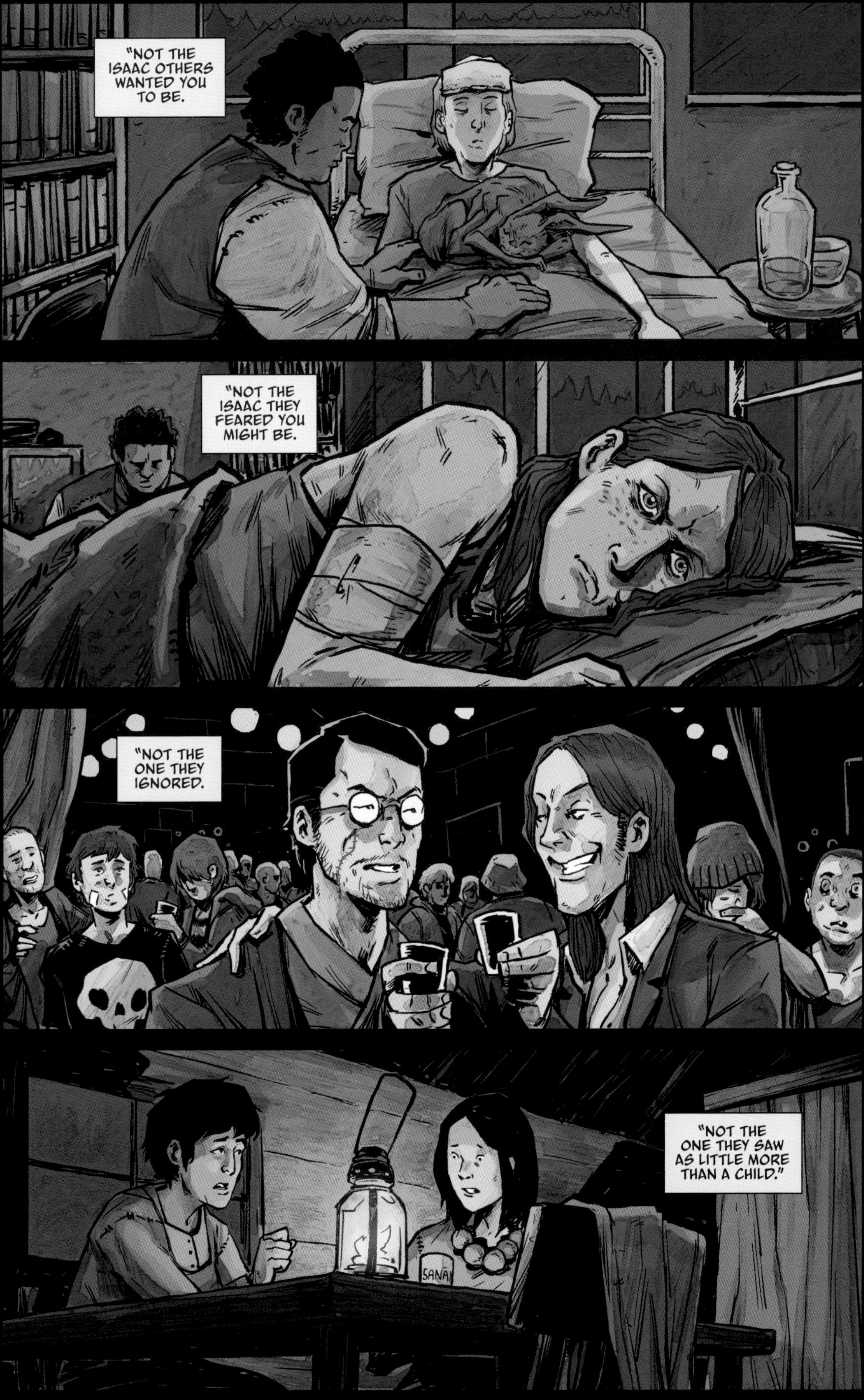
"NOT THE ISAAC OTHERS WANTED YOU TO BE.
"NOT THE ISAAC THEY FEARED YOU MIGHT BE.
"NOT THE ONE THEY IGNORED.
"NOT THE ONE THEY SAW AS LITTLE MORE THAN A CHILD."

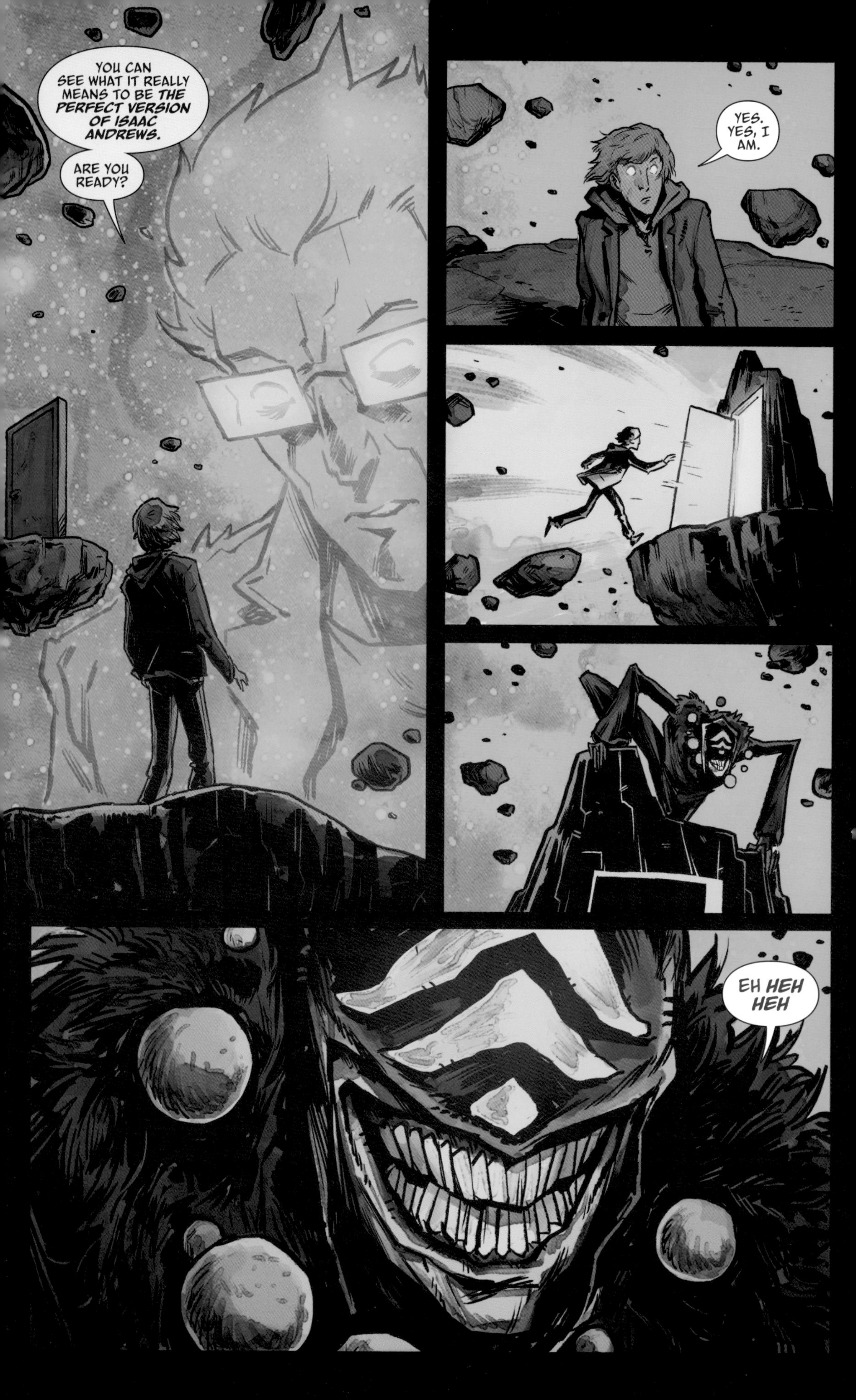
YOU CAN SEE WHAT IT REALLY MEANS TO BE THE PERFECT VERSION OF ISAAC ANDREWS.
ARE YOU READY?
YES. YES, I AM.
EH HEH HEH

CHAPTER EIGHTEEN

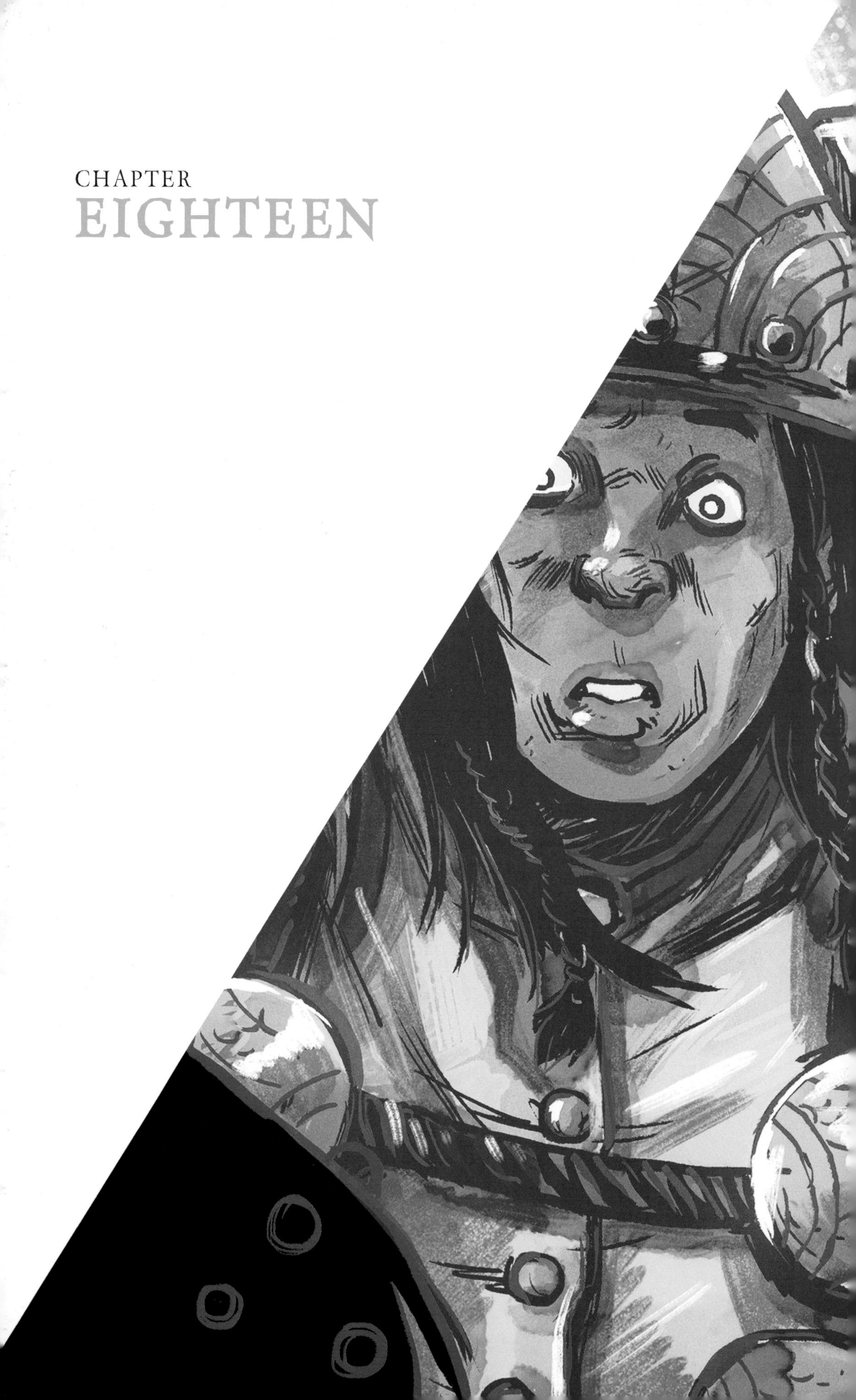

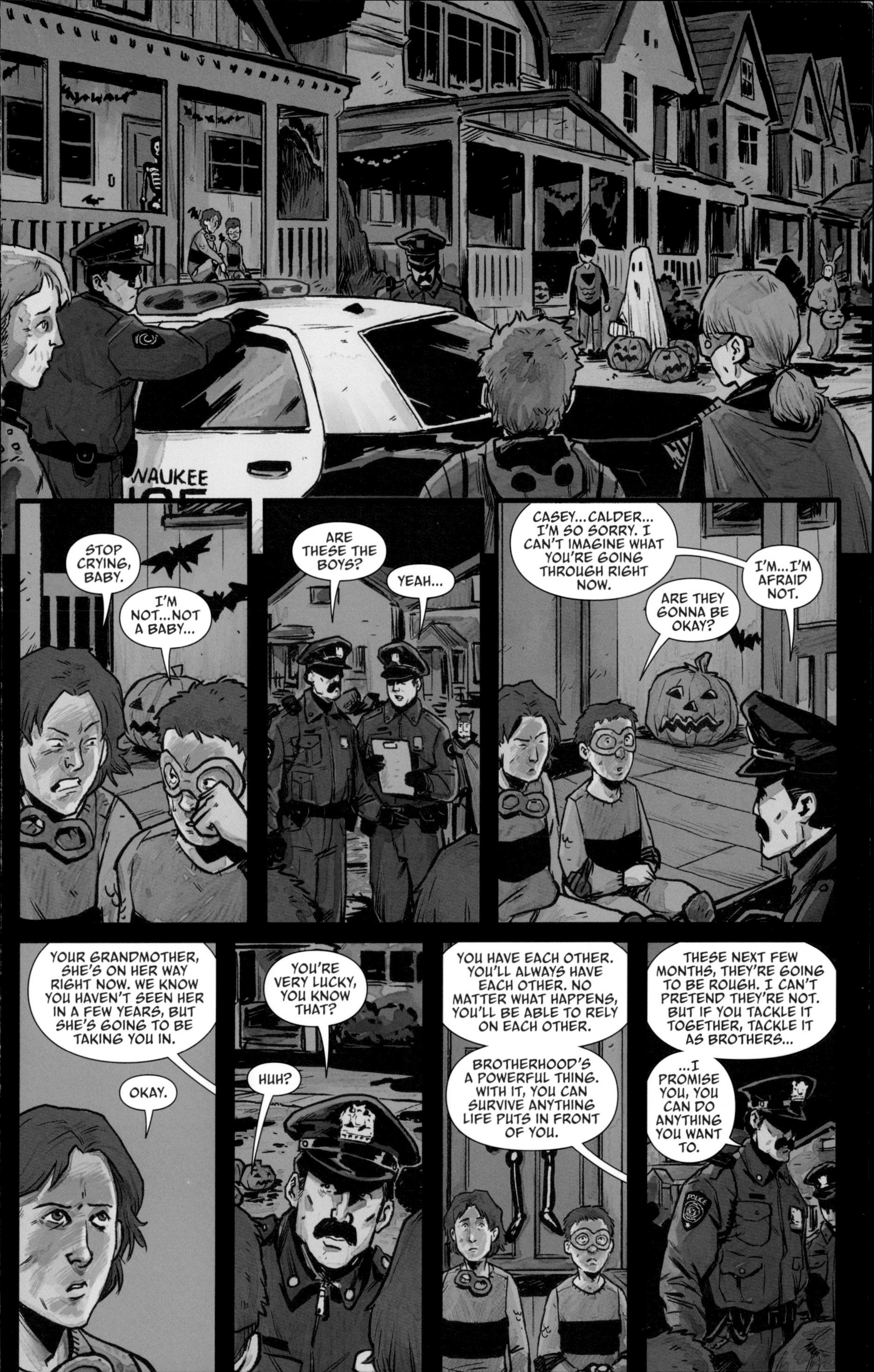
STOP CRYING, BABY.
I'M NOT...NOT A BABY...
ARE THESE THE BOYS?
YEAH...
CASEY...CALDER... I'M SO SORRY. I CAN'T IMAGINE WHAT YOU'RE GOING THROUGH RIGHT NOW.
ARE THEY GONNA BE OKAY?
I'M...I'M AFRAID NOT.
YOUR GRANDMOTHER, SHE'S ON HER WAY RIGHT NOW. WE KNOW YOU HAVEN'T SEEN HER IN A FEW YEARS, BUT SHE'S GOING TO BE TAKING YOU IN.
OKAY.
YOU'RE VERY LUCKY, YOU KNOW THAT?
HUH?
YOU HAVE EACH OTHER. YOU'LL ALWAYS HAVE EACH OTHER. NO MATTER WHAT HAPPENS, YOU'LL BE ABLE TO RELY ON EACH OTHER.
BROTHERHOOD'S A POWERFUL THING. WITH IT, YOU CAN SURVIVE ANYTHING LIFE PUTS IN FRONT OF YOU.
THESE NEXT FEW MONTHS, THEY'RE GOING TO BE ROUGH. I CAN'T PRETEND THEY'RE NOT. BUT IF YOU TACKLE IT TOGETHER, TACKLE IT AS BROTHERS...
...I PROMISE YOU, YOU CAN DO ANYTHING YOU WANT TO.

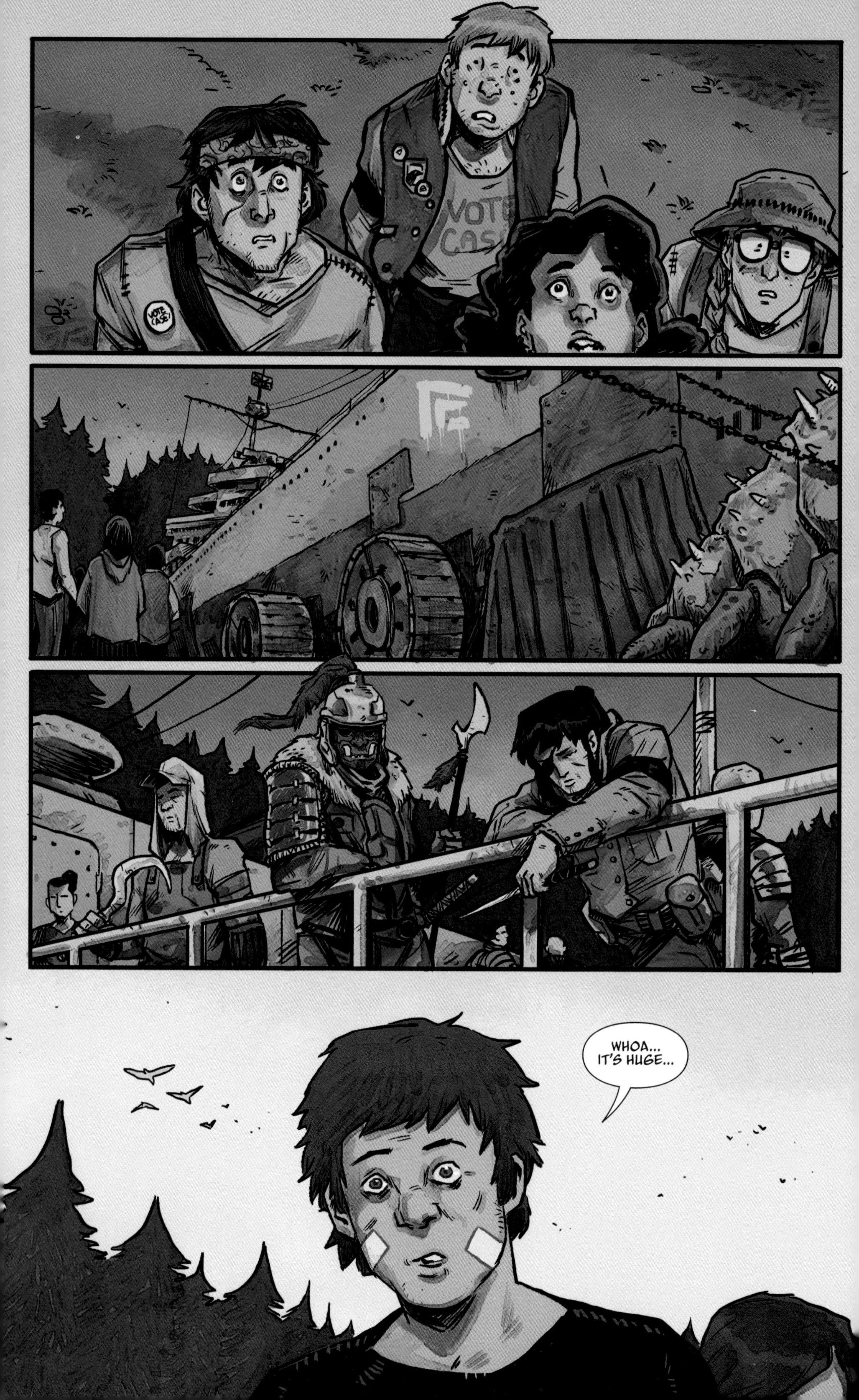
VOTE CASE
VOTE CASE
WHOA... IT'S HUGE...

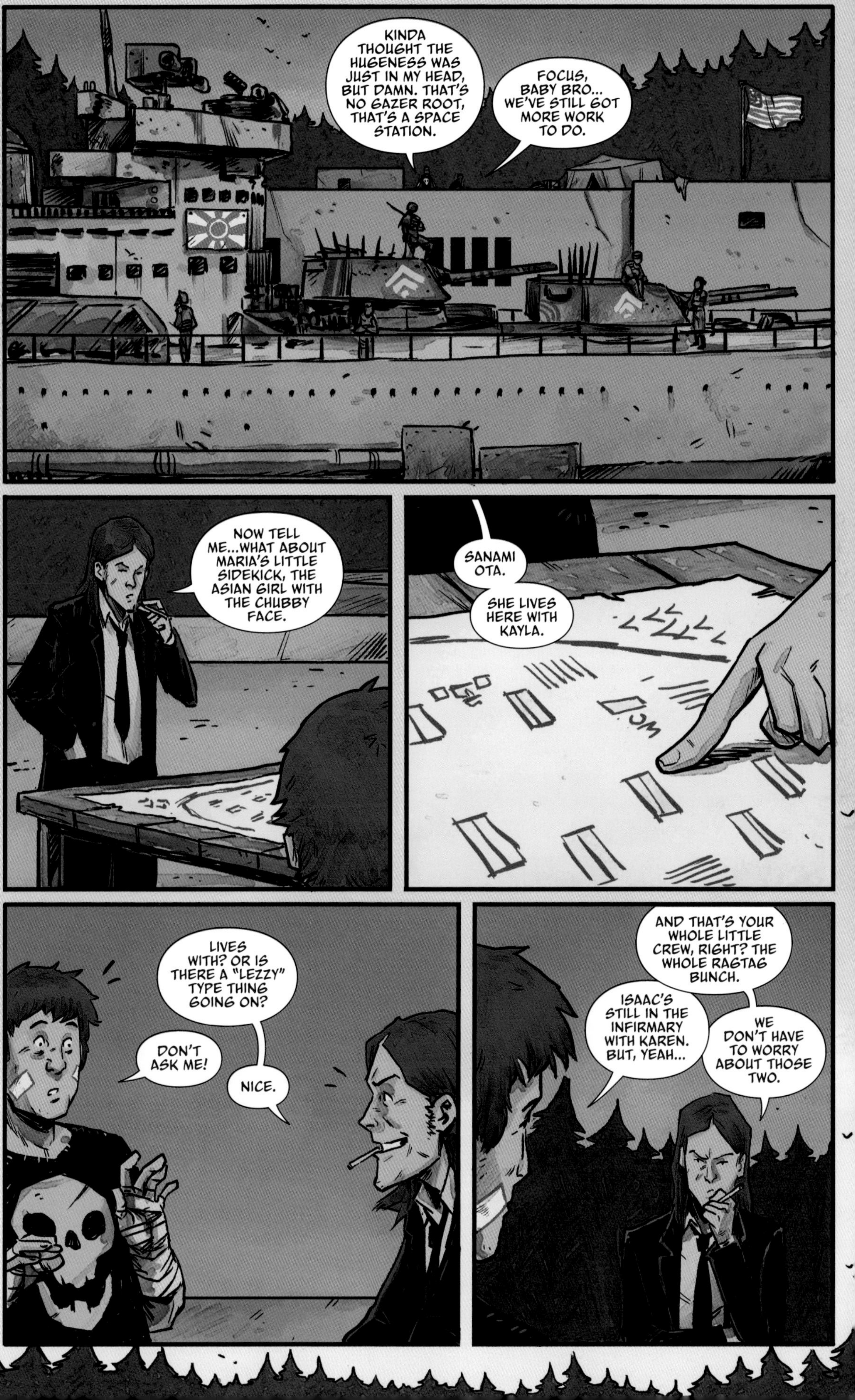
KINDA THOUGHT THE HUGENESS WAS JUST IN MY HEAD, BUT DAMN. THAT'S NO GAZER ROOT, THAT'S A SPACE STATION.
FOCUS, BABY BRO... WE'VE STILL GOT MORE WORK TO DO.
NOW TELL ME...WHAT ABOUT MARIA'S LITTLE SIDEKICK, THE ASIAN GIRL WITH THE CHUBBY FACE.
SANAMI OTA.
SHE LIVES HERE WITH KAYLA.
LIVES WITH? OR IS THERE A "LEZZY" TYPE THING GOING ON?
DON'T ASK ME!
NICE.
AND THAT'S YOUR WHOLE LITTLE CREW, RIGHT? THE WHOLE RAGTAG BUNCH.
ISAAC'S STILL IN THE INFIRMARY WITH KAREN. BUT, YEAH...
WE DON'T HAVE TO WORRY ABOUT THOSE TWO.

YOU DON'T HAVE TO WORRY ABOUT *ANY* OF THEM.

LOOK, YOU GUYS HAD THE CLOSEST RELATIONSHIP WITH THE NEW LONDON CROWD, AND WITH MARIA'S WHOLE REGIME.

I'M JUST LOOKING OUT FOR US, HERE. I'VE GOT PLANS.

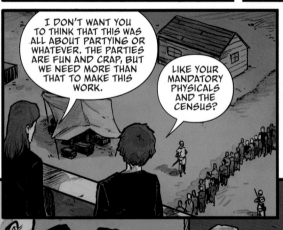

I DON'T WANT YOU TO THINK THAT THIS WAS ALL ABOUT PARTYING OR WHATEVER. THE PARTIES ARE FUN AND CRAP, BUT WE NEED MORE THAN THAT TO MAKE THIS WORK.

LIKE YOUR MANDATORY PHYSICALS AND THE CENSUS?

"WE HAVE A DOCTOR NOW, A REAL HONEST-TO-GOD DOCTOR. SOMEONE WITH A TOUCH OF 20TH CENTURY MEDICAL KNOWLEDGE."

"I'M NOT PUTTING THAT TO WASTE.

"PLUS, THEN WE CAN SEE WHO'S ACTUALLY FIT ENOUGH TO DO THE WORK THAT WE NEED DOING. I'VE BEEN TALKING TO TAISHO ALL WEEK."

HE'S GOT SOME KILLER IDEAS.

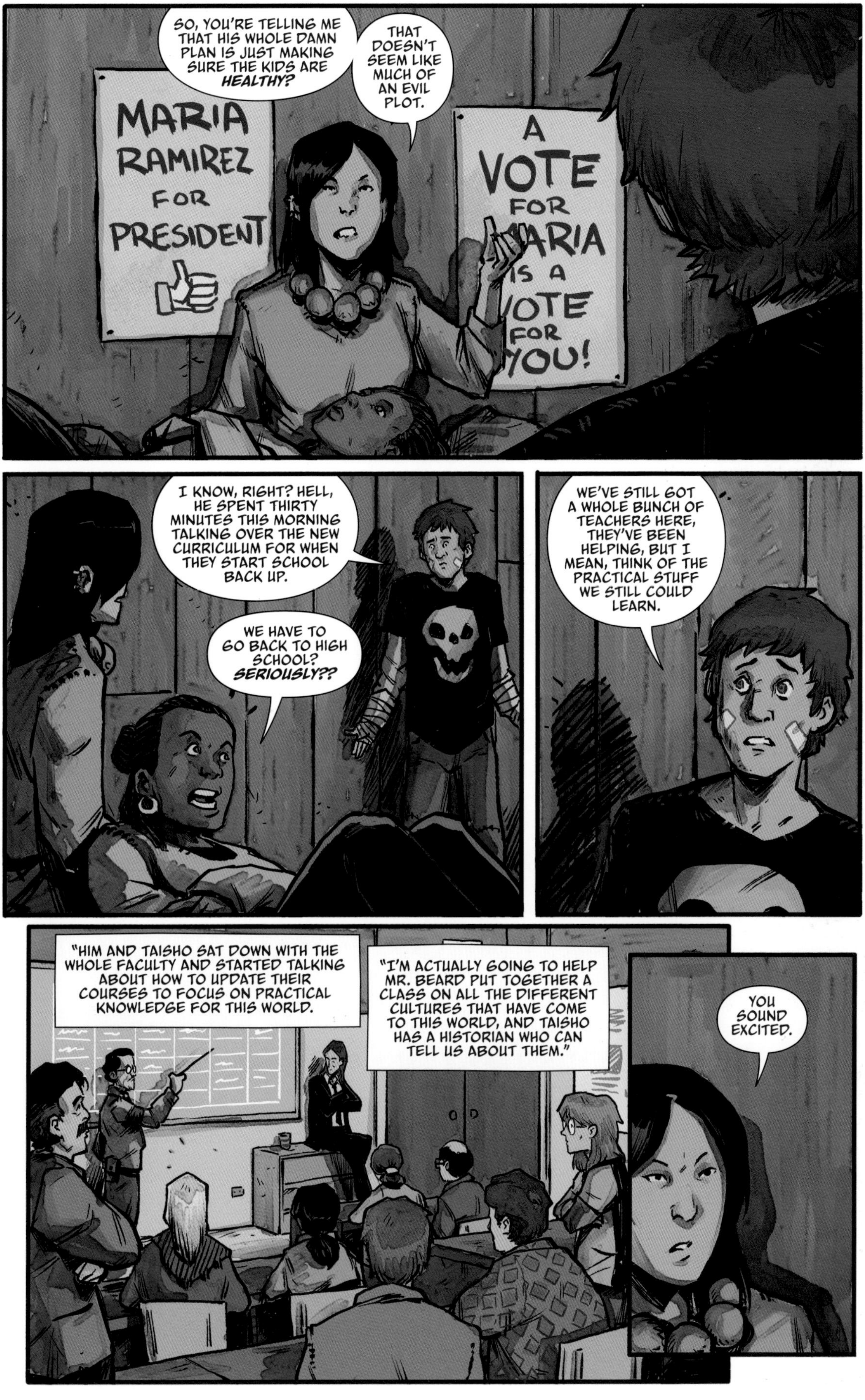

SO, YOU'RE TELLING ME THAT HIS WHOLE DAMN PLAN IS JUST MAKING SURE THE KIDS ARE *HEALTHY?*
THAT DOESN'T SEEM LIKE MUCH OF AN EVIL PLOT.
MARIA RAMIREZ FOR PRESIDENT
A VOTE FOR MARIA IS A VOTE FOR YOU!
I KNOW, RIGHT? HELL, HE SPENT THIRTY MINUTES THIS MORNING TALKING OVER THE NEW CURRICULUM FOR WHEN THEY START SCHOOL BACK UP.
WE HAVE TO GO BACK TO HIGH SCHOOL? *SERIOUSLY??*
WE'VE STILL GOT A WHOLE BUNCH OF TEACHERS HERE, THEY'VE BEEN HELPING, BUT I MEAN, THINK OF THE PRACTICAL STUFF WE STILL COULD LEARN.
"HIM AND TAISHO SAT DOWN WITH THE WHOLE FACULTY AND STARTED TALKING ABOUT HOW TO UPDATE THEIR COURSES TO FOCUS ON PRACTICAL KNOWLEDGE FOR THIS WORLD.
"I'M ACTUALLY GOING TO HELP MR. BEARD PUT TOGETHER A CLASS ON ALL THE DIFFERENT CULTURES THAT HAVE COME TO THIS WORLD, AND TAISHO HAS A HISTORIAN WHO CAN TELL US ABOUT THEM."
YOU SOUND EXCITED.

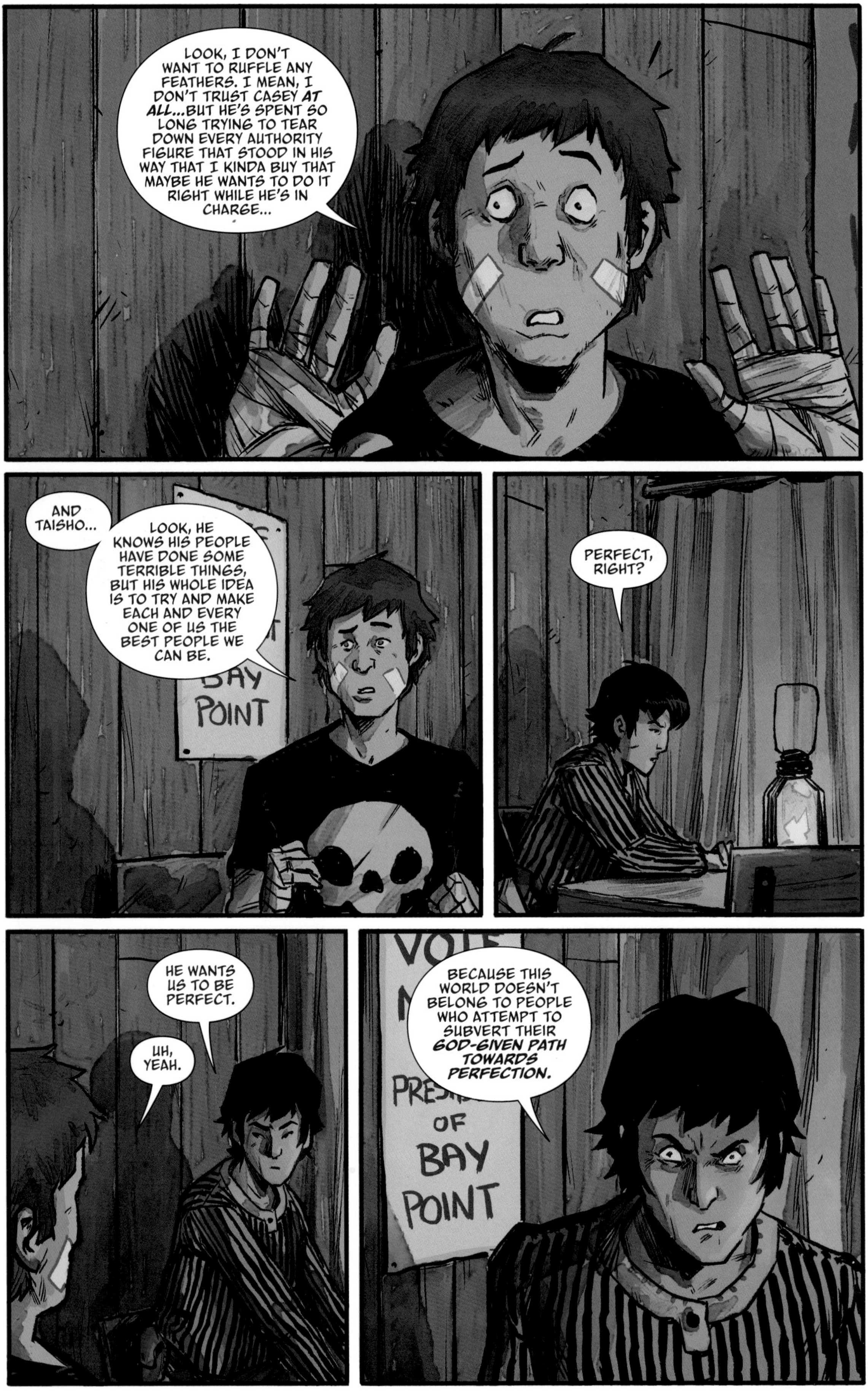
LOOK, I DON'T WANT TO RUFFLE ANY FEATHERS. I MEAN, I DON'T TRUST CASEY AT ALL...BUT HE'S SPENT SO LONG TRYING TO TEAR DOWN EVERY AUTHORITY FIGURE THAT STOOD IN HIS WAY THAT I KINDA BUY THAT MAYBE HE WANTS TO DO IT RIGHT WHILE HE'S IN CHARGE...
AND TAISHO...
LOOK, HE KNOWS HIS PEOPLE HAVE DONE SOME TERRIBLE THINGS, BUT HIS WHOLE IDEA IS TO TRY AND MAKE EACH AND EVERY ONE OF US THE BEST PEOPLE WE CAN BE.
BAY POINT
PERFECT, RIGHT?
HE WANTS US TO BE PERFECT.
UH, YEAH.
BECAUSE THIS WORLD DOESN'T BELONG TO PEOPLE WHO ATTEMPT TO SUBVERT THEIR GOD-GIVEN PATH TOWARDS PERFECTION.
OF
BAY
POINT

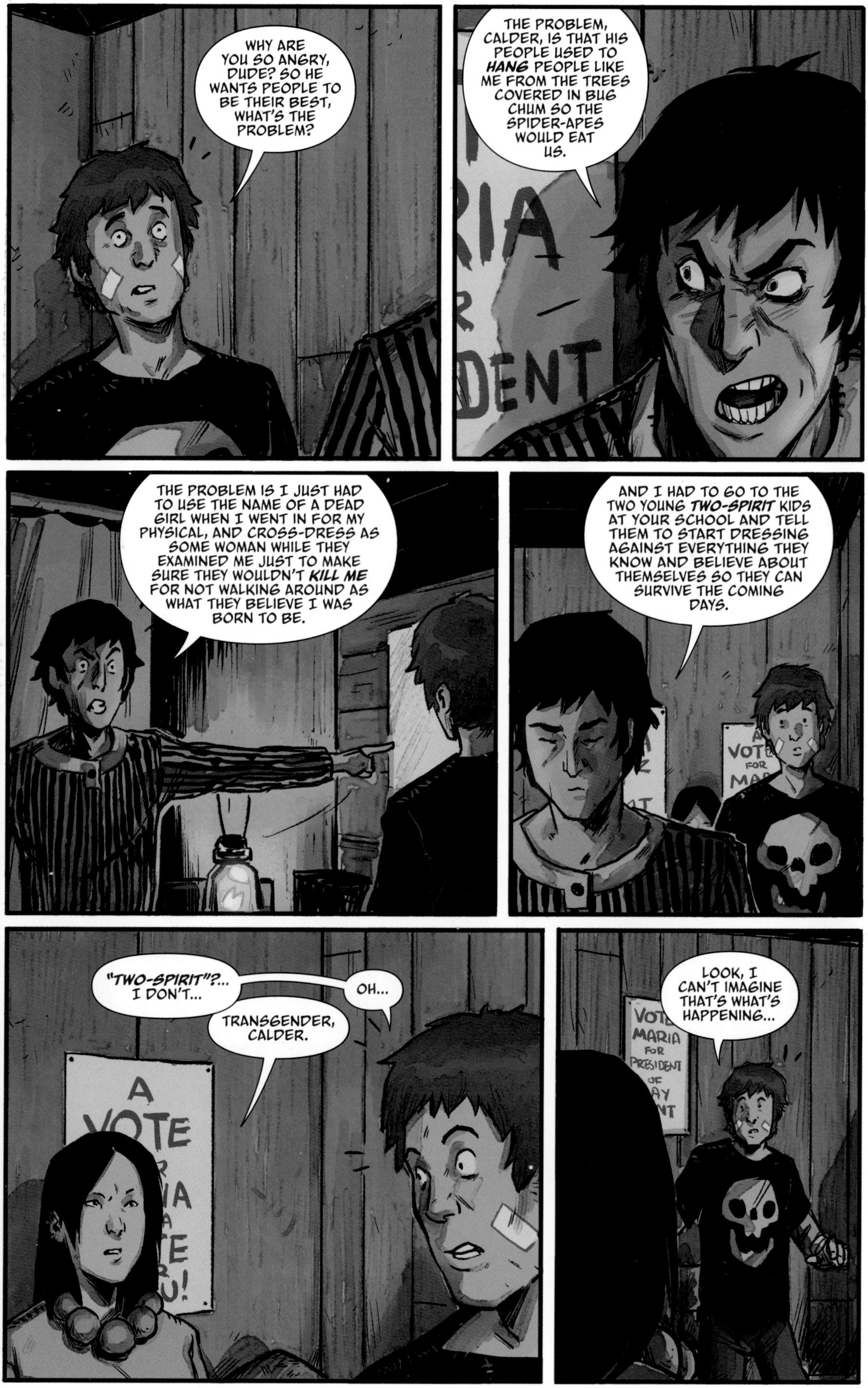
WHY ARE YOU SO ANGRY, DUDE? SO HE WANTS PEOPLE TO BE THEIR BEST, WHAT'S THE PROBLEM?
THE PROBLEM, CALDER, IS THAT HIS PEOPLE USED TO HANG PEOPLE LIKE ME FROM THE TREES COVERED IN BUG CHUM SO THE SPIDER-APES WOULD EAT US.
THE PROBLEM IS I JUST HAD TO USE THE NAME OF A DEAD GIRL WHEN I WENT IN FOR MY PHYSICAL, AND CROSS-DRESS AS SOME WOMAN WHILE THEY EXAMINED ME JUST TO MAKE SURE THEY WOULDN'T KILL ME FOR NOT WALKING AROUND AS WHAT THEY BELIEVE I WAS BORN TO BE.
AND I HAD TO GO TO THE TWO YOUNG TWO-SPIRIT KIDS AT YOUR SCHOOL AND TELL THEM TO START DRESSING AGAINST EVERYTHING THEY KNOW AND BELIEVE ABOUT THEMSELVES SO THEY CAN SURVIVE THE COMING DAYS.
"TWO-SPIRIT"?... I DON'T...
TRANSGENDER, CALDER.
OH...
A VOTE
LOOK, I CAN'T IMAGINE THAT'S WHAT'S HAPPENING...
VOTE MARIA FOR PRESIDENT OF

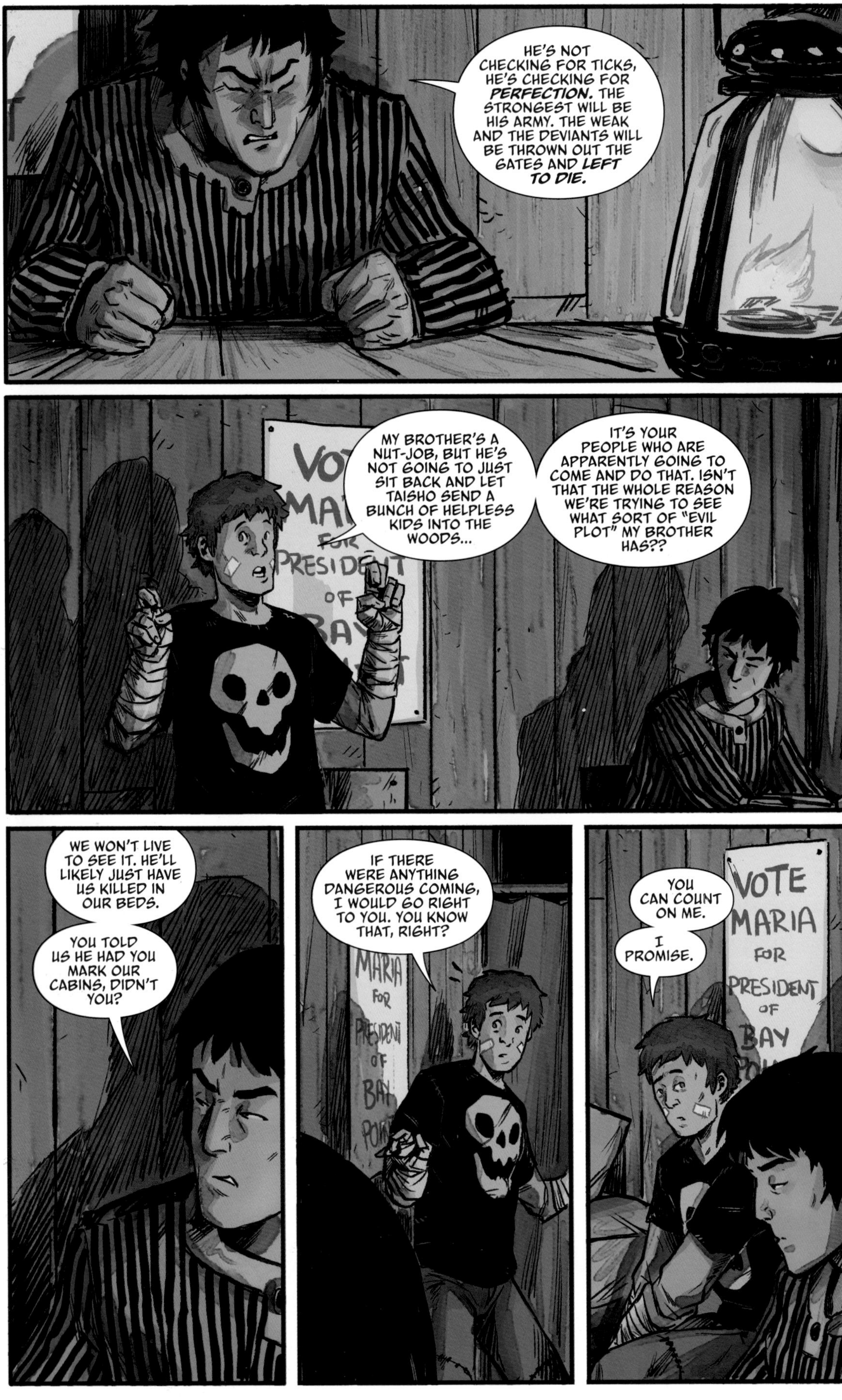
HE'S NOT CHECKING FOR TICKS, HE'S CHECKING FOR **PERFECTION.** THE STRONGEST WILL BE HIS ARMY. THE WEAK AND THE DEVIANTS WILL BE THROWN OUT THE GATES AND ***LEFT TO DIE.***
VOTE MARIA ~~FOR~~ PRESIDENT OF BAY
MY BROTHER'S A NUT-JOB, BUT HE'S NOT GOING TO JUST SIT BACK AND LET TAISHO SEND A BUNCH OF HELPLESS KIDS INTO THE WOODS...
IT'S YOUR PEOPLE WHO ARE APPARENTLY GOING TO COME AND DO THAT. ISN'T THAT THE WHOLE REASON WE'RE TRYING TO SEE WHAT SORT OF "EVIL PLOT" MY BROTHER HAS??
WE WON'T LIVE TO SEE IT. HE'LL LIKELY JUST HAVE US KILLED IN OUR BEDS.
YOU TOLD US HE HAD YOU MARK OUR CABINS, DIDN'T YOU?
IF THERE WERE ANYTHING DANGEROUS COMING, I WOULD GO RIGHT TO YOU. YOU KNOW THAT, RIGHT?
MARIA FOR PRESIDENT OF BAY POINT
YOU CAN COUNT ON ME.
I PROMISE.
VOTE MARIA FOR PRESIDENT OF BAY

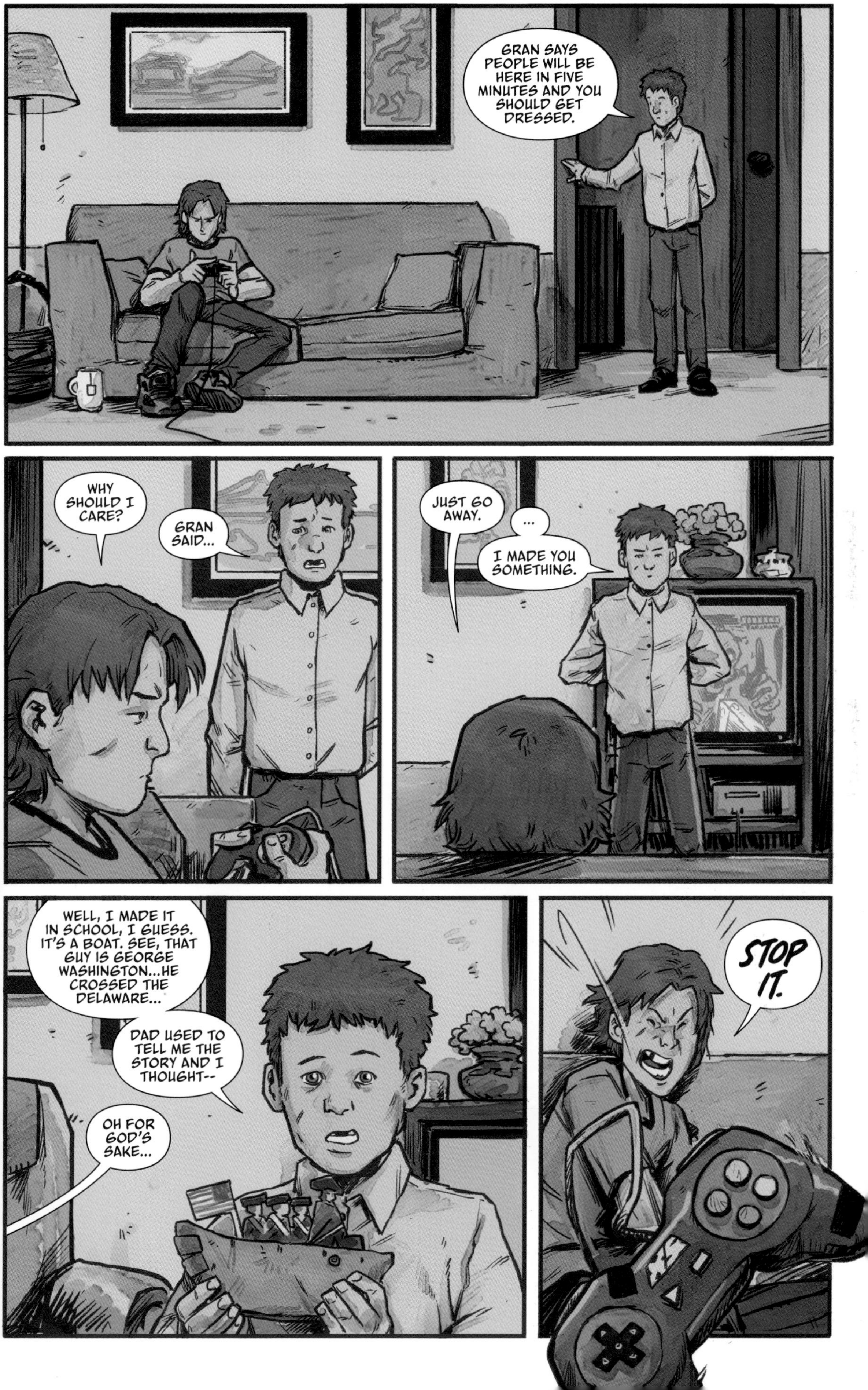
GRAN SAYS PEOPLE WILL BE HERE IN FIVE MINUTES AND YOU SHOULD GET DRESSED.
WHY SHOULD I CARE?
GRAN SAID...
JUST GO AWAY.
...
I MADE YOU SOMETHING.
WELL, I MADE IT IN SCHOOL, I GUESS. IT'S A BOAT. SEE, THAT GUY IS GEORGE WASHINGTON...HE CROSSED THE DELAWARE...
DAD USED TO TELL ME THE STORY AND I THOUGHT--
OH FOR GOD'S SAKE...
STOP IT.

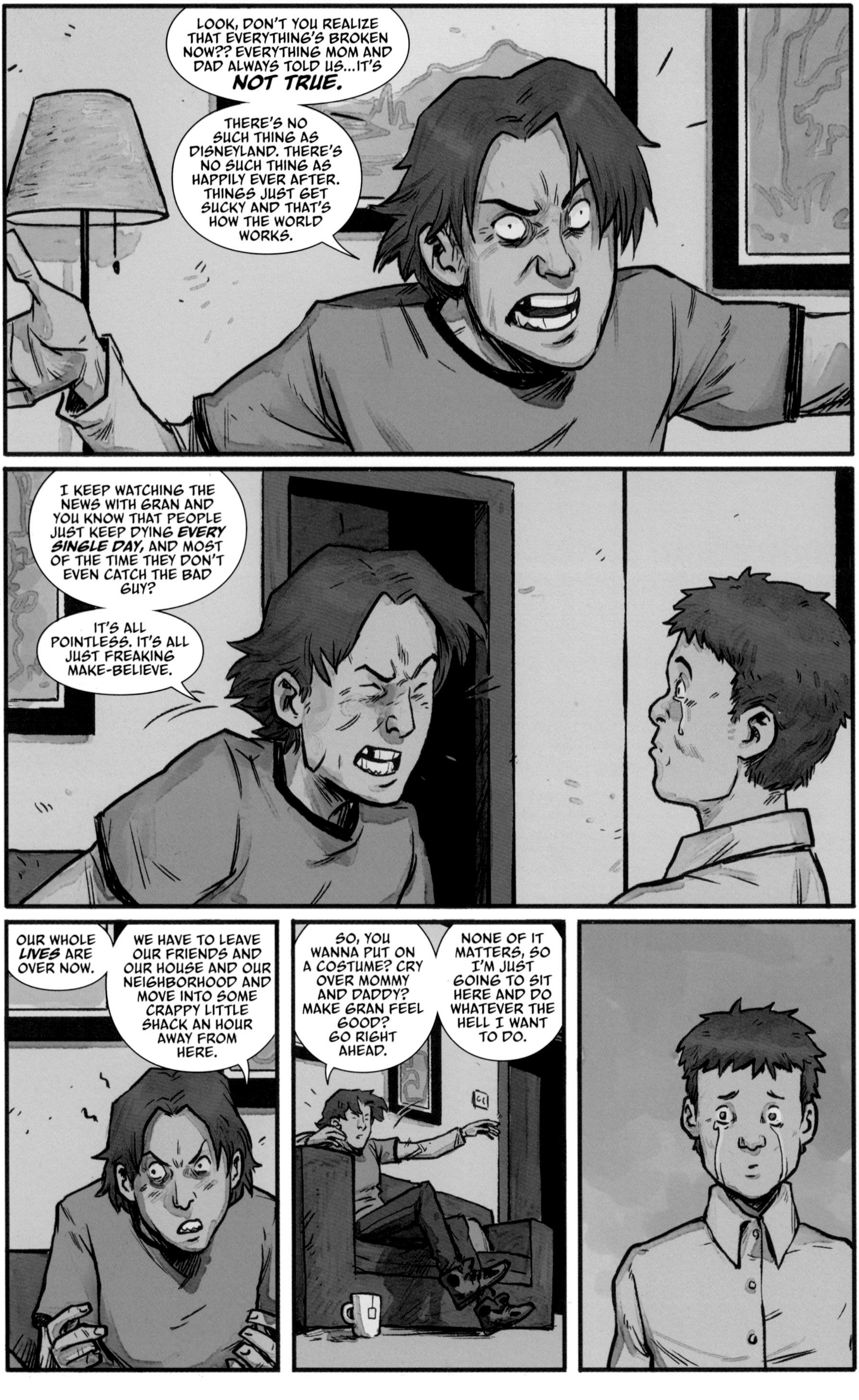
LOOK, DON'T YOU REALIZE THAT EVERYTHING'S BROKEN NOW?? EVERYTHING MOM AND DAD ALWAYS TOLD US...IT'S **NOT TRUE.**
THERE'S NO SUCH THING AS DISNEYLAND. THERE'S NO SUCH THING AS HAPPILY EVER AFTER. THINGS JUST GET SUCKY AND THAT'S HOW THE WORLD WORKS.
I KEEP WATCHING THE NEWS WITH GRAN AND YOU KNOW THAT PEOPLE JUST KEEP DYING ***EVERY SINGLE DAY,*** AND MOST OF THE TIME THEY DON'T EVEN CATCH THE BAD GUY?
IT'S ALL POINTLESS. IT'S ALL JUST FREAKING MAKE-BELIEVE.
OUR WHOLE ***LIVES*** ARE OVER NOW.
WE HAVE TO LEAVE OUR FRIENDS AND OUR HOUSE AND OUR NEIGHBORHOOD AND MOVE INTO SOME CRAPPY LITTLE SHACK AN HOUR AWAY FROM HERE.
SO, YOU WANNA PUT ON A COSTUME? CRY OVER MOMMY AND DADDY? MAKE GRAN FEEL GOOD? GO RIGHT AHEAD.
NONE OF IT MATTERS, SO I'M JUST GOING TO SIT HERE AND DO WHATEVER THE HELL I WANT TO DO.

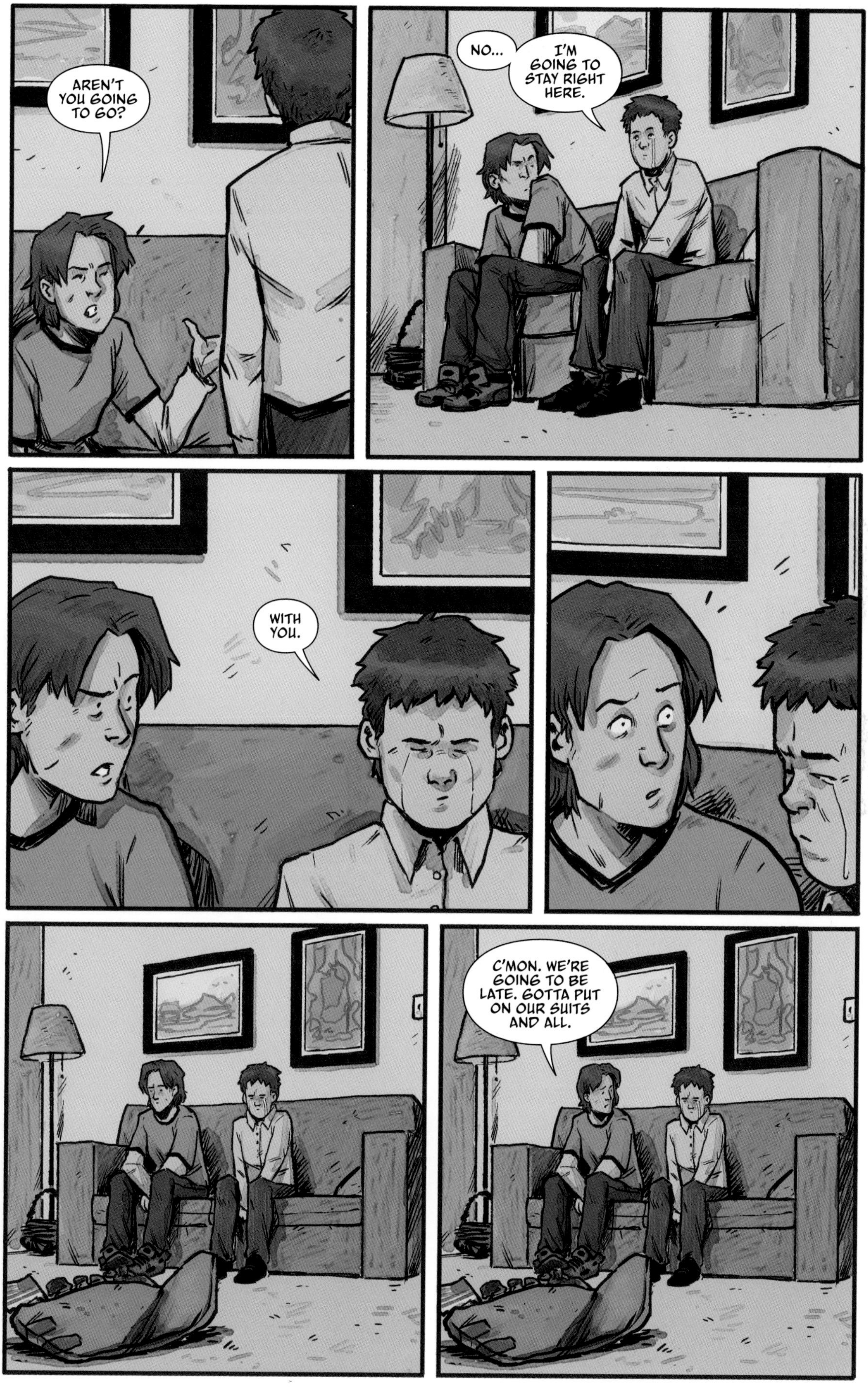
AREN'T YOU GOING TO GO?
NO...
I'M GOING TO STAY RIGHT HERE.
WITH YOU.
C'MON. WE'RE GOING TO BE LATE. GOTTA PUT ON OUR SUITS AND ALL.

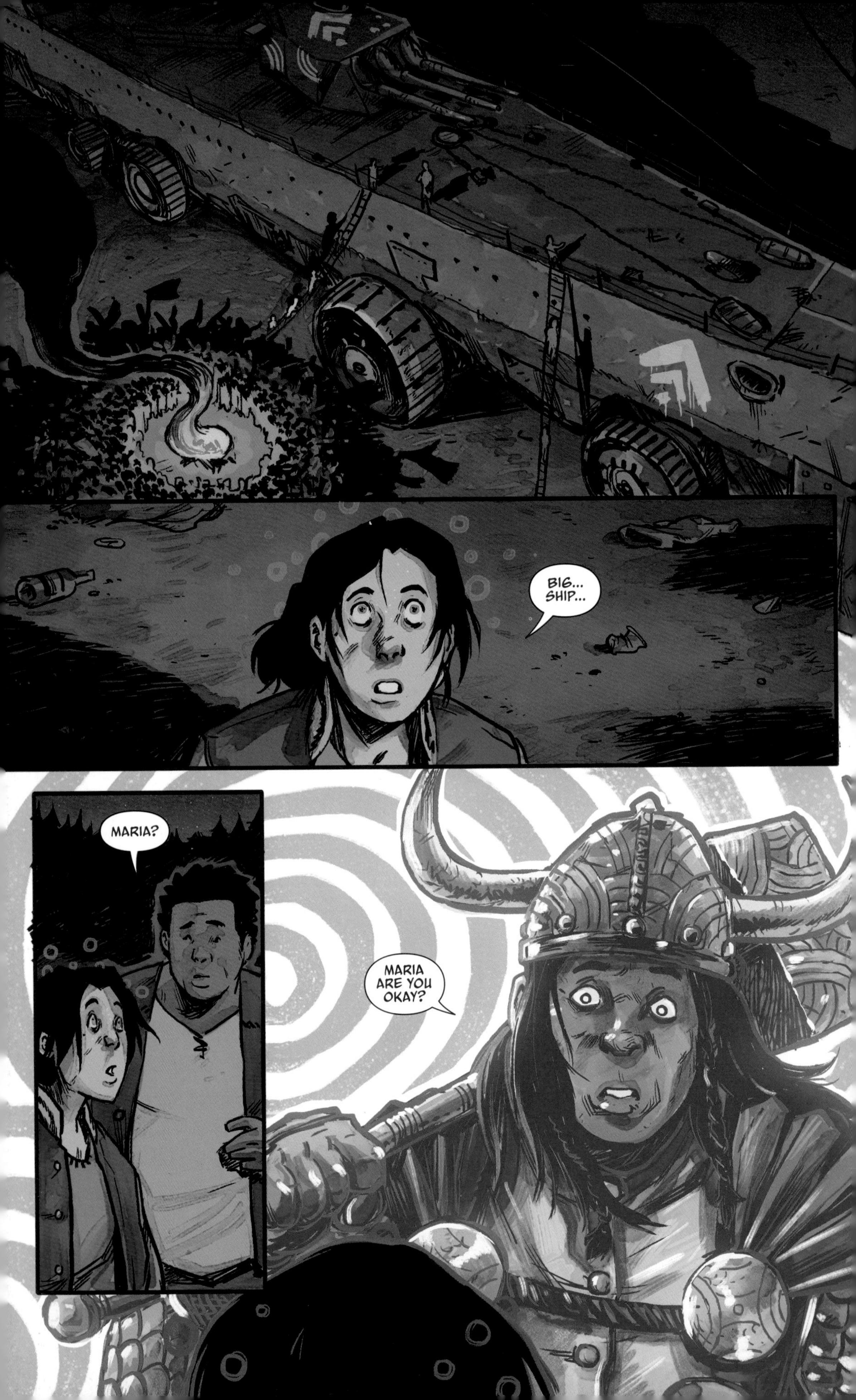
BIG...
SHIP...
MARIA?
MARIA
ARE YOU
OKAY?

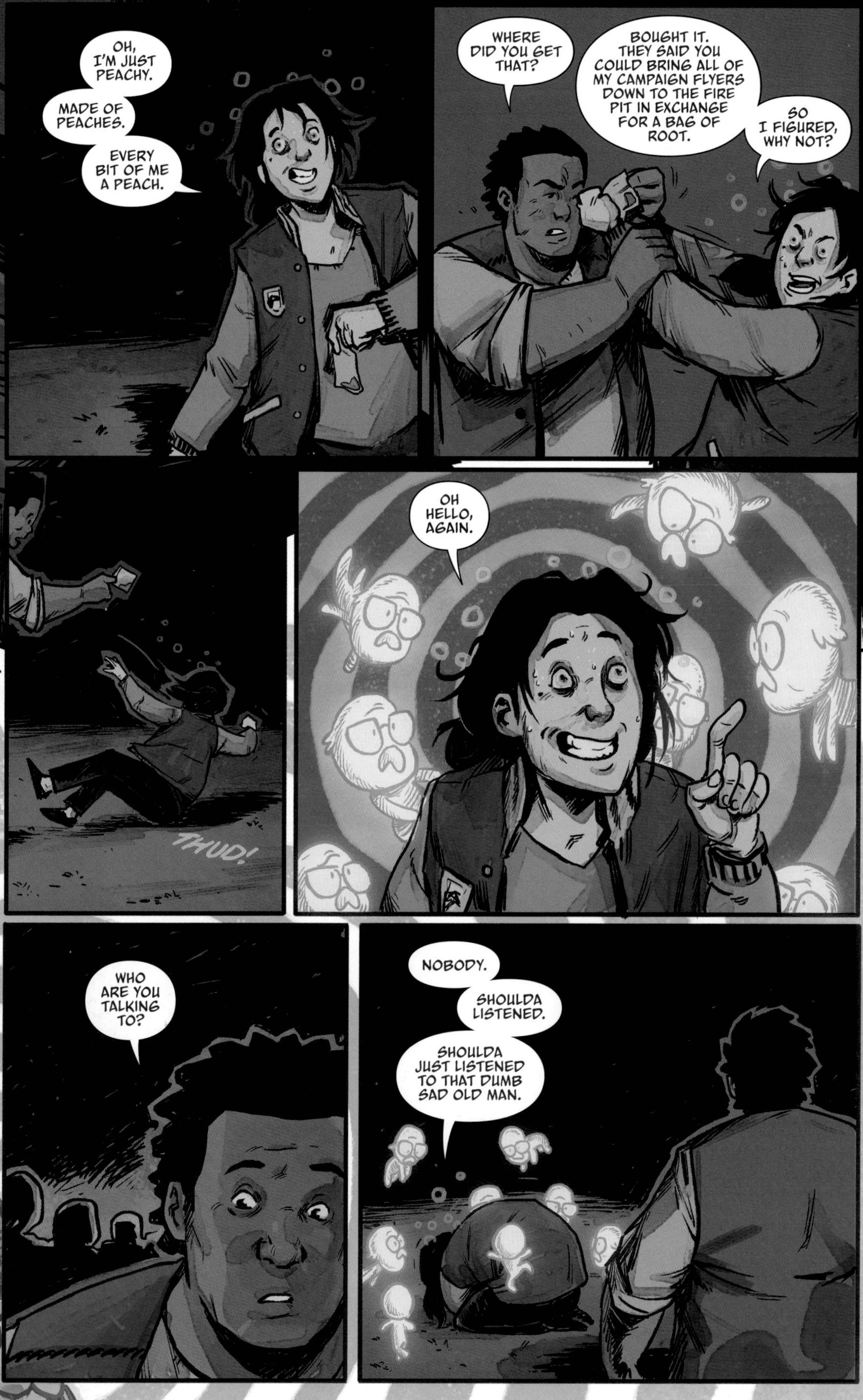
OH, I'M JUST PEACHY.
MADE OF PEACHES.
EVERY BIT OF ME A PEACH.
WHERE DID YOU GET THAT?
BOUGHT IT. THEY SAID YOU COULD BRING ALL OF MY CAMPAIGN FLYERS DOWN TO THE FIRE PIT IN EXCHANGE FOR A BAG OF ROOT.
SO I FIGURED, WHY NOT?
THUD!
OH HELLO, AGAIN.
WHO ARE YOU TALKING TO?
NOBODY.
SHOULDA LISTENED.
SHOULDA JUST LISTENED TO THAT DUMB SAD OLD MAN.

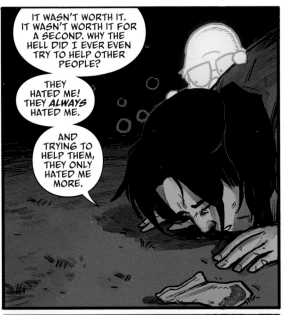

IT WASN'T WORTH IT. IT WASN'T WORTH IT FOR A SECOND. WHY THE HELL DID I EVER EVEN TRY TO HELP OTHER PEOPLE?

THEY HATED ME! THEY *ALWAYS* HATED ME.

AND TRYING TO HELP THEM, THEY ONLY HATED ME MORE.

I DON'T HATE YOU.

YOU BARELY KNOW ME.

ASK KAREN, SHE KNOWS ME. KNOWS I'M JUST A GARBAGE PERSON. DOM...DOM STORMED OUT EARLIER. I SAID SOME PRETTY NASTY STUFF TO HIM.

I DON'T KNOW WHY IT'S SO HARD TO JUST BE HAPPY...WHY IT'S SO HARD TO JUST LIVE.

I DON'T KNOW EITHER.

I DON'T EVEN KNOW WHY I STILL GO IN TO CHECK ON ISAAC EVERY DAY...EVEN IF HE WAS BETTER, WE ALREADY ENDED THINGS.

AND NOW HE'S JUST GONE. I HEARD HIM SAY SOMETHING, AND IT SOUNDED LIKE MY NAME...

BUT THEN AGAIN, IT ALSO SOUNDED LIKE HE SAID ADRIAN.

YOU SHOULD TRY SOME OF THIS STUFF. IT'S GREAT.

MAYBE IF YOU TAKE ME DOWN THERE TO BURN YOU'LL GET A BIG BAG. HEH.

THAT'S OKAY.

I JUST KEPT TRYING TO MAKE THINGS BETTER, AND IT JUST ALL FELL APART IN A SECOND. IN JUST ONE SECOND.

EVERYTHING THAT MATTERED TO ME MEANT NOTHING. EVERYTHING IS MEANINGLESS.

LET'S GET YOU TO SLEEP.

OKAY.

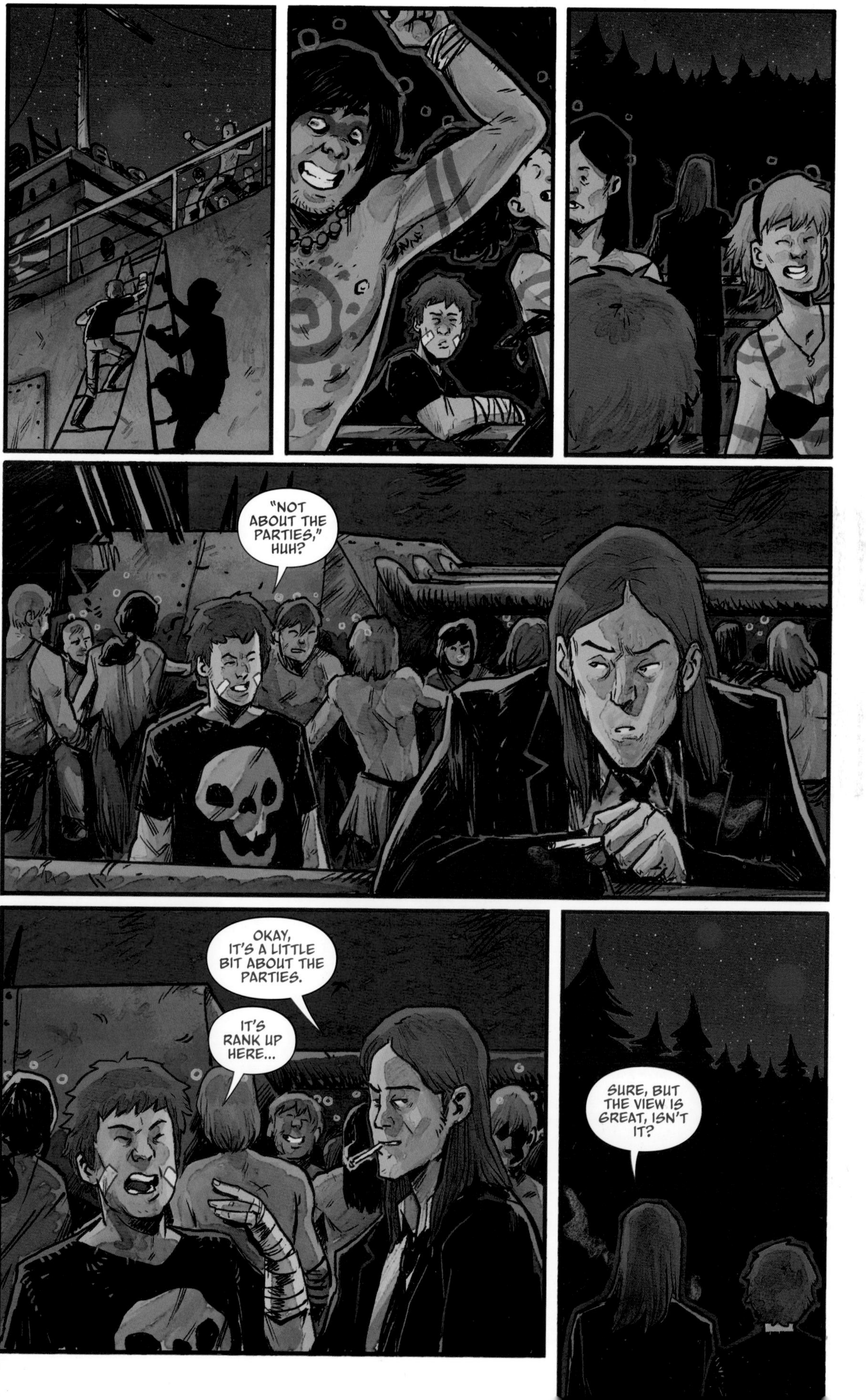
"NOT ABOUT THE PARTIES," HUH?
OKAY, IT'S A LITTLE BIT ABOUT THE PARTIES.
IT'S RANK UP HERE...
SURE, BUT THE VIEW IS GREAT, ISN'T IT?

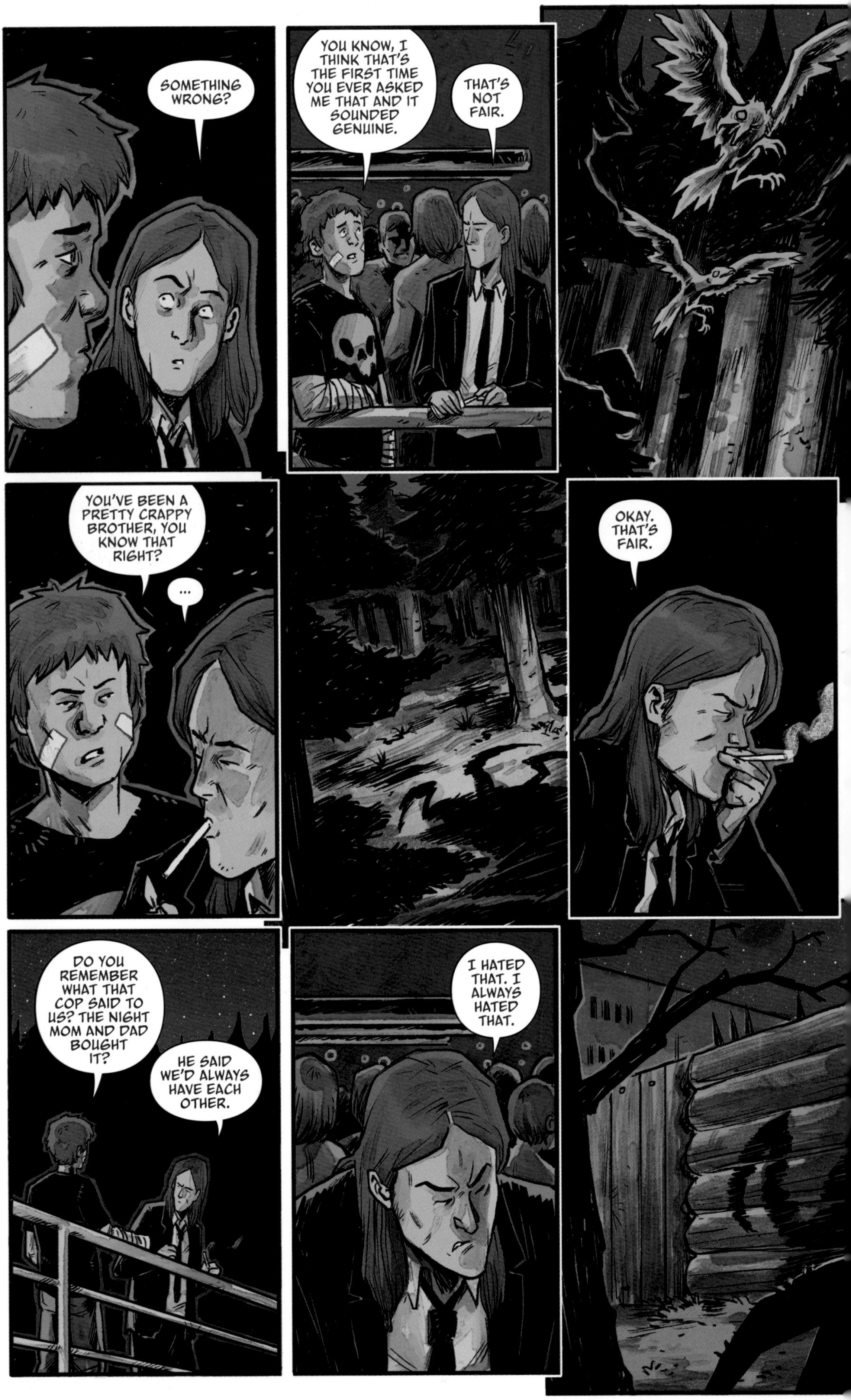
SOMETHING WRONG?
YOU KNOW, I THINK THAT'S THE FIRST TIME YOU EVER ASKED ME THAT AND IT SOUNDED GENUINE.
THAT'S NOT FAIR.
YOU'VE BEEN A PRETTY CRAPPY BROTHER, YOU KNOW THAT RIGHT?
...
OKAY. THAT'S FAIR.
DO YOU REMEMBER WHAT THAT COP SAID TO US? THE NIGHT MOM AND DAD BOUGHT IT?
HE SAID WE'D ALWAYS HAVE EACH OTHER.
I HATED THAT. I ALWAYS HATED THAT.

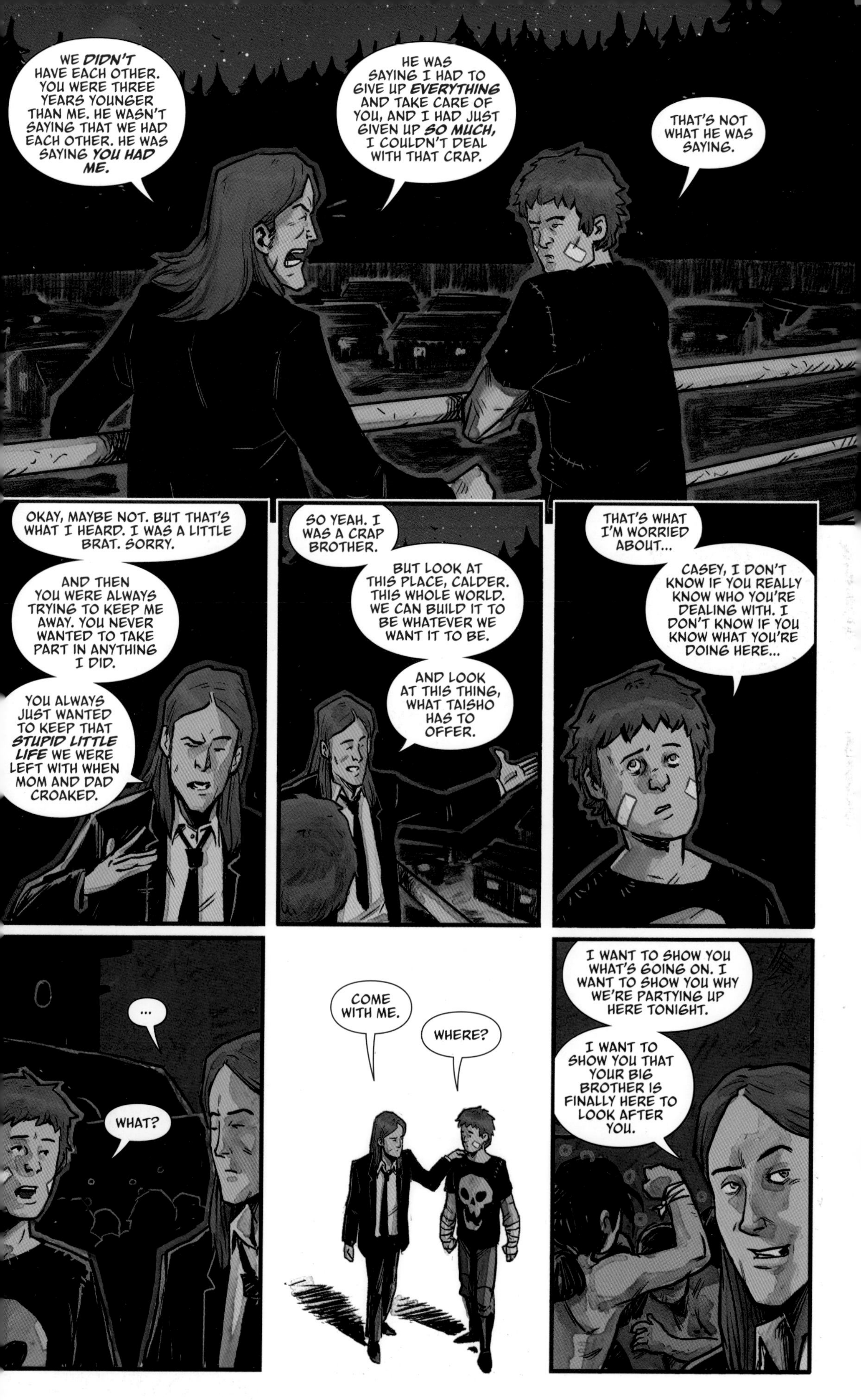
WE DIDN'T HAVE EACH OTHER. YOU WERE THREE YEARS YOUNGER THAN ME. HE WASN'T SAYING THAT WE HAD EACH OTHER. HE WAS SAYING YOU HAD ME.
HE WAS SAYING I HAD TO GIVE UP EVERYTHING AND TAKE CARE OF YOU, AND I HAD JUST GIVEN UP SO MUCH, I COULDN'T DEAL WITH THAT CRAP.
THAT'S NOT WHAT HE WAS SAYING.
OKAY, MAYBE NOT. BUT THAT'S WHAT I HEARD. I WAS A LITTLE BRAT. SORRY.
AND THEN YOU WERE ALWAYS TRYING TO KEEP ME AWAY. YOU NEVER WANTED TO TAKE PART IN ANYTHING I DID.
YOU ALWAYS JUST WANTED TO KEEP THAT STUPID LITTLE LIFE WE WERE LEFT WITH WHEN MOM AND DAD CROAKED.
SO YEAH. I WAS A CRAP BROTHER.
BUT LOOK AT THIS PLACE, CALDER. THIS WHOLE WORLD. WE CAN BUILD IT TO BE WHATEVER WE WANT IT TO BE.
AND LOOK AT THIS THING, WHAT TAISHO HAS TO OFFER.
THAT'S WHAT I'M WORRIED ABOUT...
CASEY, I DON'T KNOW IF YOU REALLY KNOW WHO YOU'RE DEALING WITH. I DON'T KNOW IF YOU KNOW WHAT YOU'RE DOING HERE...
...
WHAT?
COME WITH ME.
WHERE?
I WANT TO SHOW YOU WHAT'S GOING ON. I WANT TO SHOW YOU WHY WE'RE PARTYING UP HERE TONIGHT.
I WANT TO SHOW YOU THAT YOUR BIG BROTHER IS FINALLY HERE TO LOOK AFTER YOU.

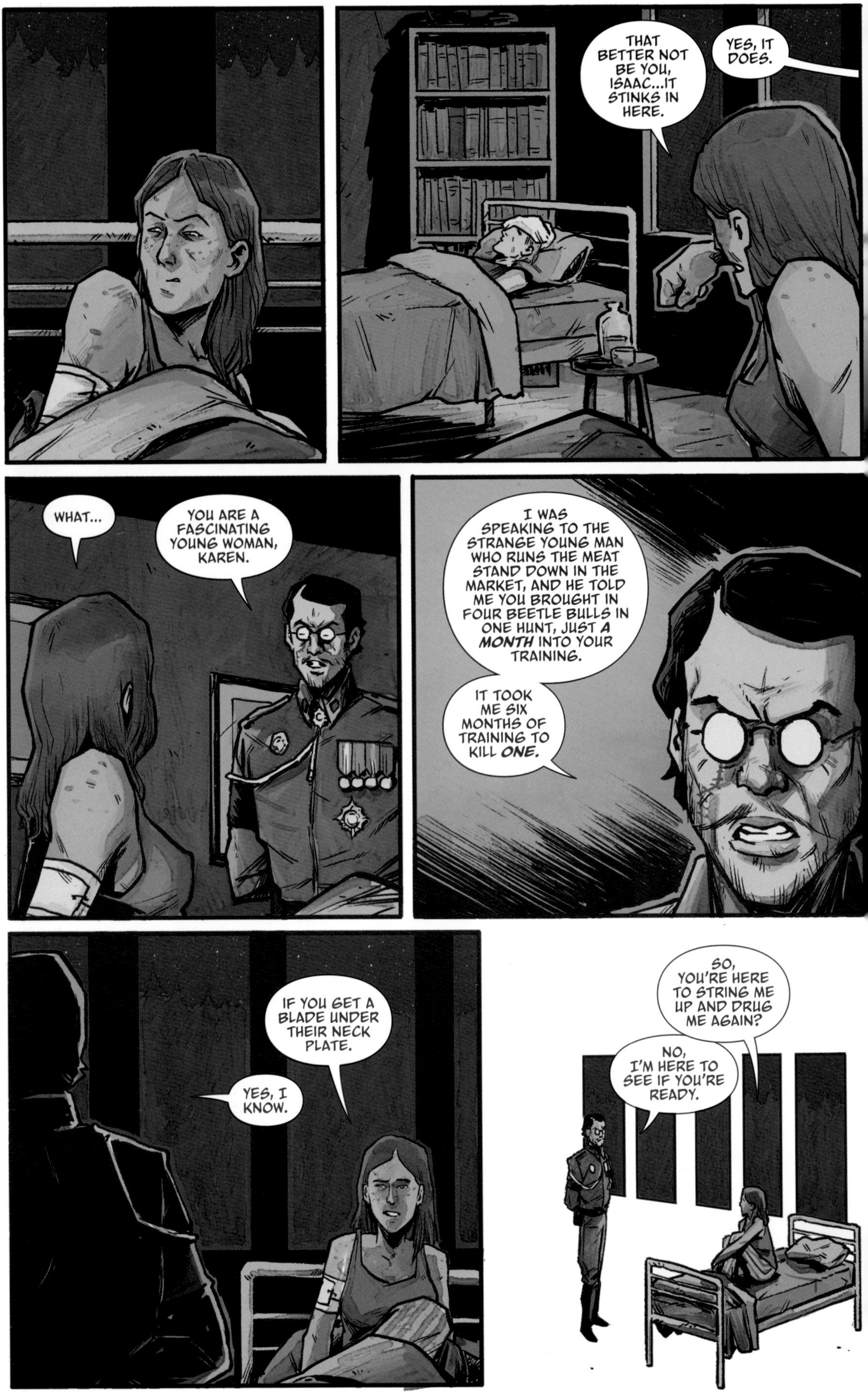
THAT BETTER NOT BE YOU, ISAAC...IT STINKS IN HERE.
YES, IT DOES.
WHAT...
YOU ARE A FASCINATING YOUNG WOMAN, KAREN.
I WAS SPEAKING TO THE STRANGE YOUNG MAN WHO RUNS THE MEAT STAND DOWN IN THE MARKET, AND HE TOLD ME YOU BROUGHT IN FOUR BEETLE BULLS IN ONE HUNT, JUST A MONTH INTO YOUR TRAINING.
IT TOOK ME SIX MONTHS OF TRAINING TO KILL ONE.
IF YOU GET A BLADE UNDER THEIR NECK PLATE.
YES, I KNOW.
SO, YOU'RE HERE TO STRING ME UP AND DRUG ME AGAIN?
NO, I'M HERE TO SEE IF YOU'RE READY.

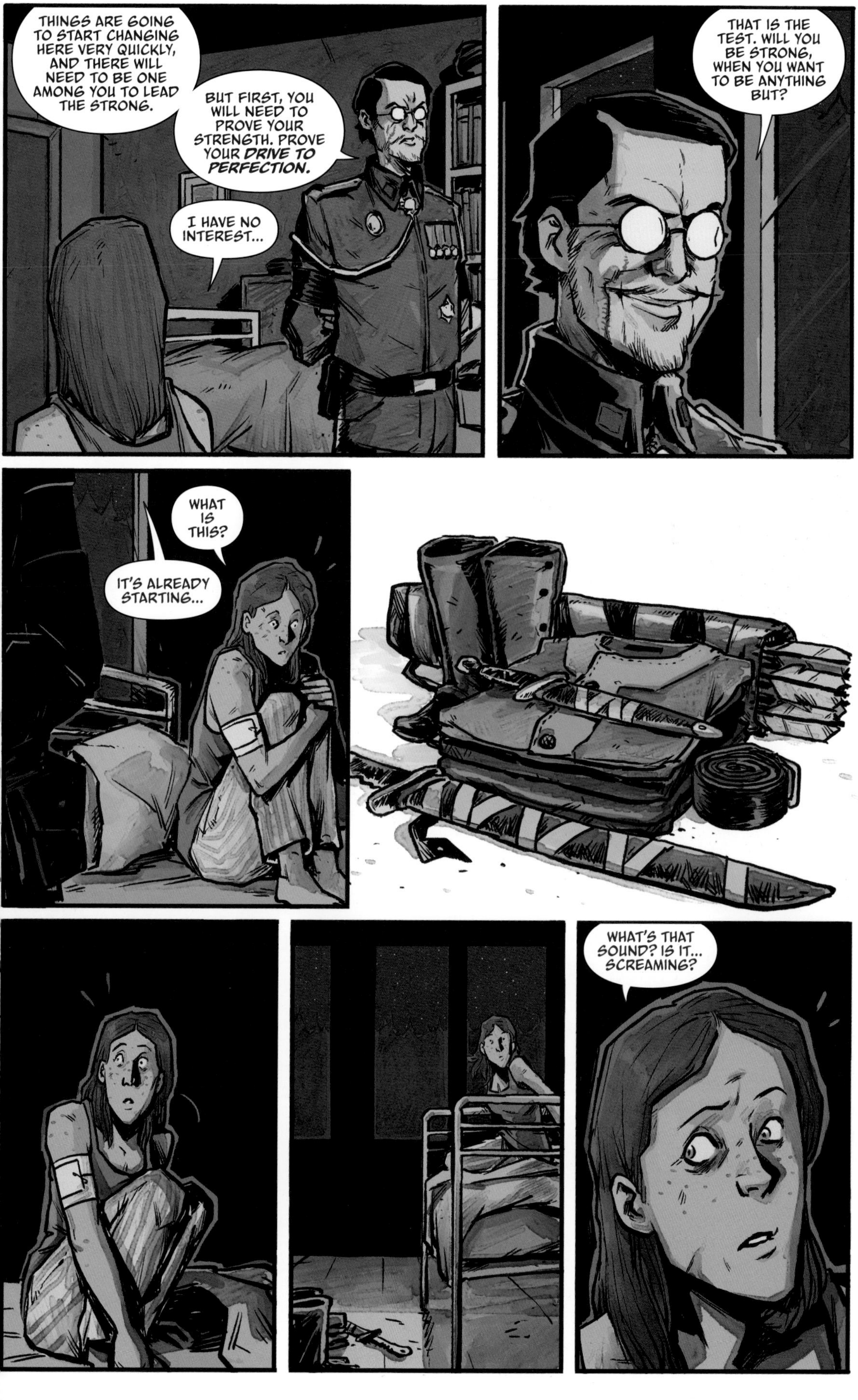
THINGS ARE GOING TO START CHANGING HERE VERY QUICKLY, AND THERE WILL NEED TO BE ONE AMONG YOU TO LEAD THE STRONG.
BUT FIRST, YOU WILL NEED TO PROVE YOUR STRENGTH. PROVE YOUR *DRIVE TO PERFECTION.*
I HAVE NO INTEREST...
THAT IS THE TEST. WILL YOU BE STRONG, WHEN YOU WANT TO BE ANYTHING BUT?
WHAT IS THIS?
IT'S ALREADY STARTING...
WHAT'S THAT SOUND? IS IT... SCREAMING?

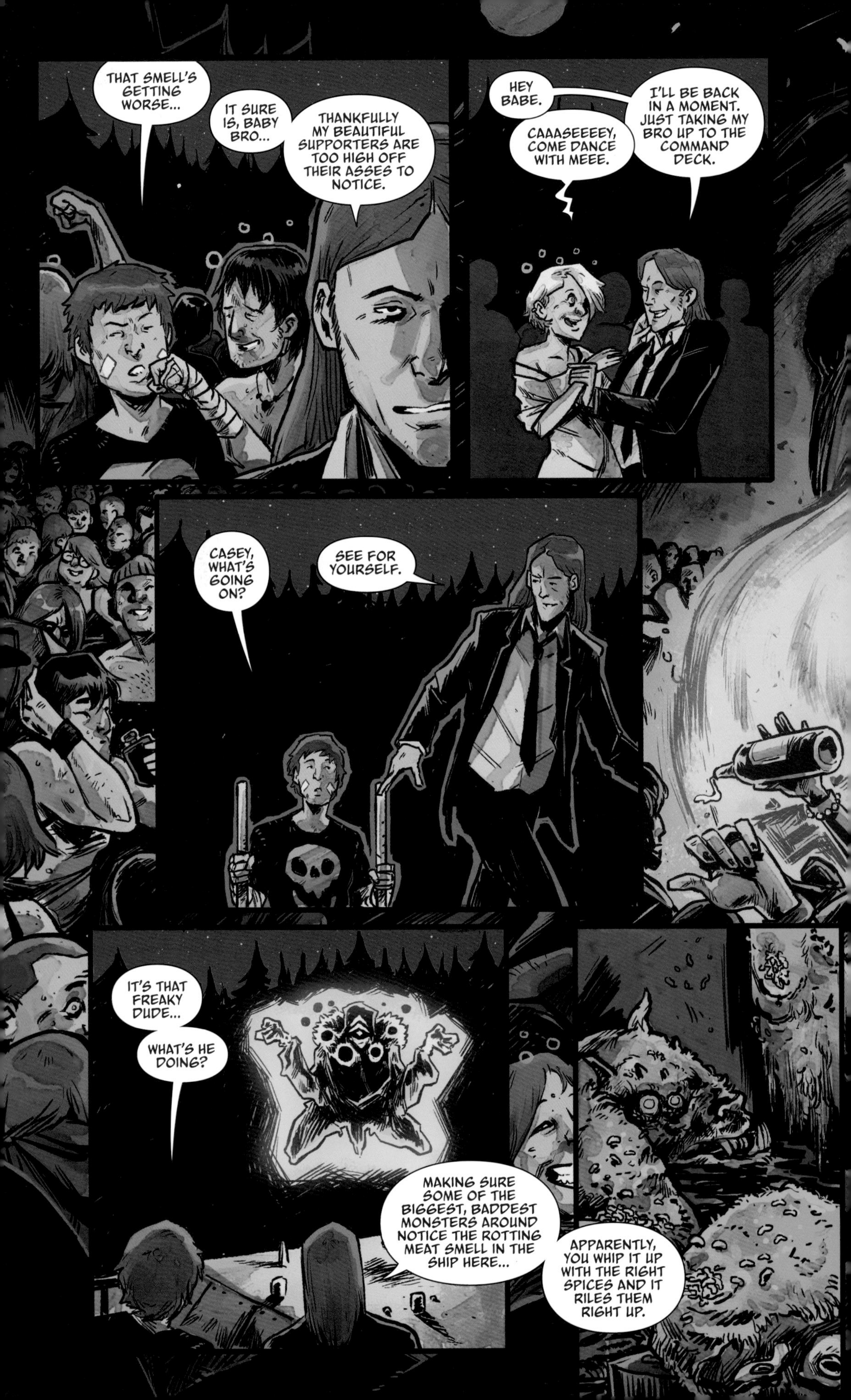
THAT SMELL'S GETTING WORSE...
IT SURE IS, BABY BRO...
THANKFULLY MY BEAUTIFUL SUPPORTERS ARE TOO HIGH OFF THEIR ASSES TO NOTICE.
HEY BABE.
CAAASEEEEY, COME DANCE WITH MEEE.
I'LL BE BACK IN A MOMENT. JUST TAKING MY BRO UP TO THE COMMAND DECK.
CASEY, WHAT'S GOING ON?
SEE FOR YOURSELF.
IT'S THAT FREAKY DUDE...
WHAT'S HE DOING?
MAKING SURE SOME OF THE BIGGEST, BADDEST MONSTERS AROUND NOTICE THE ROTTING MEAT SMELL IN THE SHIP HERE...
APPARENTLY, YOU WHIP IT UP WITH THE RIGHT SPICES AND IT RILES THEM RIGHT UP.

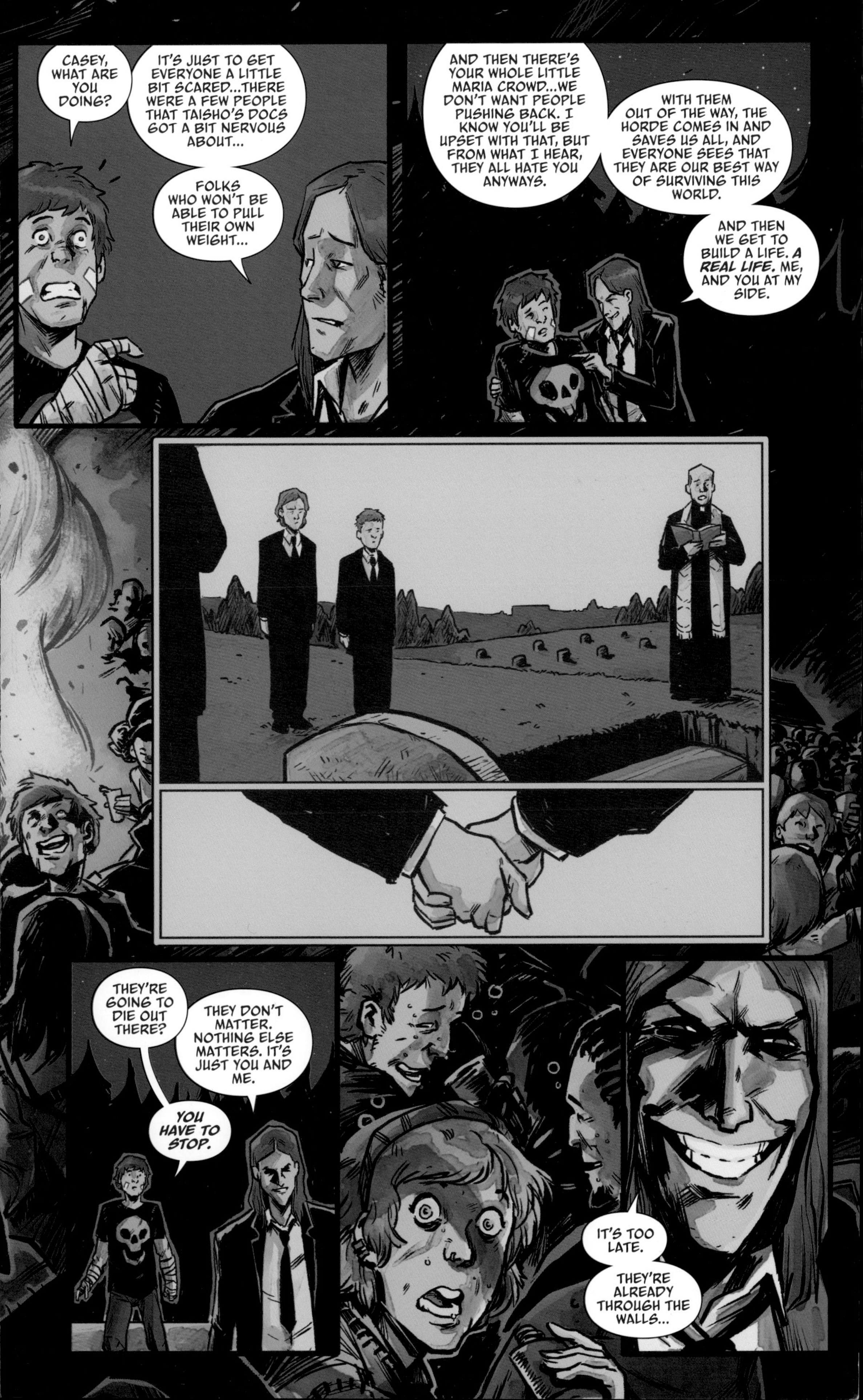
CASEY, WHAT ARE YOU DOING?
IT'S JUST TO GET EVERYONE A LITTLE BIT SCARED...THERE WERE A FEW PEOPLE THAT TAISHO'S DOCS GOT A BIT NERVOUS ABOUT...
FOLKS WHO WON'T BE ABLE TO PULL THEIR OWN WEIGHT...
AND THEN THERE'S YOUR WHOLE LITTLE MARIA CROWD...WE DON'T WANT PEOPLE PUSHING BACK. I KNOW YOU'LL BE UPSET WITH THAT, BUT FROM WHAT I HEAR, THEY ALL HATE YOU ANYWAYS.
WITH THEM OUT OF THE WAY, THE HORDE COMES IN AND SAVES US ALL, AND EVERYONE SEES THAT THEY ARE OUR BEST WAY OF SURVIVING THIS WORLD.
AND THEN WE GET TO BUILD A LIFE. A *REAL LIFE.* ME, AND YOU AT MY SIDE.
THEY'RE GOING TO DIE OUT THERE?
THEY DON'T MATTER. NOTHING ELSE MATTERS. IT'S JUST YOU AND ME.
YOU HAVE TO STOP.
IT'S TOO LATE.
THEY'RE ALREADY THROUGH THE WALLS...

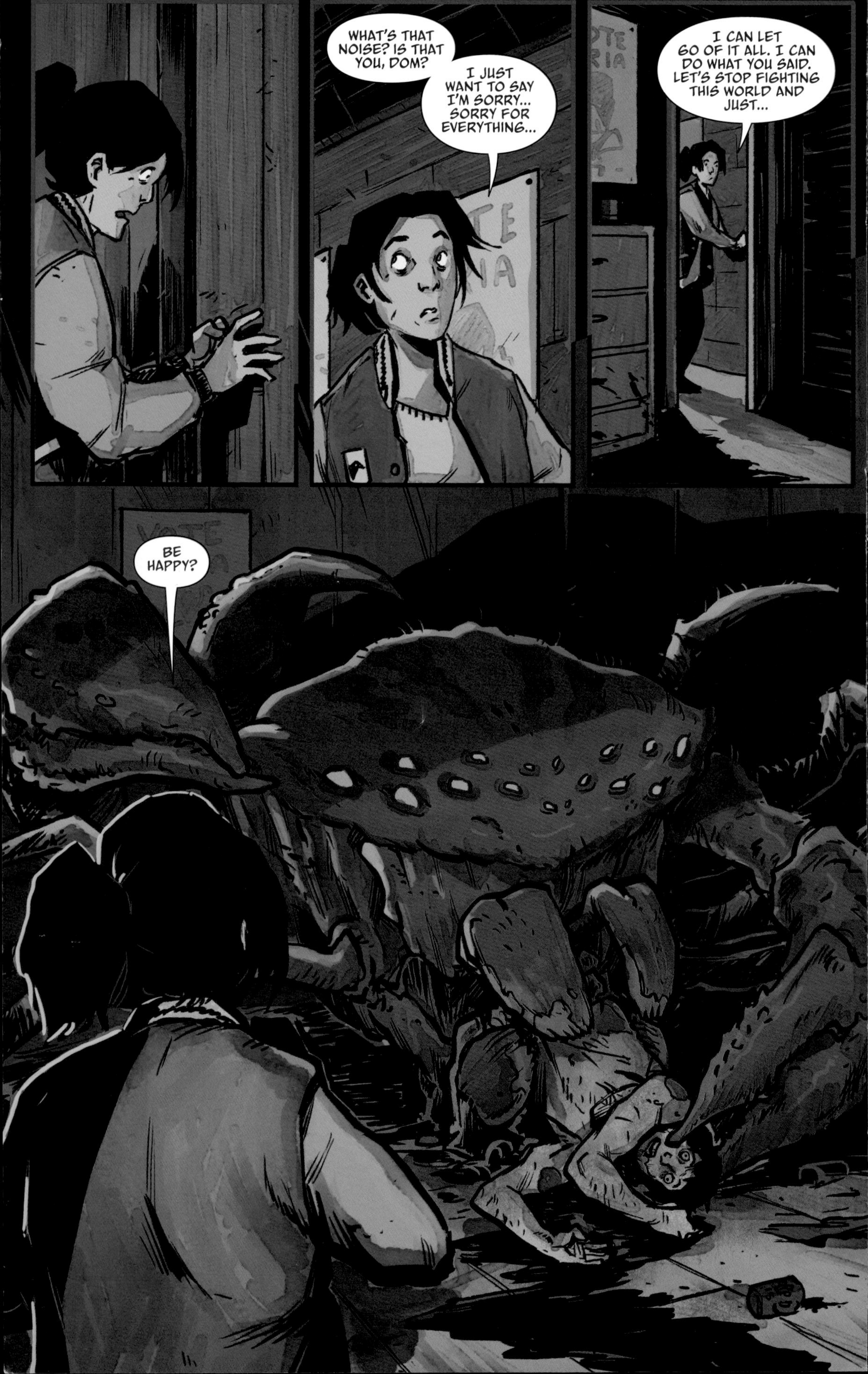
WHAT'S THAT NOISE? IS THAT YOU, DOM?
I JUST WANT TO SAY I'M SORRY... SORRY FOR EVERYTHING...
I CAN LET GO OF IT ALL. I CAN DO WHAT YOU SAID. LET'S STOP FIGHTING THIS WORLD AND JUST...
BE HAPPY?

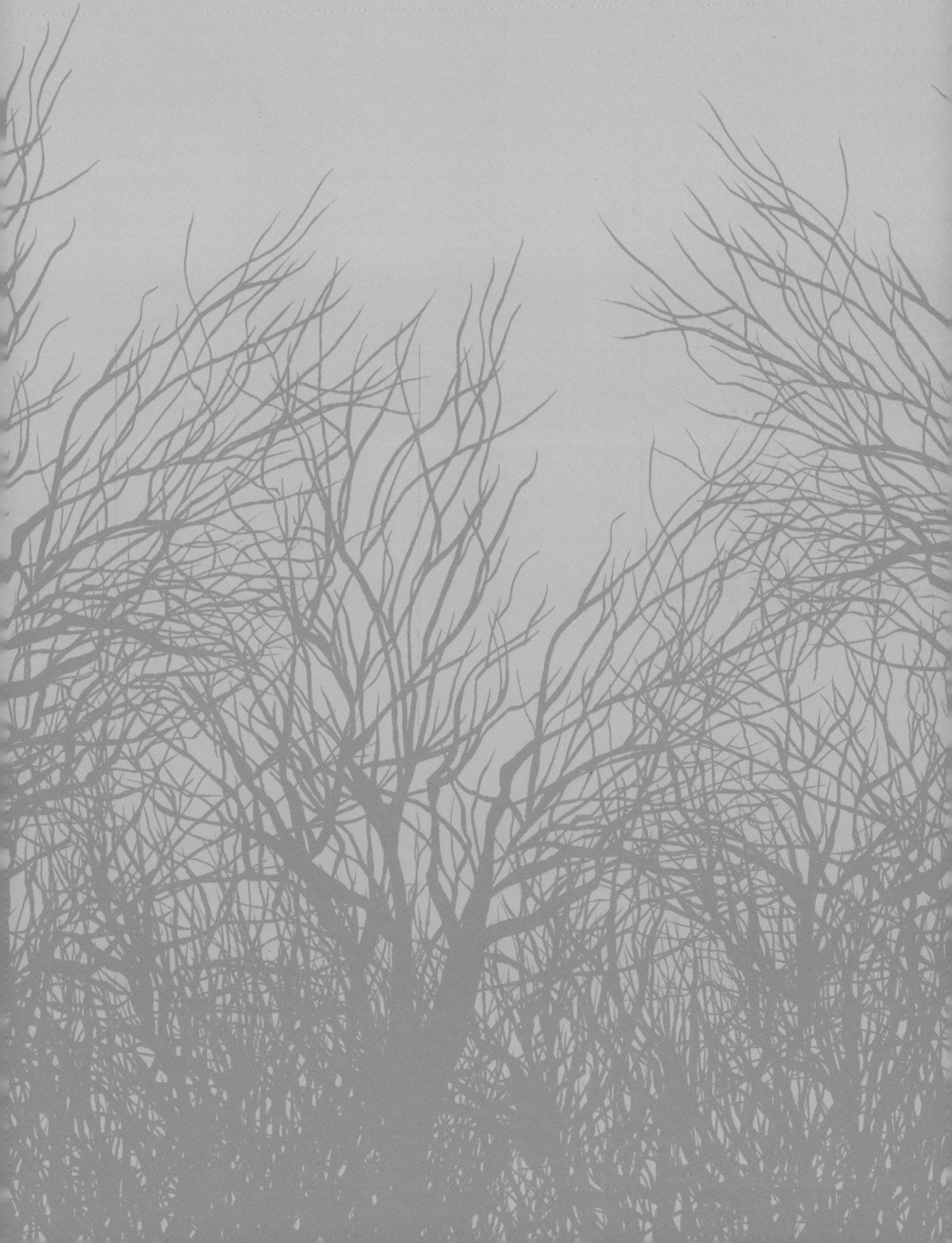

CHAPTER NINETEEN

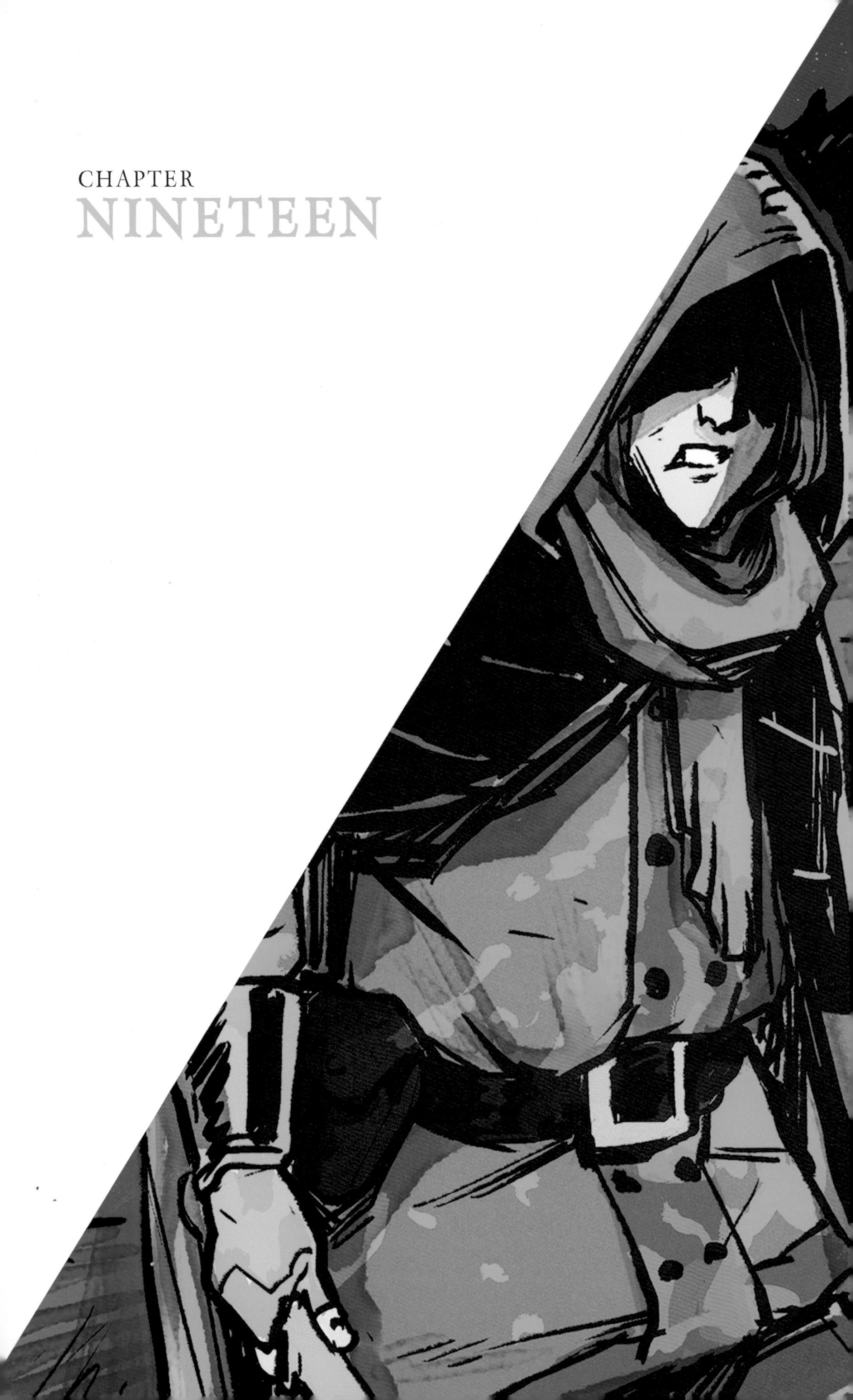

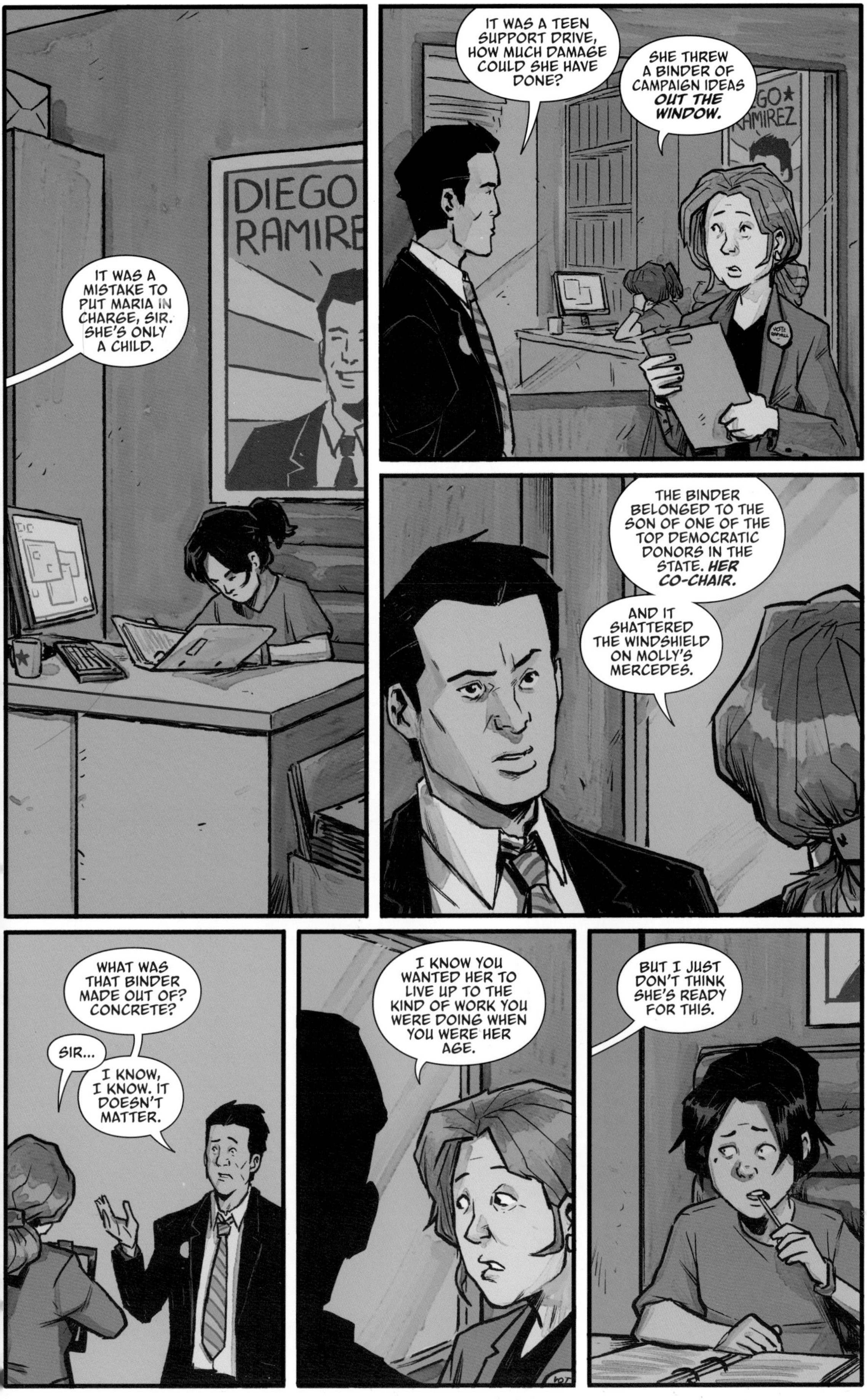

DIEGO RAMIRE
IT WAS A MISTAKE TO PUT MARIA IN CHARGE, SIR. SHE'S ONLY A CHILD.
IT WAS A TEEN SUPPORT DRIVE, HOW MUCH DAMAGE COULD SHE HAVE DONE?
SHE THREW A BINDER OF CAMPAIGN IDEAS ***OUT THE WINDOW.***
DIEGO RAMIREZ
THE BINDER BELONGED TO THE SON OF ONE OF THE TOP DEMOCRATIC DONORS IN THE STATE. ***HER CO-CHAIR.***
AND IT SHATTERED THE WINDSHIELD ON MOLLY'S MERCEDES.
WHAT WAS THAT BINDER MADE OUT OF? CONCRETE?
SIR...
I KNOW, I KNOW. IT DOESN'T MATTER.
I KNOW YOU WANTED HER TO LIVE UP TO THE KIND OF WORK YOU WERE DOING WHEN YOU WERE HER AGE.
BUT I JUST DON'T THINK SHE'S READY FOR THIS.

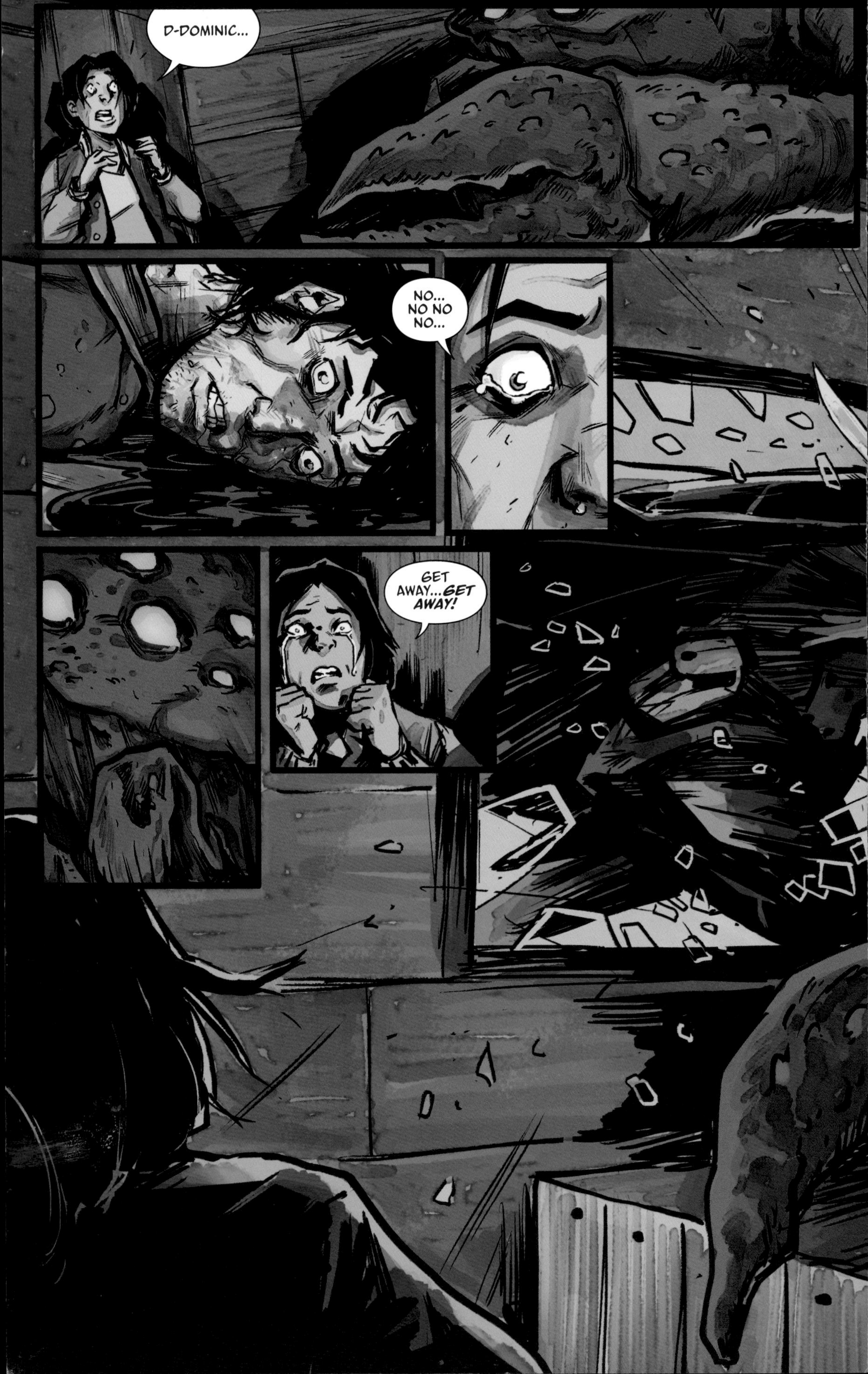
D-DOMINIC...
NO... NO NO NO...
GET AWAY...GET AWAY!

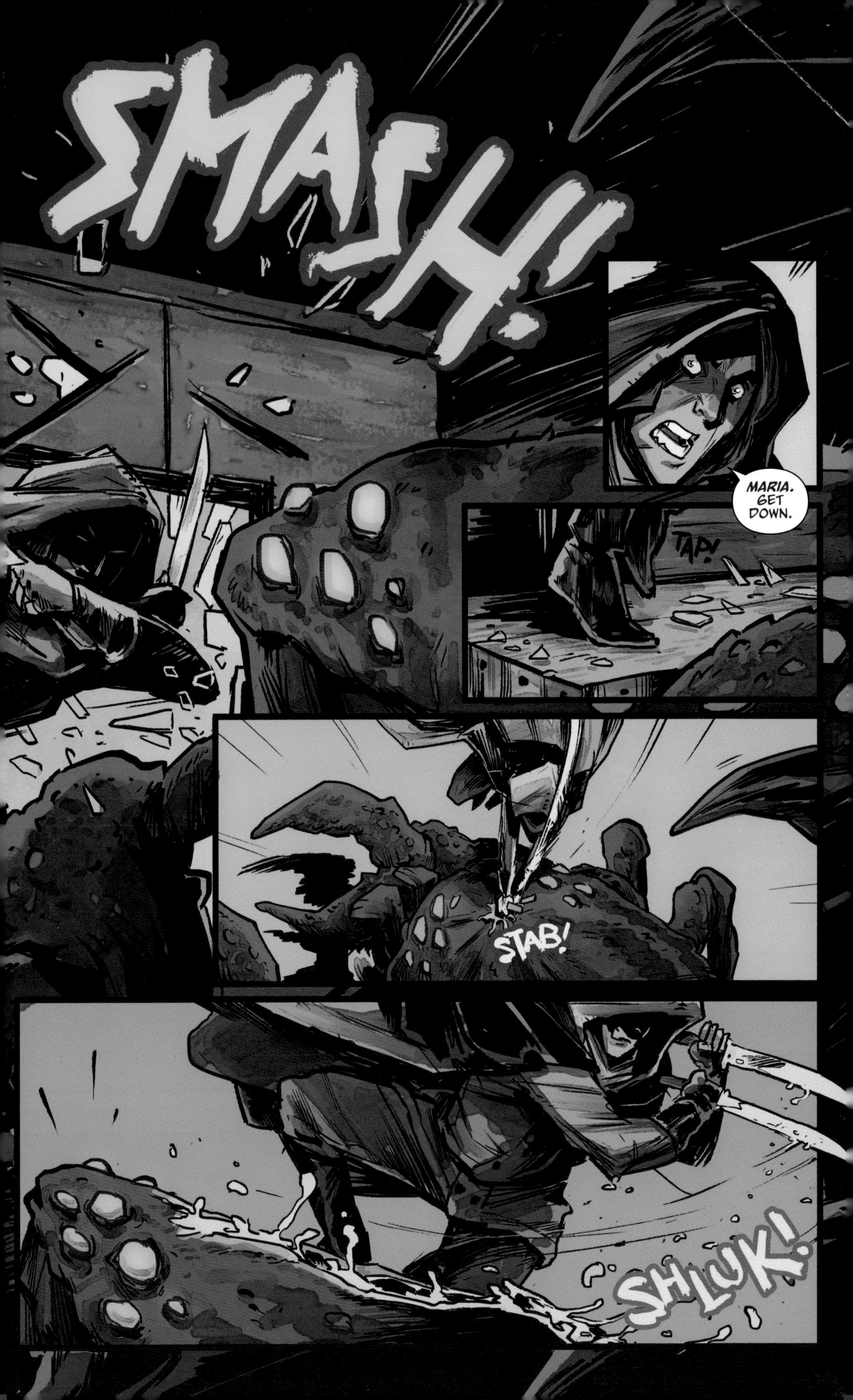
SMASH!
MARIA. GET DOWN.
TAP!
STAB!
SHLUK!

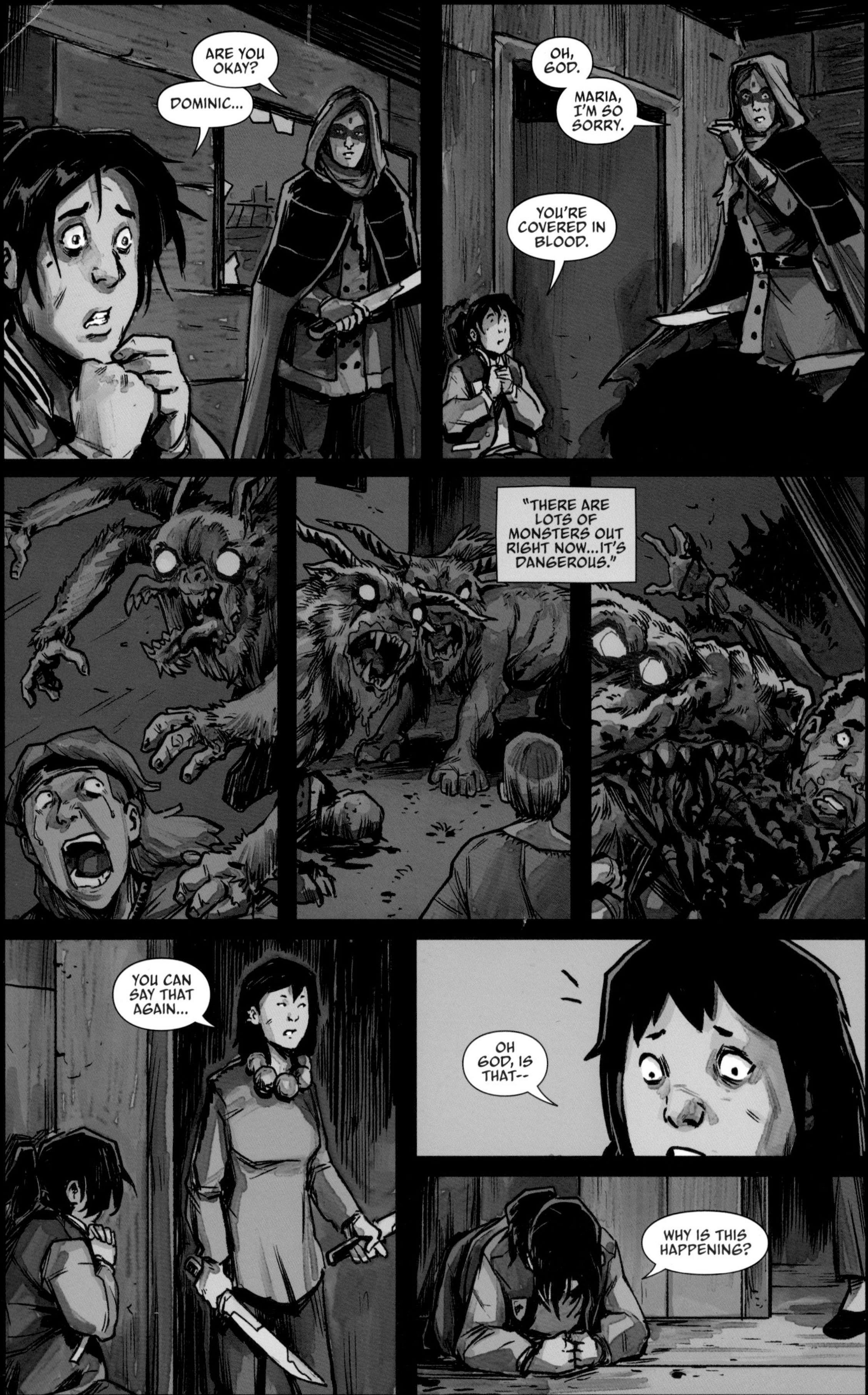
ARE YOU OKAY?
DOMINIC...
OH, GOD.
MARIA, I'M SO SORRY.
YOU'RE COVERED IN BLOOD.
"THERE ARE LOTS OF MONSTERS OUT RIGHT NOW...IT'S DANGEROUS."
YOU CAN SAY THAT AGAIN...
OH GOD, IS THAT--
WHY IS THIS HAPPENING?

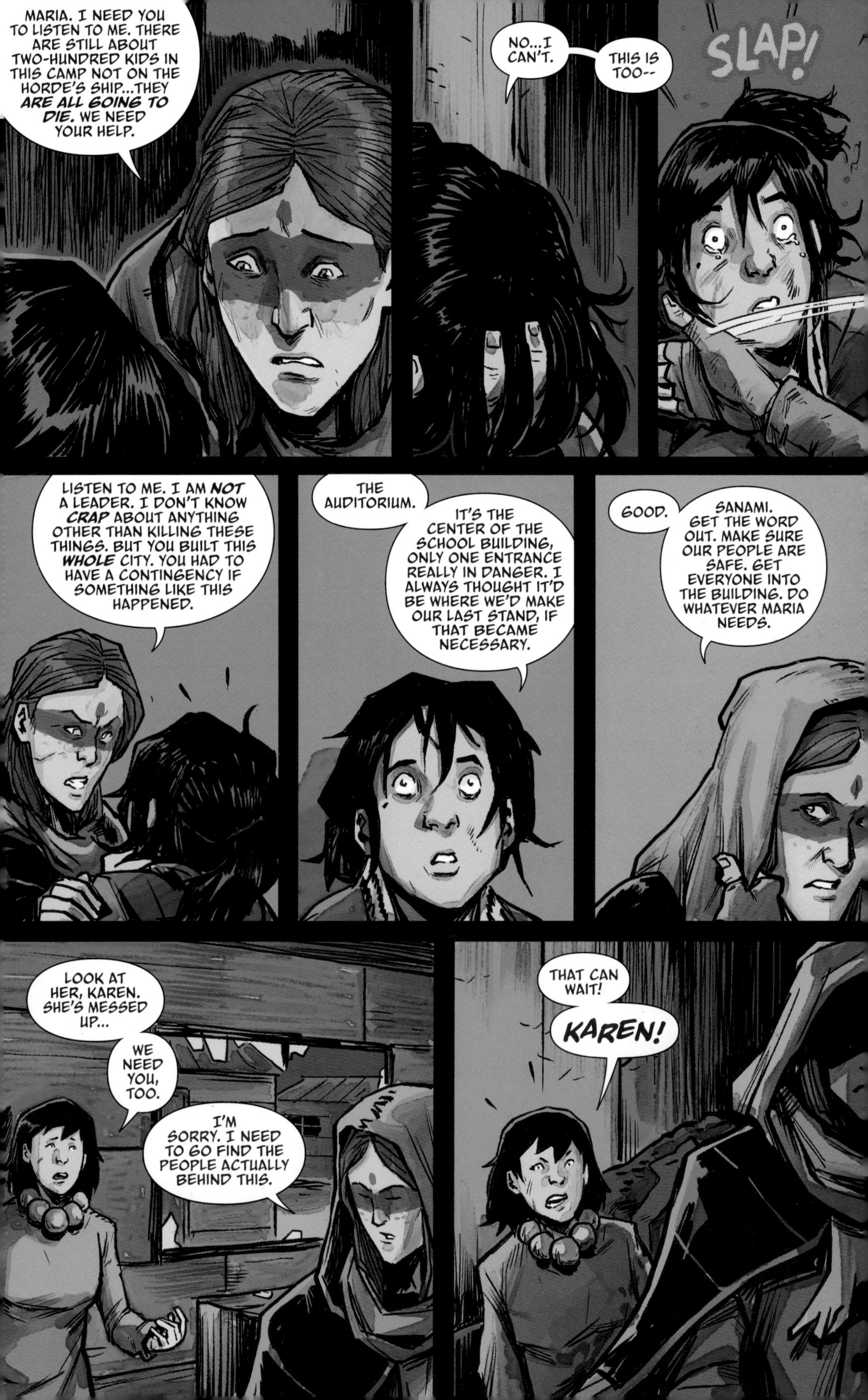
MARIA. I NEED YOU TO LISTEN TO ME. THERE ARE STILL ABOUT TWO-HUNDRED KIDS IN THIS CAMP NOT ON THE HORDE'S SHIP...THEY ARE ALL GOING TO DIE. WE NEED YOUR HELP.
NO...I CAN'T.
THIS IS TOO--
SLAP!
LISTEN TO ME. I AM NOT A LEADER. I DON'T KNOW CRAP ABOUT ANYTHING OTHER THAN KILLING THESE THINGS. BUT YOU BUILT THIS WHOLE CITY. YOU HAD TO HAVE A CONTINGENCY IF SOMETHING LIKE THIS HAPPENED.
THE AUDITORIUM.
IT'S THE CENTER OF THE SCHOOL BUILDING, ONLY ONE ENTRANCE REALLY IN DANGER. I ALWAYS THOUGHT IT'D BE WHERE WE'D MAKE OUR LAST STAND, IF THAT BECAME NECESSARY.
GOOD.
SANAMI. GET THE WORD OUT. MAKE SURE OUR PEOPLE ARE SAFE. GET EVERYONE INTO THE BUILDING. DO WHATEVER MARIA NEEDS.
LOOK AT HER, KAREN. SHE'S MESSED UP...
WE NEED YOU, TOO.
I'M SORRY. I NEED TO GO FIND THE PEOPLE ACTUALLY BEHIND THIS.
THAT CAN WAIT!
KAREN!

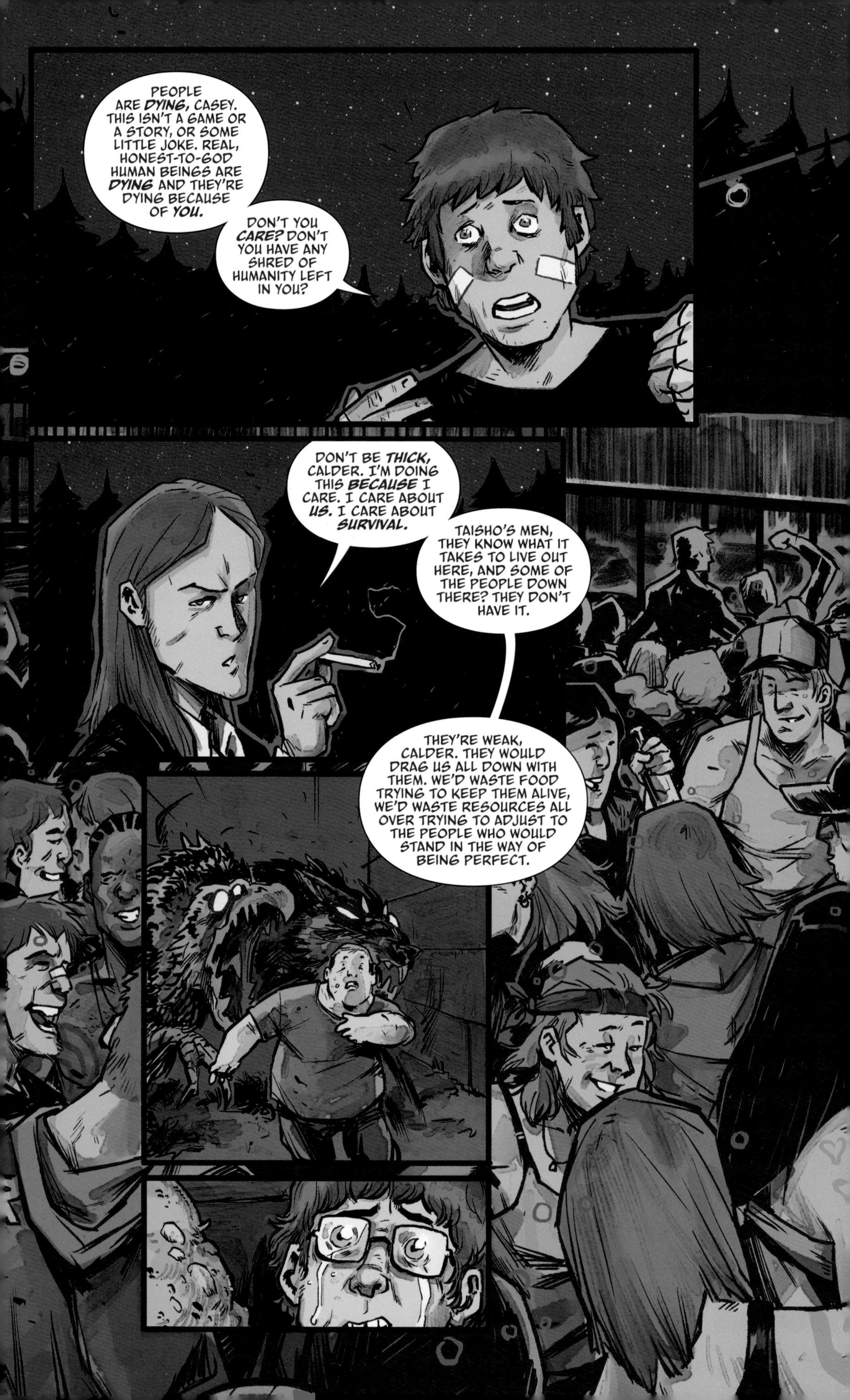
PEOPLE ARE DYING, CASEY. THIS ISN'T A GAME OR A STORY, OR SOME LITTLE JOKE. REAL, HONEST-TO-GOD HUMAN BEINGS ARE DYING AND THEY'RE DYING BECAUSE OF YOU.
DON'T YOU CARE? DON'T YOU HAVE ANY SHRED OF HUMANITY LEFT IN YOU?
DON'T BE THICK, CALDER. I'M DOING THIS BECAUSE I CARE. I CARE ABOUT US. I CARE ABOUT SURVIVAL.
TAISHO'S MEN, THEY KNOW WHAT IT TAKES TO LIVE OUT HERE, AND SOME OF THE PEOPLE DOWN THERE? THEY DON'T HAVE IT.
THEY'RE WEAK, CALDER. THEY WOULD DRAG US ALL DOWN WITH THEM. WE'D WASTE FOOD TRYING TO KEEP THEM ALIVE, WE'D WASTE RESOURCES ALL OVER TRYING TO ADJUST TO THE PEOPLE WHO WOULD STAND IN THE WAY OF BEING PERFECT.

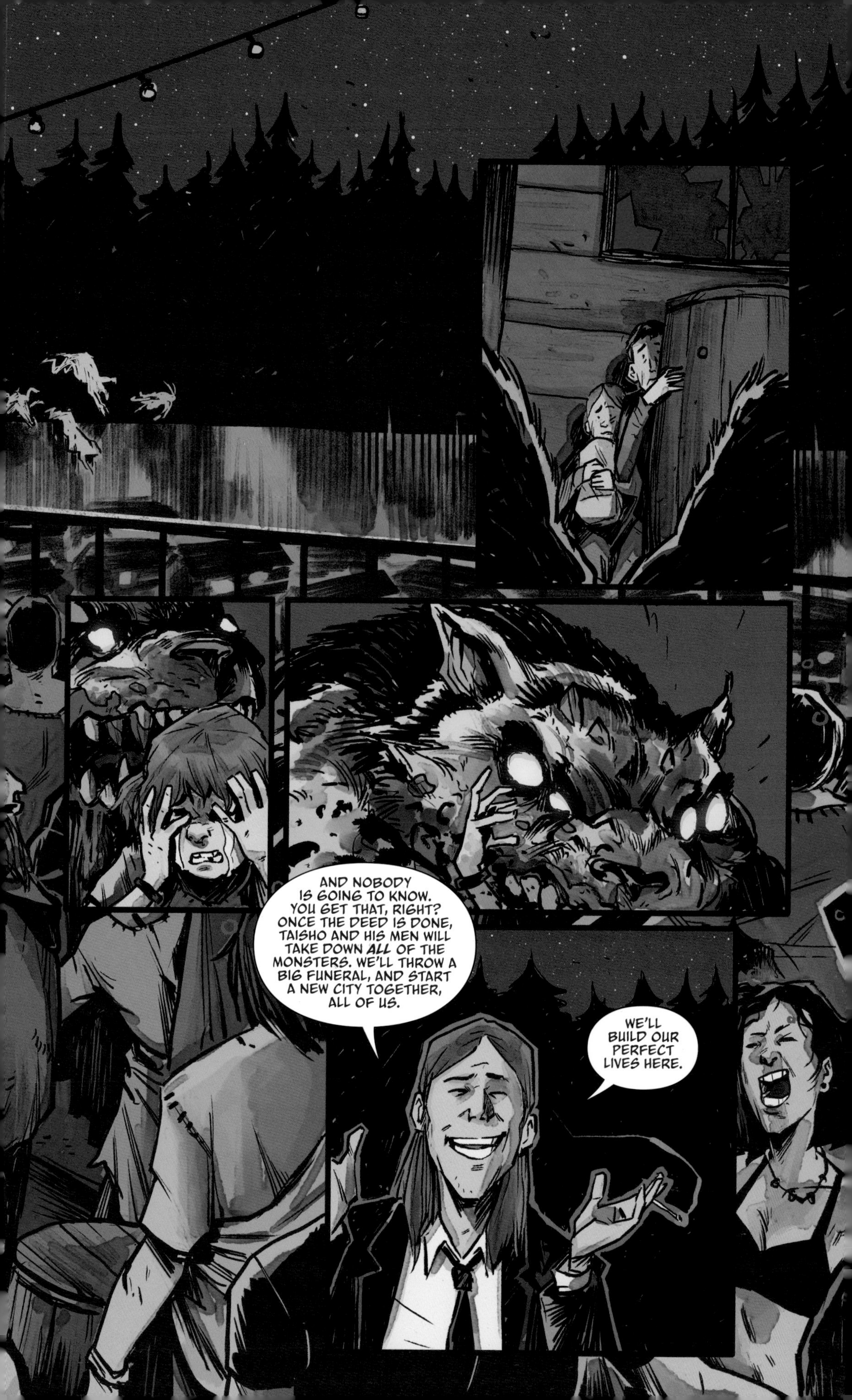
AND NOBODY IS GOING TO KNOW. YOU GET THAT, RIGHT? ONCE THE DEED IS DONE, TAISHO AND HIS MEN WILL TAKE DOWN *ALL* OF THE MONSTERS. WE'LL THROW A BIG FUNERAL, AND START A NEW CITY TOGETHER, ALL OF US.
WE'LL BUILD OUR PERFECT LIVES HERE.

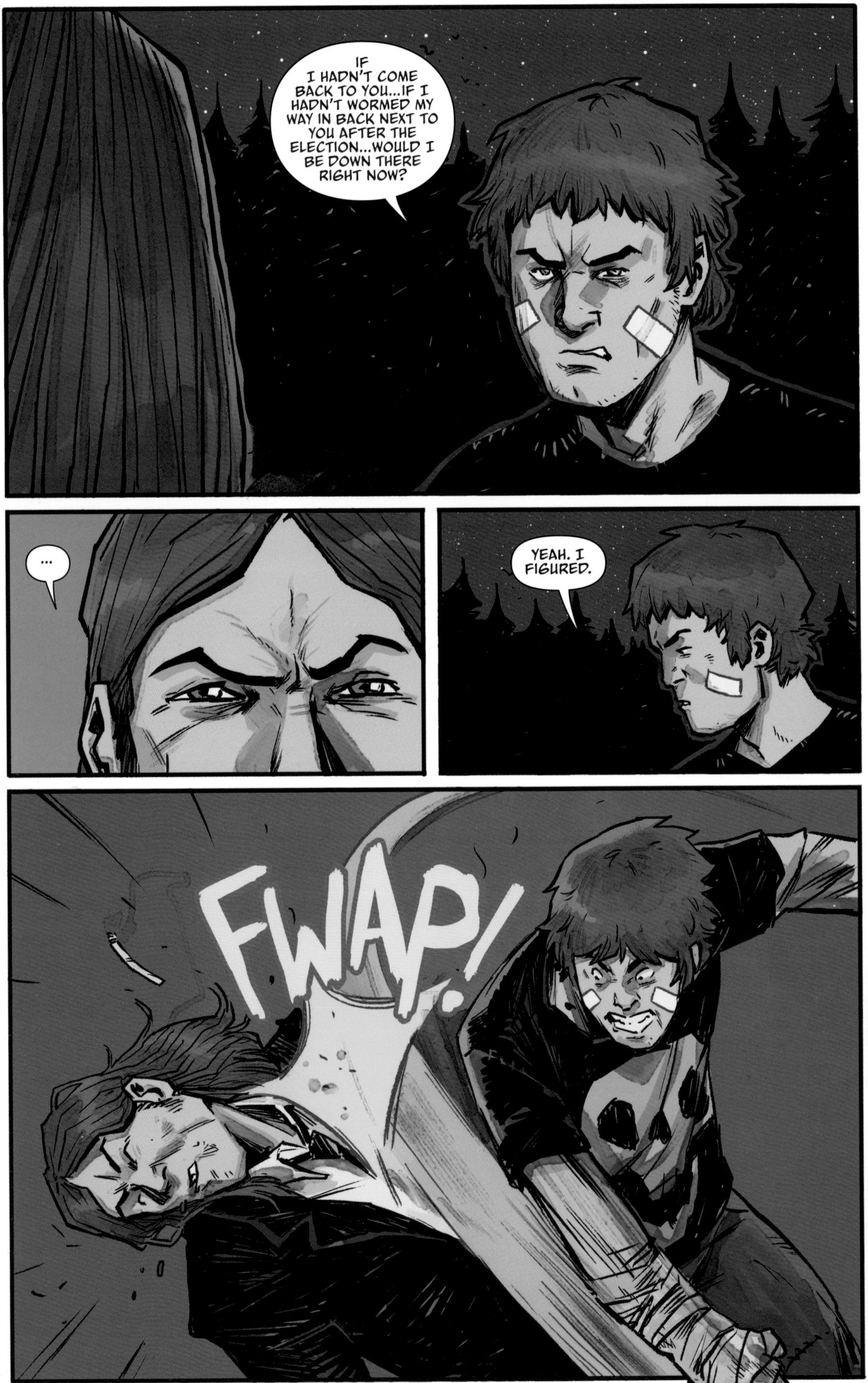
IF I HADN'T COME BACK TO YOU...IF I HADN'T WORMED MY WAY IN BACK NEXT TO YOU AFTER THE ELECTION...WOULD I BE DOWN THERE RIGHT NOW?
...
YEAH. I FIGURED.
FWAP!

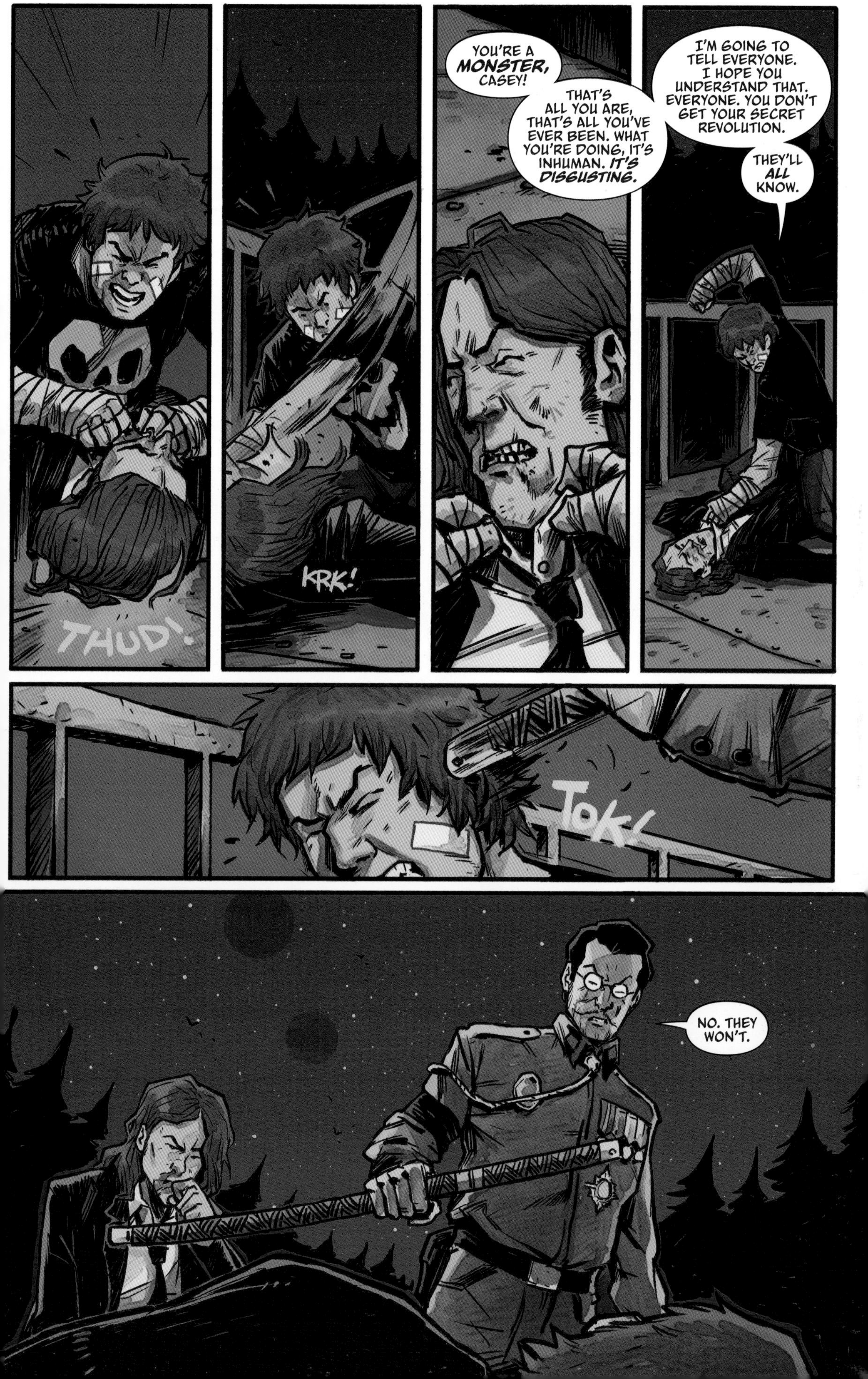
THUD!
KRK!
YOU'RE A MONSTER, CASEY!
THAT'S ALL YOU ARE, THAT'S ALL YOU'VE EVER BEEN. WHAT YOU'RE DOING, IT'S INHUMAN. IT'S DISGUSTING.
I'M GOING TO TELL EVERYONE. I HOPE YOU UNDERSTAND THAT. EVERYONE. YOU DON'T GET YOUR SECRET REVOLUTION.
THEY'LL ALL KNOW.
TOK!
NO. THEY WON'T.

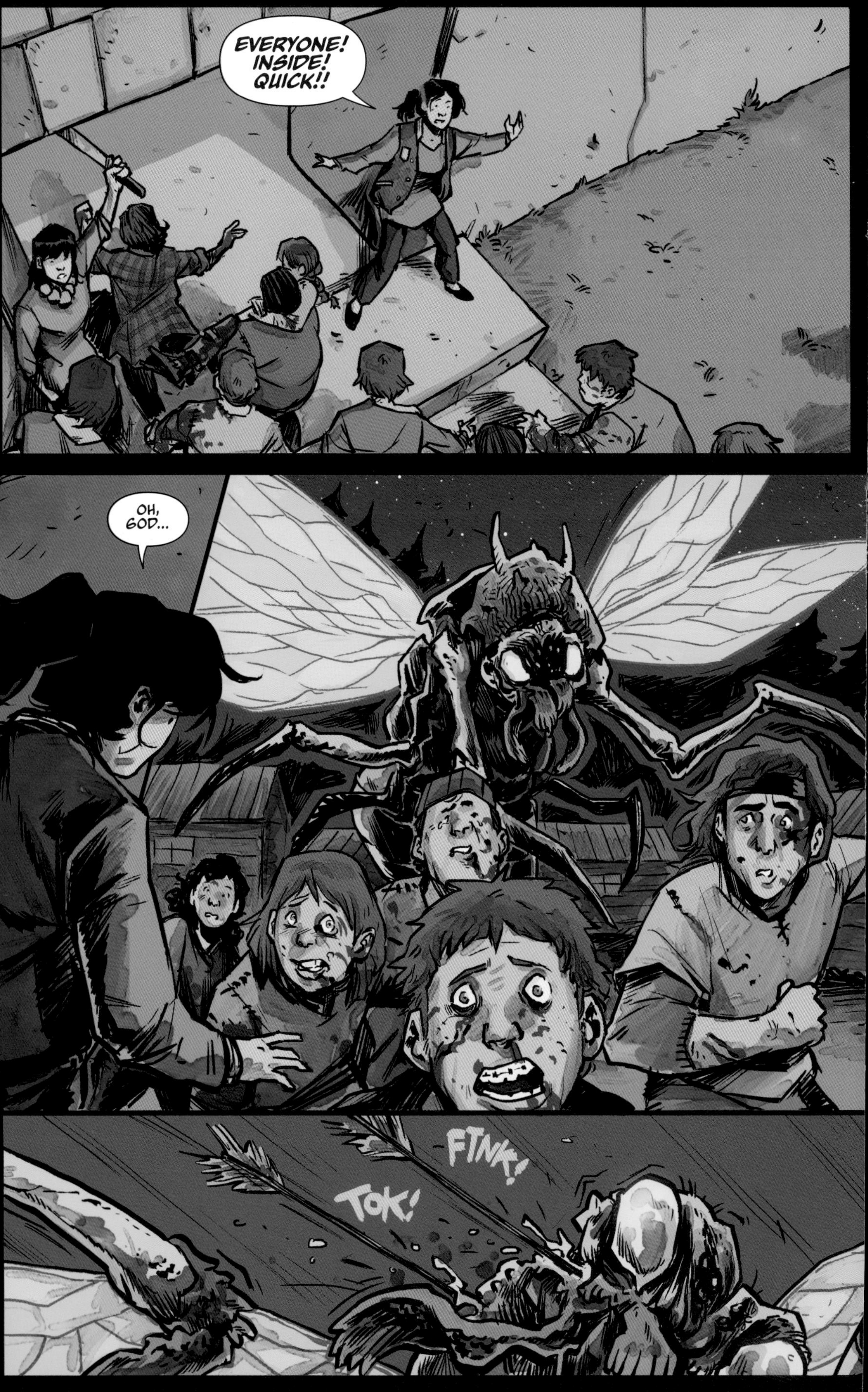
EVERYONE! INSIDE! QUICK!!
OH, GOD...
FTNK!
TOK!

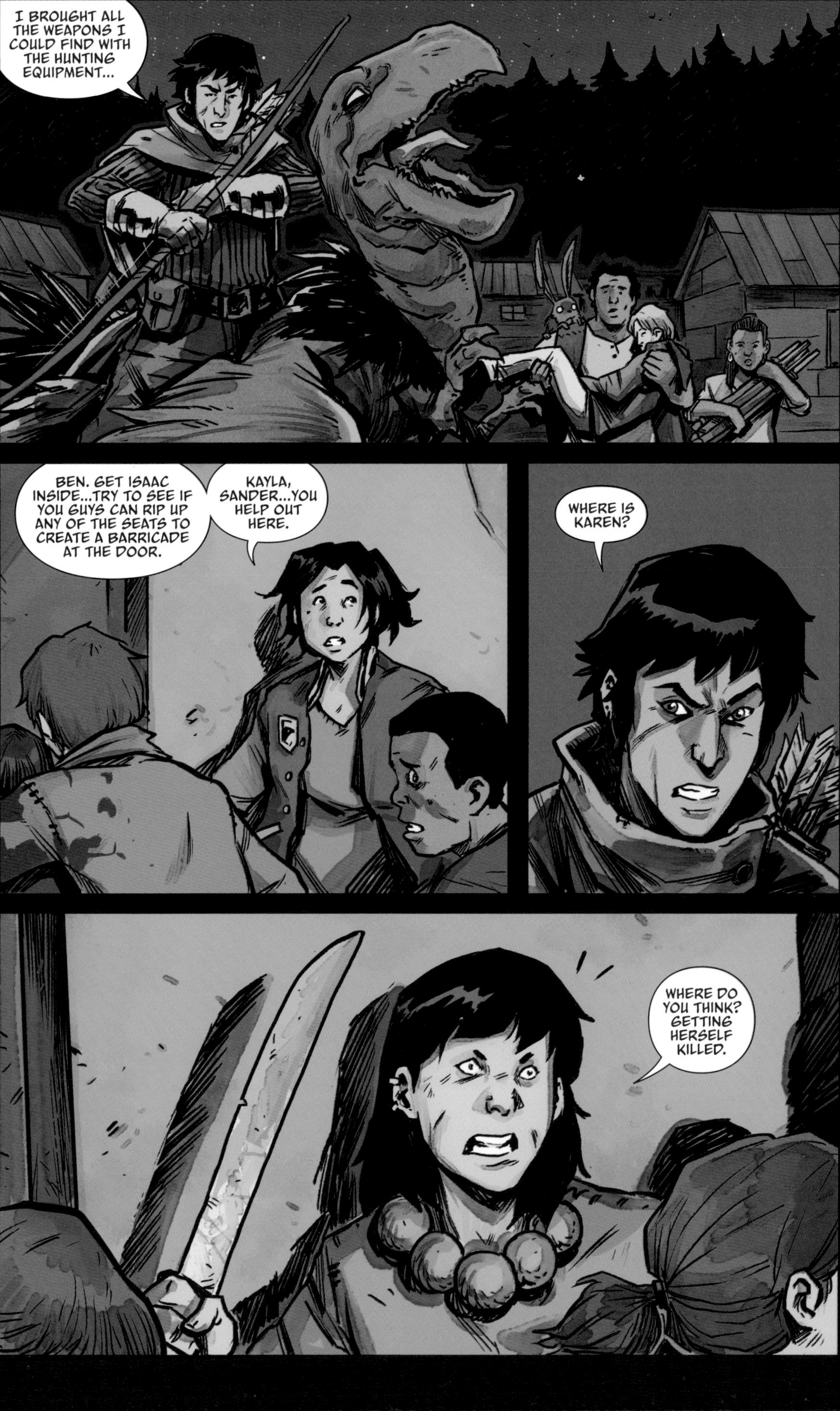
I BROUGHT ALL THE WEAPONS I COULD FIND WITH THE HUNTING EQUIPMENT...
BEN. GET ISAAC INSIDE...TRY TO SEE IF YOU GUYS CAN RIP UP ANY OF THE SEATS TO CREATE A BARRICADE AT THE DOOR.
KAYLA, SANDER...YOU HELP OUT HERE.
WHERE IS KAREN?
WHERE DO YOU THINK? GETTING HERSELF KILLED.

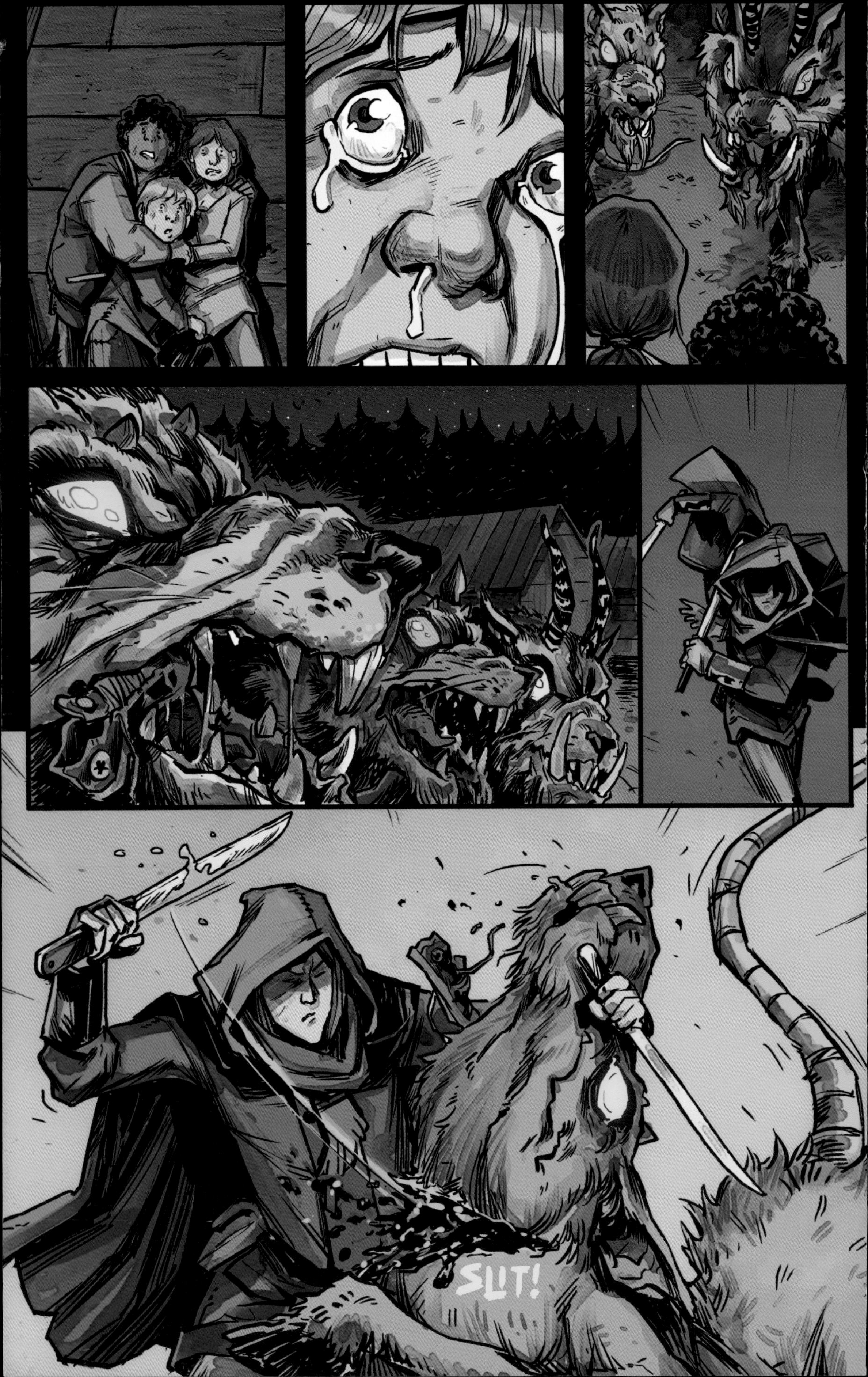
SLIT!

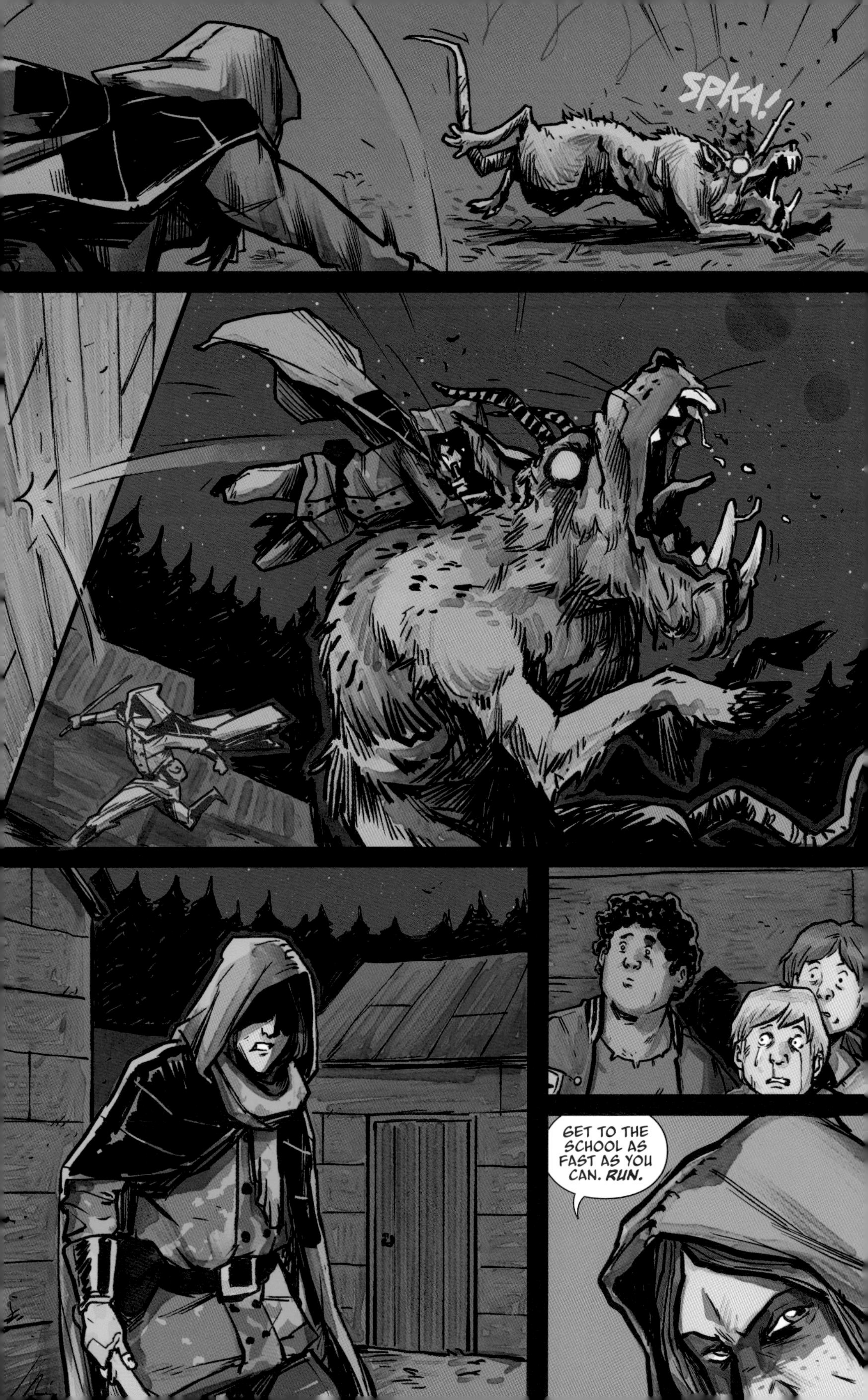
SPKA!
GET TO THE SCHOOL AS FAST AS YOU CAN. *RUN.*

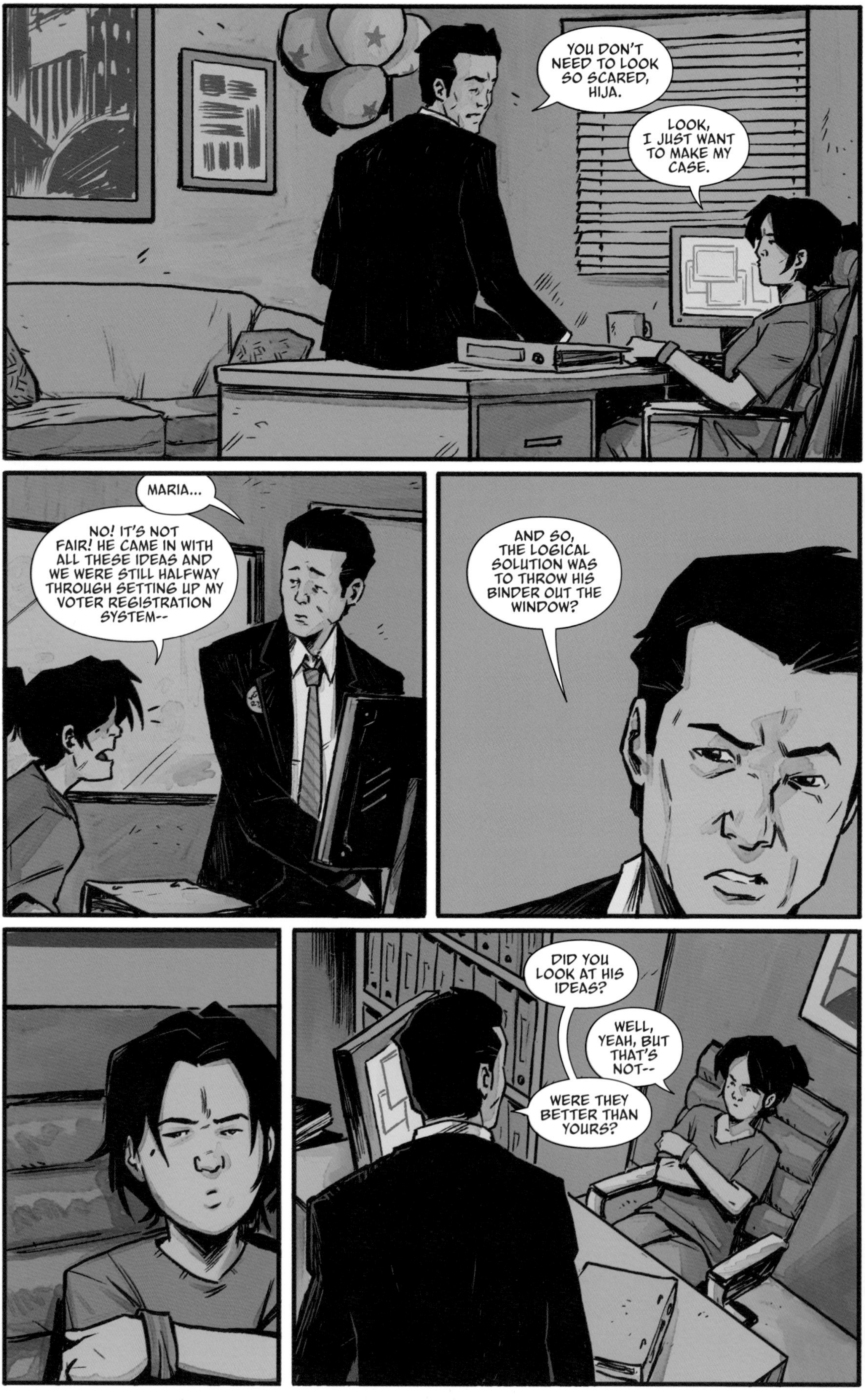
YOU DON'T NEED TO LOOK SO SCARED, HIJA.
LOOK, I JUST WANT TO MAKE MY CASE.
MARIA...
NO! IT'S NOT FAIR! HE CAME IN WITH ALL THESE IDEAS AND WE WERE STILL HALFWAY THROUGH SETTING UP MY VOTER REGISTRATION SYSTEM--
AND SO, THE LOGICAL SOLUTION WAS TO THROW HIS BINDER OUT THE WINDOW?
DID YOU LOOK AT HIS IDEAS?
WELL, YEAH, BUT THAT'S NOT--
WERE THEY BETTER THAN YOURS?

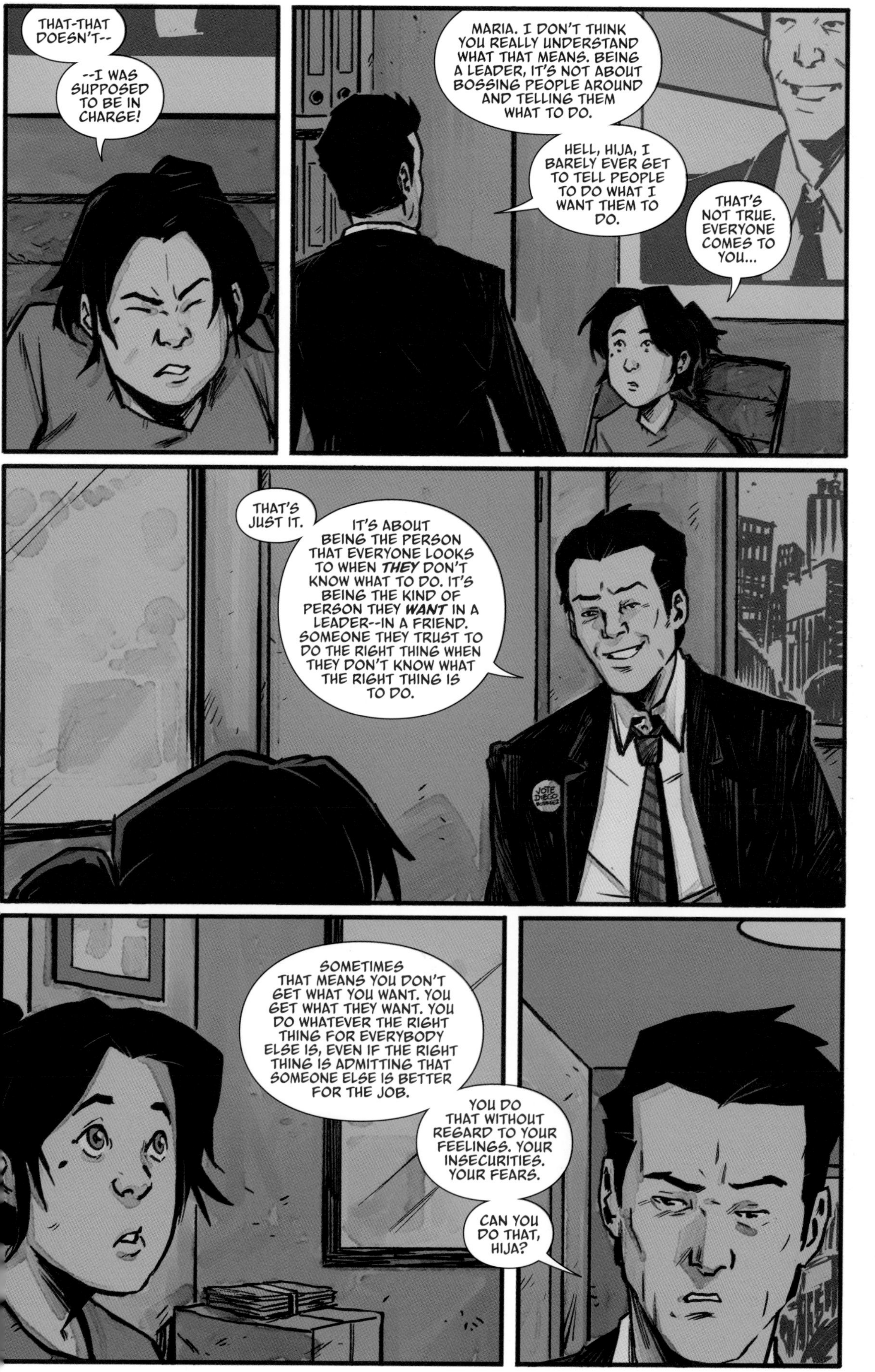

THAT-THAT DOESN'T--
--I WAS SUPPOSED TO BE IN CHARGE!
MARIA. I DON'T THINK YOU REALLY UNDERSTAND WHAT THAT MEANS. BEING A LEADER, IT'S NOT ABOUT BOSSING PEOPLE AROUND AND TELLING THEM WHAT TO DO.
HELL, HIJA, I BARELY EVER GET TO TELL PEOPLE TO DO WHAT I WANT THEM TO DO.
THAT'S NOT TRUE. EVERYONE COMES TO YOU...
THAT'S JUST IT.
IT'S ABOUT BEING THE PERSON THAT EVERYONE LOOKS TO WHEN THEY DON'T KNOW WHAT TO DO. IT'S BEING THE KIND OF PERSON THEY WANT IN A LEADER--IN A FRIEND. SOMEONE THEY TRUST TO DO THE RIGHT THING WHEN THEY DON'T KNOW WHAT THE RIGHT THING IS TO DO.
VOTE DIEGO
SOMETIMES THAT MEANS YOU DON'T GET WHAT YOU WANT. YOU GET WHAT THEY WANT. YOU DO WHATEVER THE RIGHT THING FOR EVERYBODY ELSE IS, EVEN IF THE RIGHT THING IS ADMITTING THAT SOMEONE ELSE IS BETTER FOR THE JOB.
YOU DO THAT WITHOUT REGARD TO YOUR FEELINGS. YOUR INSECURITIES. YOUR FEARS.
CAN YOU DO THAT, HIJA?

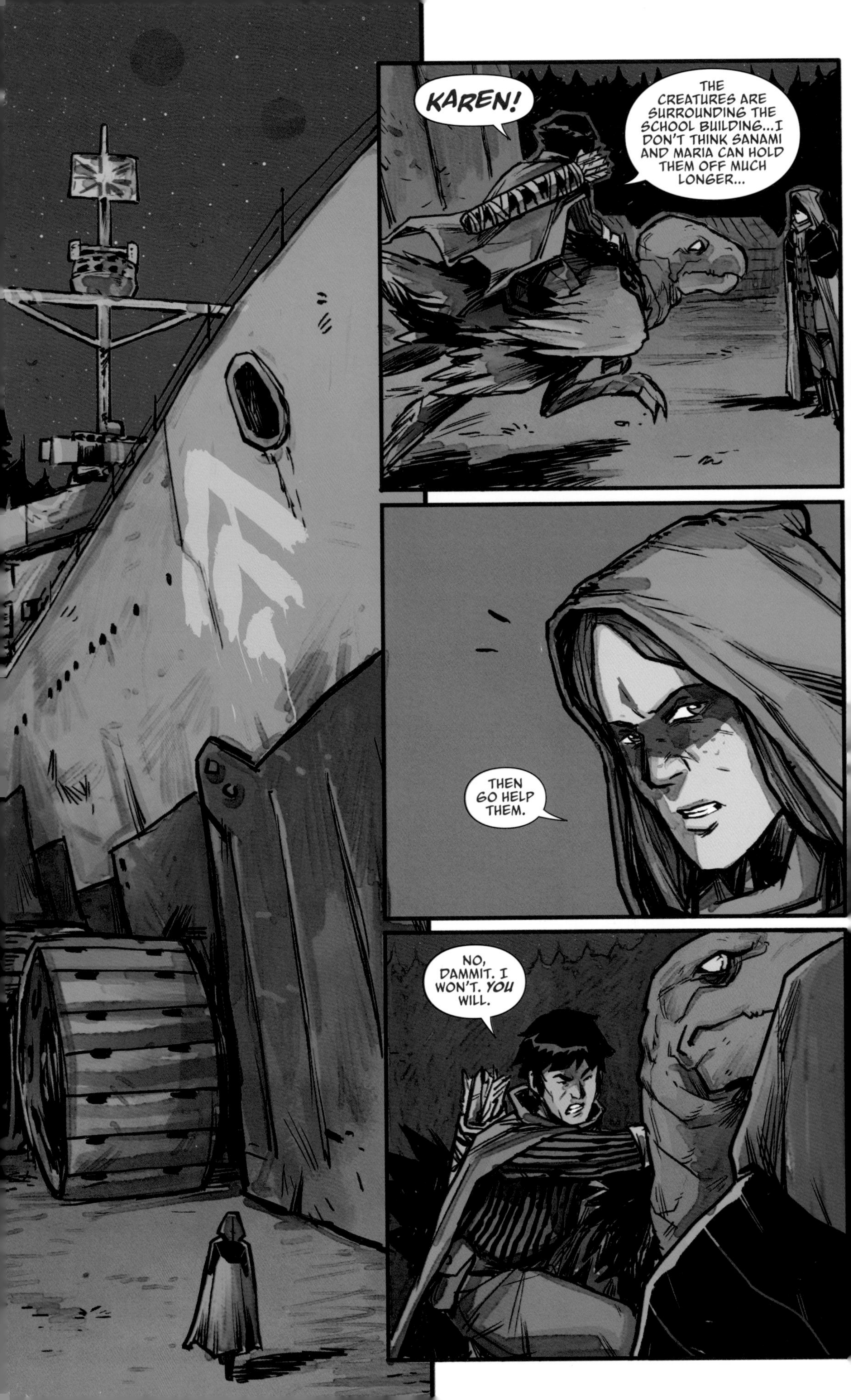
KAREN!
THE CREATURES ARE SURROUNDING THE SCHOOL BUILDING...I DON'T THINK SANAMI AND MARIA CAN HOLD THEM OFF MUCH LONGER...
THEN GO HELP THEM.
NO, DAMMIT. I WON'T. *YOU* WILL.

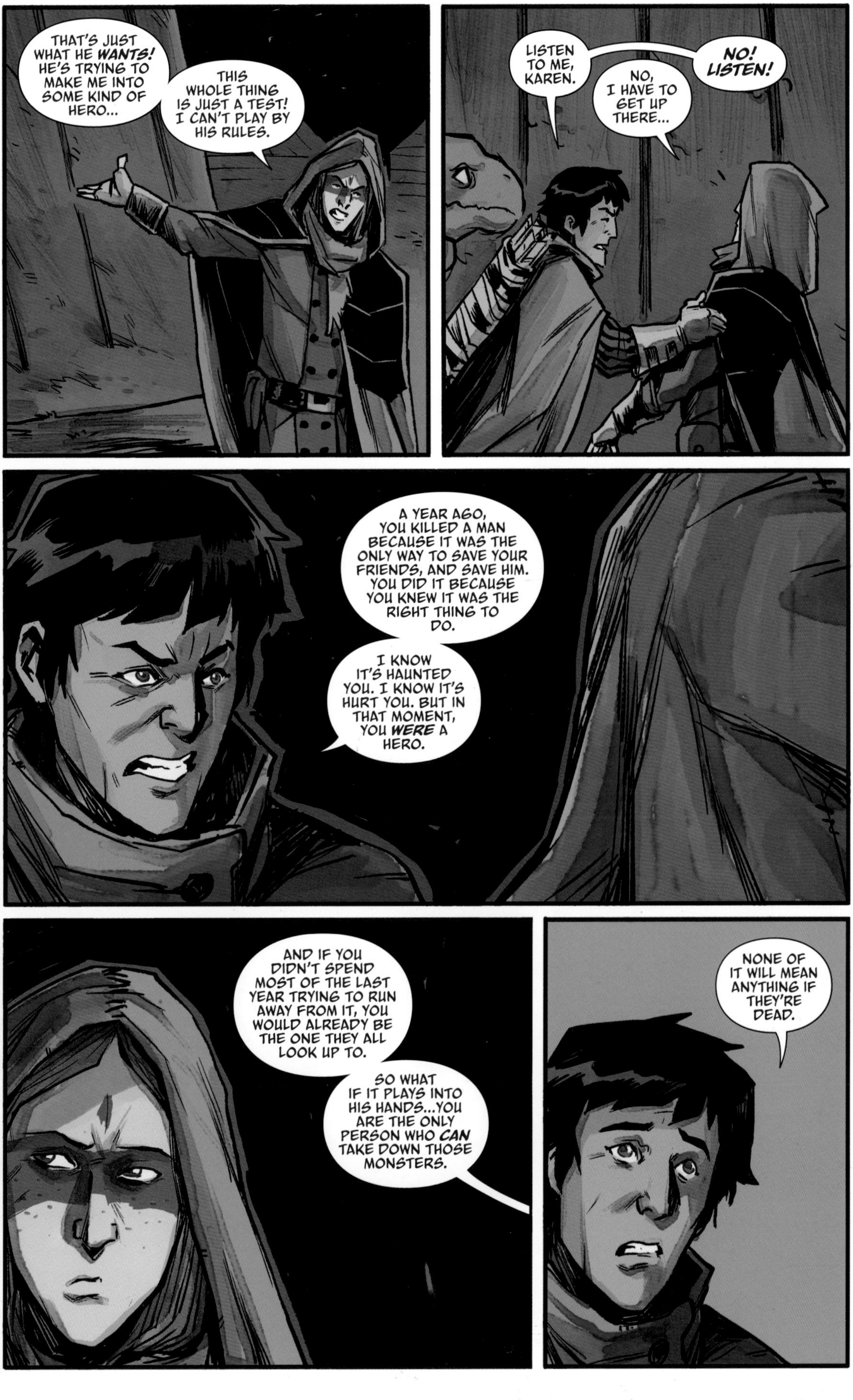
THAT'S JUST WHAT HE *WANTS!* HE'S TRYING TO MAKE ME INTO SOME KIND OF HERO...
THIS WHOLE THING IS JUST A TEST! I CAN'T PLAY BY HIS RULES.
LISTEN TO ME, KAREN.
NO, I HAVE TO GET UP THERE...
NO! LISTEN!
A YEAR AGO, YOU KILLED A MAN BECAUSE IT WAS THE ONLY WAY TO SAVE YOUR FRIENDS, AND SAVE HIM. YOU DID IT BECAUSE YOU KNEW IT WAS THE RIGHT THING TO DO.
I KNOW IT'S HAUNTED YOU. I KNOW IT'S HURT YOU. BUT IN THAT MOMENT, YOU *WERE* A HERO.
AND IF YOU DIDN'T SPEND MOST OF THE LAST YEAR TRYING TO RUN AWAY FROM IT, YOU WOULD ALREADY BE THE ONE THEY ALL LOOK UP TO.
SO WHAT IF IT PLAYS INTO HIS HANDS...YOU ARE THE ONLY PERSON WHO *CAN* TAKE DOWN THOSE MONSTERS.
NONE OF IT WILL MEAN ANYTHING IF THEY'RE DEAD.

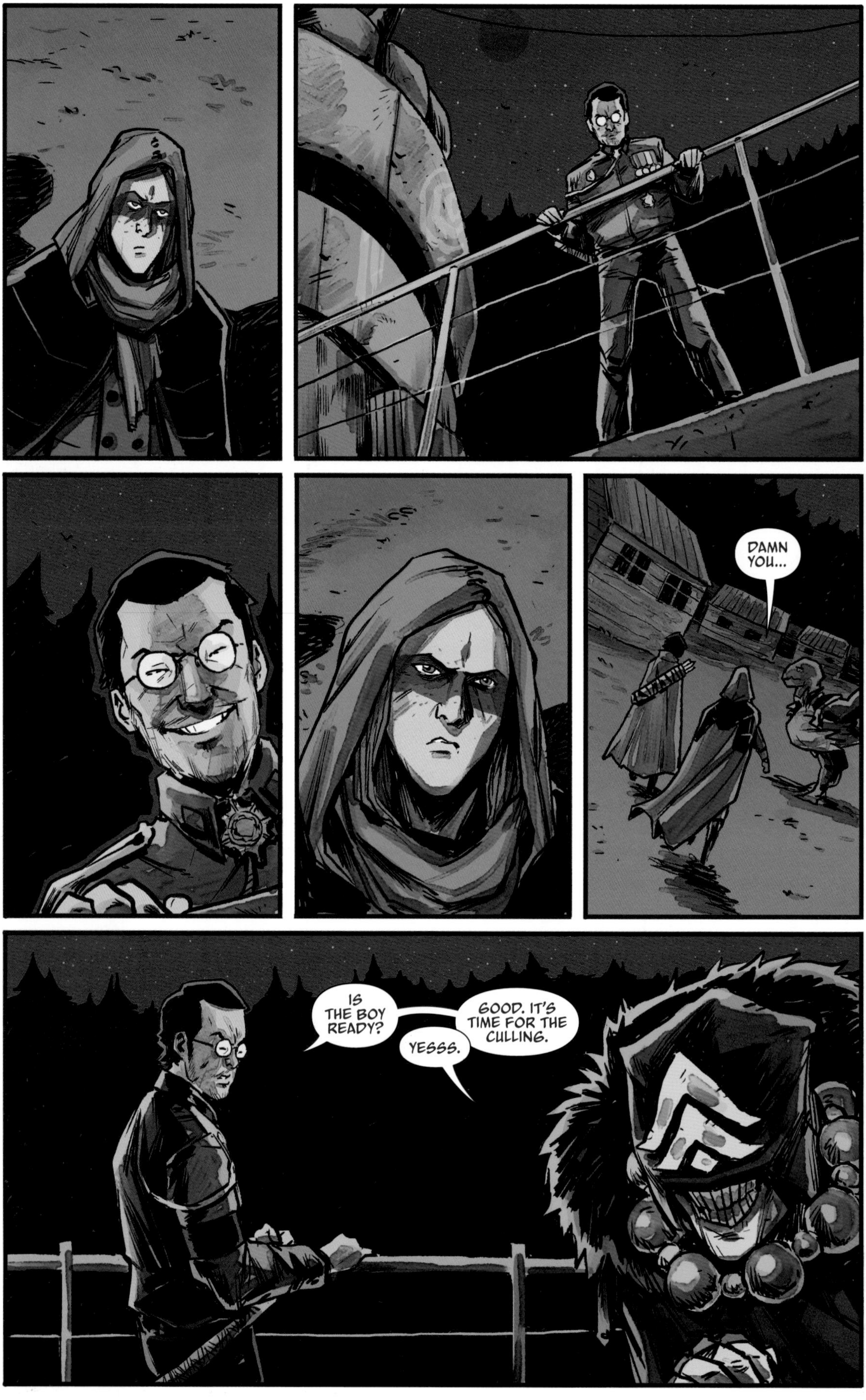
DAMN YOU...
IS THE BOY READY?
YESSS.
GOOD. IT'S TIME FOR THE CULLING.

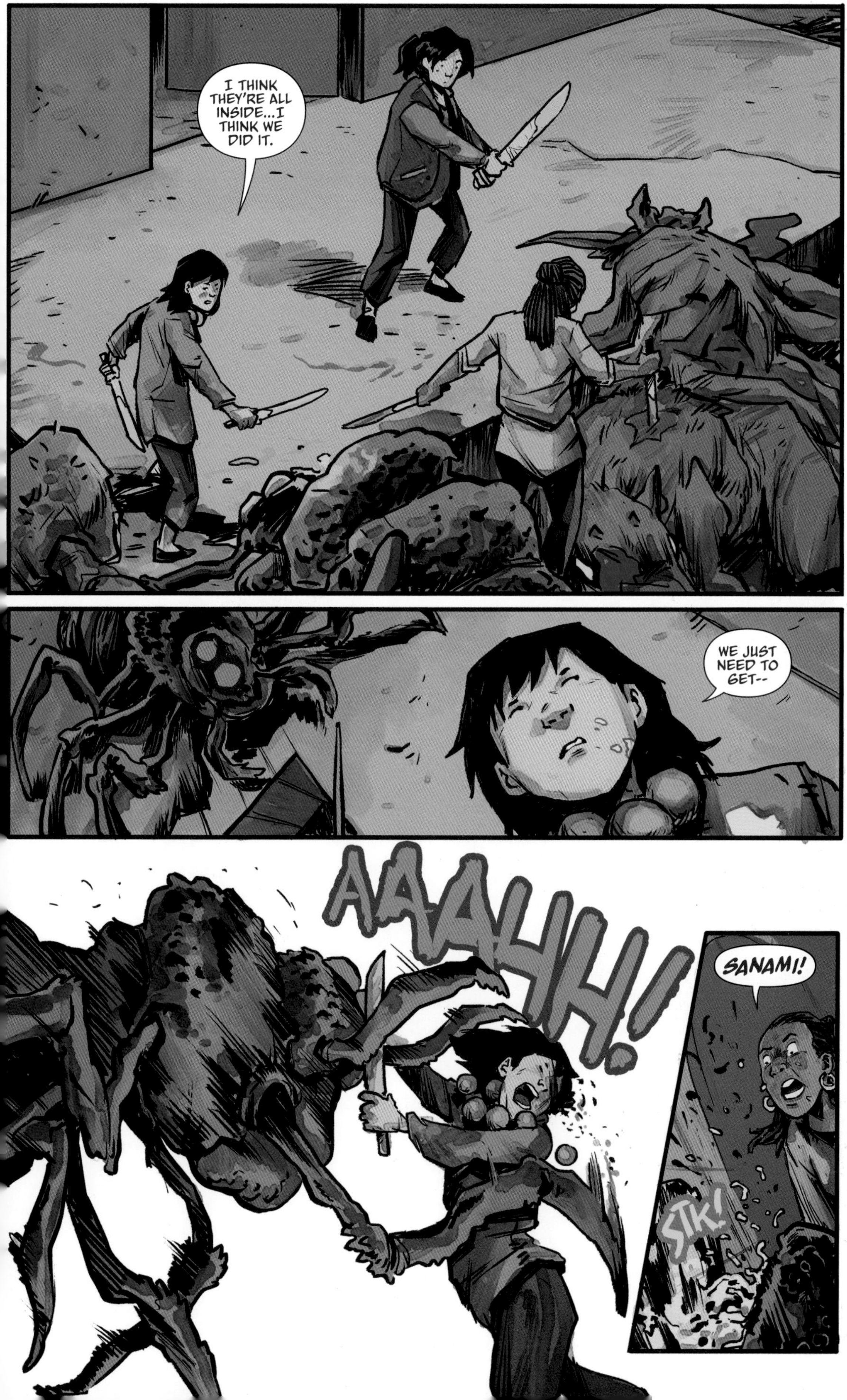
I THINK THEY'RE ALL INSIDE...I THINK WE DID IT.
WE JUST NEED TO GET--
AAAHH!
SANAMI!
STK!

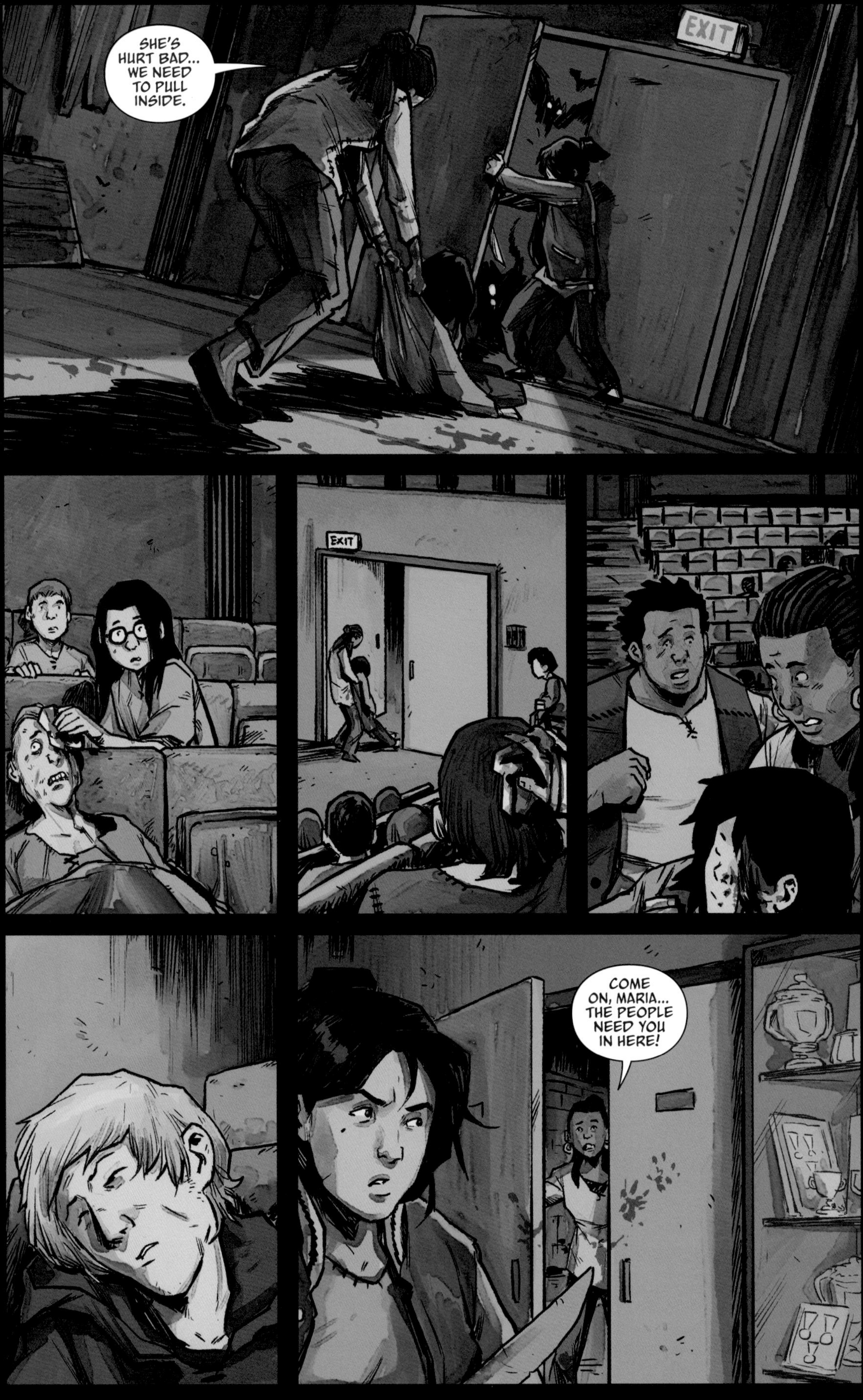
SHE'S HURT BAD... WE NEED TO PULL INSIDE.
EXIT
EXIT
COME ON, MARIA... THE PEOPLE NEED YOU IN HERE!

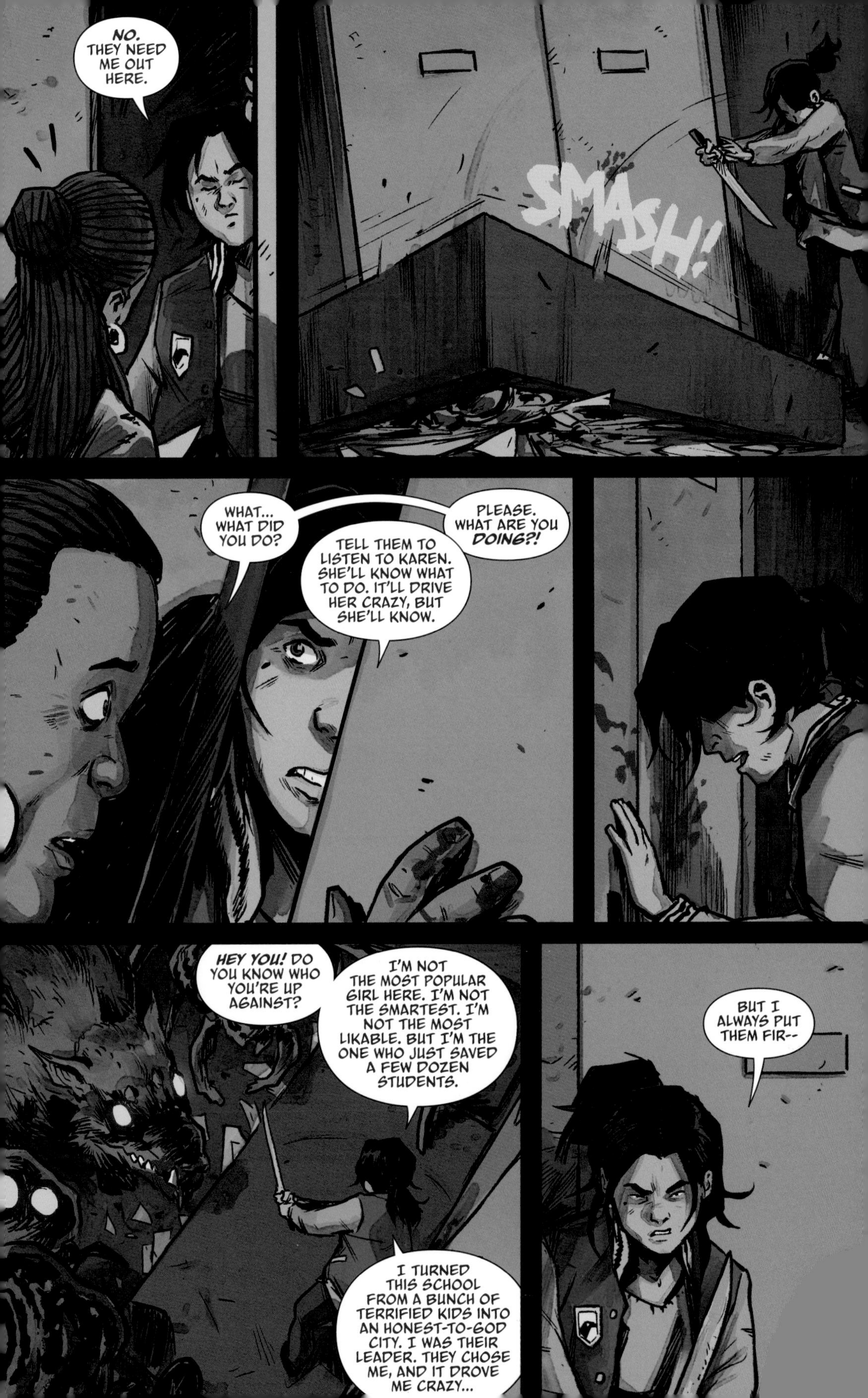
NO. THEY NEED ME OUT HERE.
SMASH!
WHAT... WHAT DID YOU DO?
PLEASE. WHAT ARE YOU DOING?!
TELL THEM TO LISTEN TO KAREN. SHE'LL KNOW WHAT TO DO. IT'LL DRIVE HER CRAZY, BUT SHE'LL KNOW.
HEY YOU! DO YOU KNOW WHO YOU'RE UP AGAINST?
I'M NOT THE MOST POPULAR GIRL HERE. I'M NOT THE SMARTEST. I'M NOT THE MOST LIKABLE. BUT I'M THE ONE WHO JUST SAVED A FEW DOZEN STUDENTS.
I TURNED THIS SCHOOL FROM A BUNCH OF TERRIFIED KIDS INTO AN HONEST-TO-GOD CITY. I WAS THEIR LEADER. THEY CHOSE ME, AND IT DROVE ME CRAZY...
BUT I ALWAYS PUT THEM FIR--

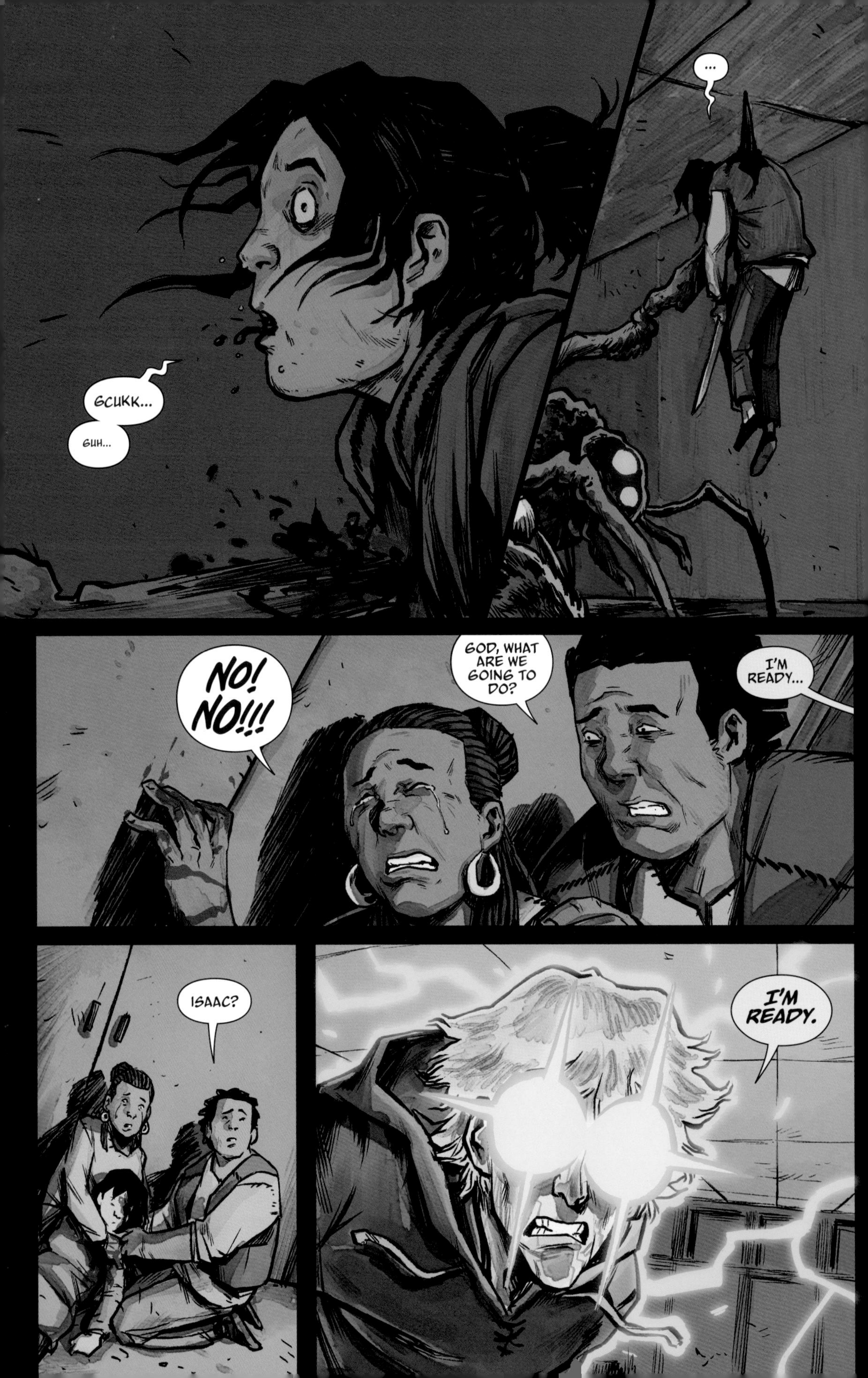
...
GCUKK...
GUH...
NO! NO!!!
GOD, WHAT ARE WE GOING TO DO?
I'M READY...
ISAAC?
I'M READY.

CHAPTER TWENTY

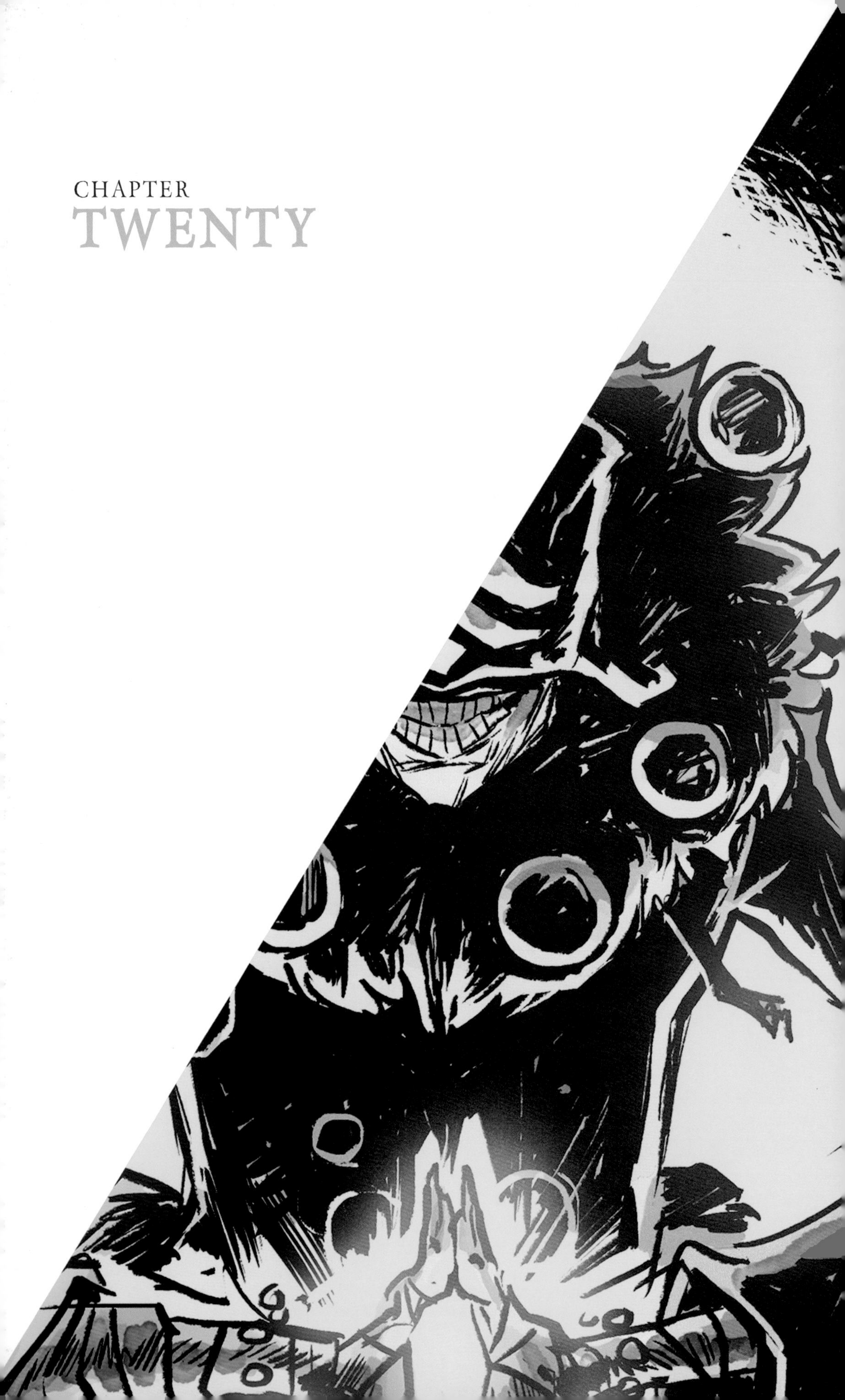

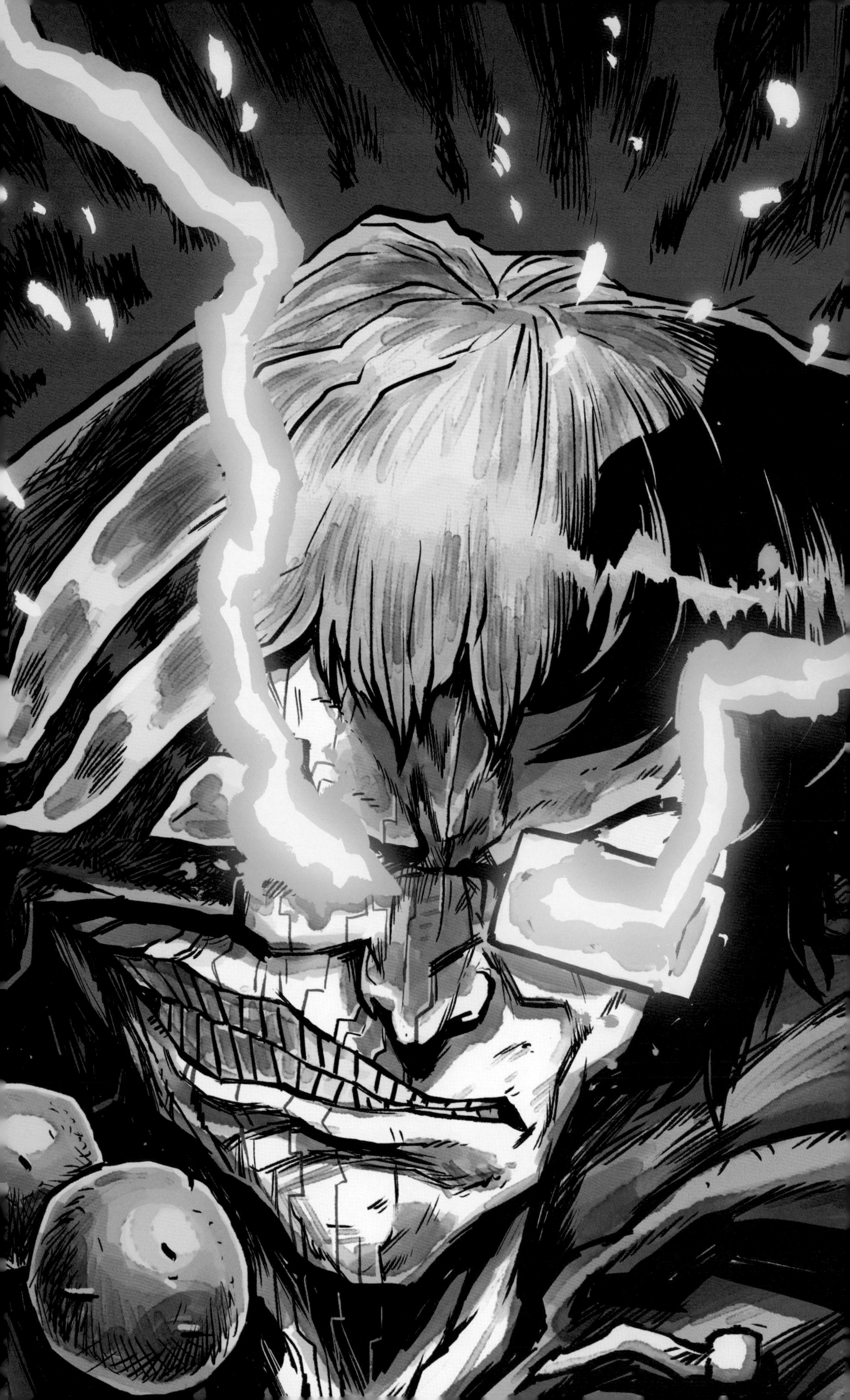

NOW.

FWOOSH!

ISAAC?!

AAAAAAA

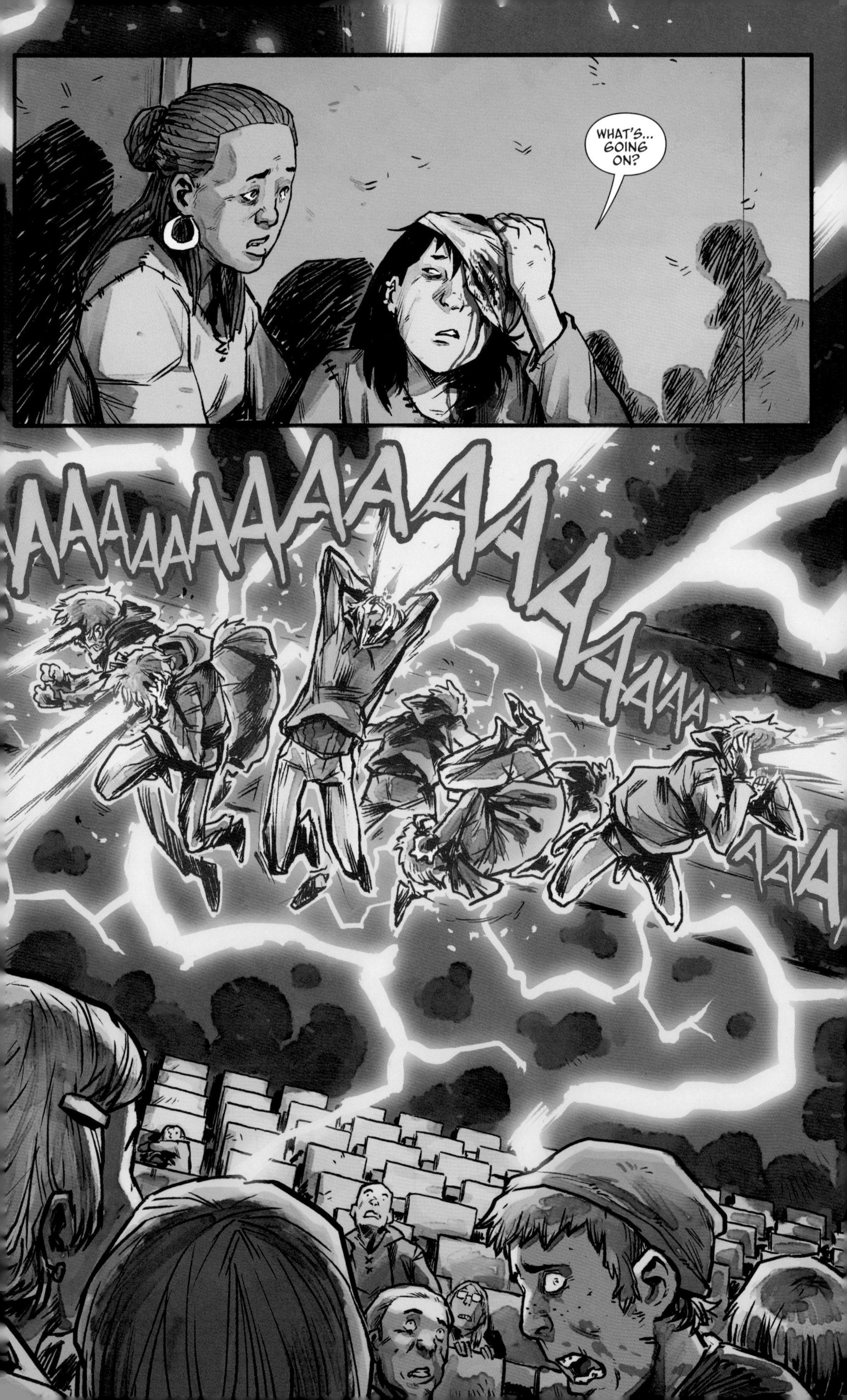
WHAT'S... GOING ON?
AAAAAAAAAAAAAAAAAAAAAAAAA

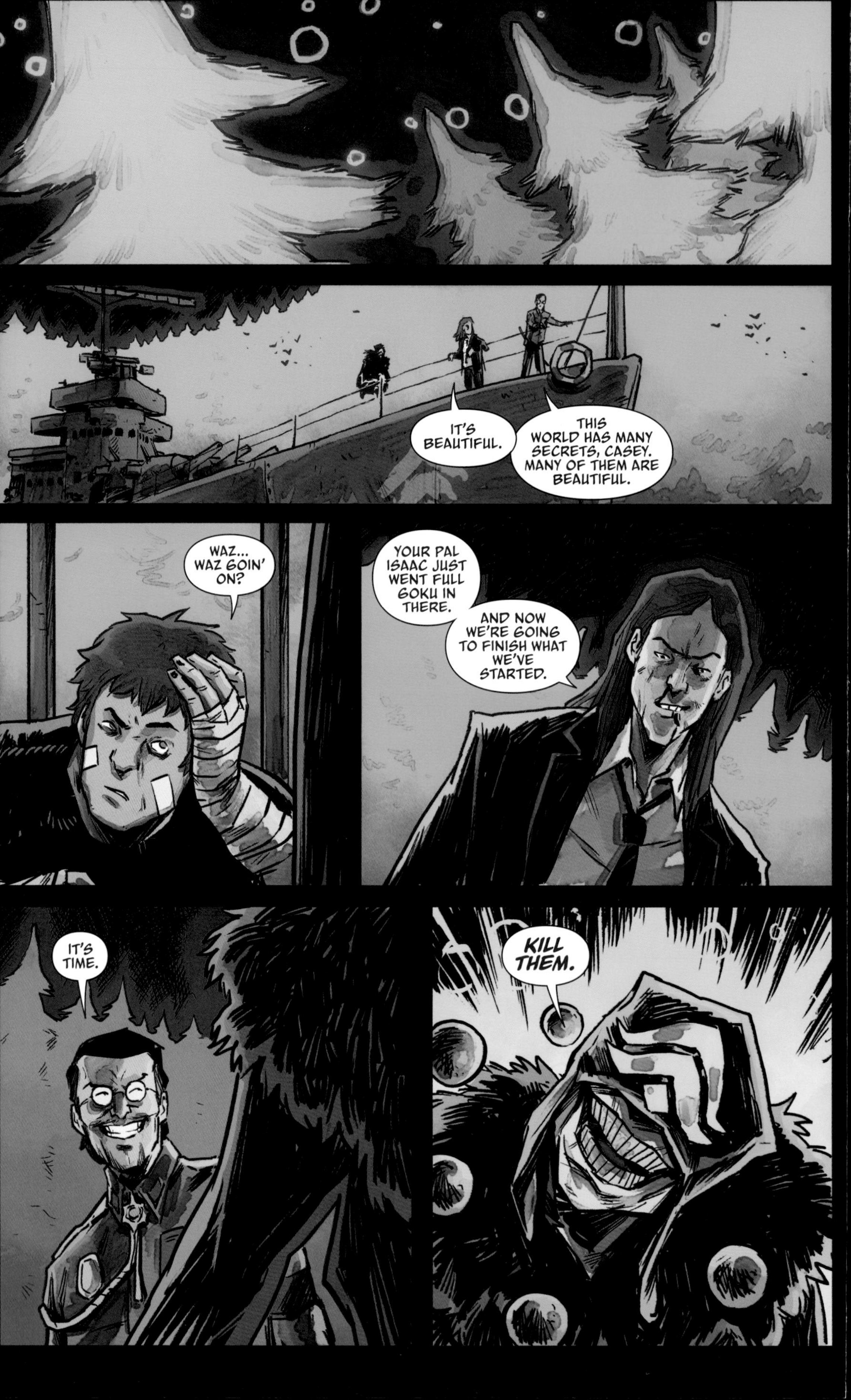
IT'S BEAUTIFUL.
THIS WORLD HAS MANY SECRETS, CASEY. MANY OF THEM ARE BEAUTIFUL.
WAZ... WAZ GOIN' ON?
YOUR PAL ISAAC JUST WENT FULL GOKU IN THERE.
AND NOW WE'RE GOING TO FINISH WHAT WE'VE STARTED.
IT'S TIME.
KILL THEM.

VOOM!

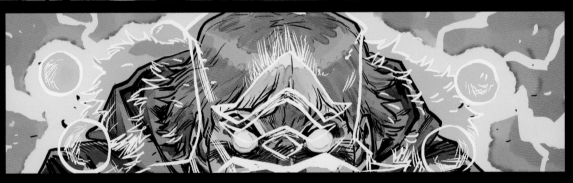

ISAAC...YOU DON'T HAVE TO DO THIS.

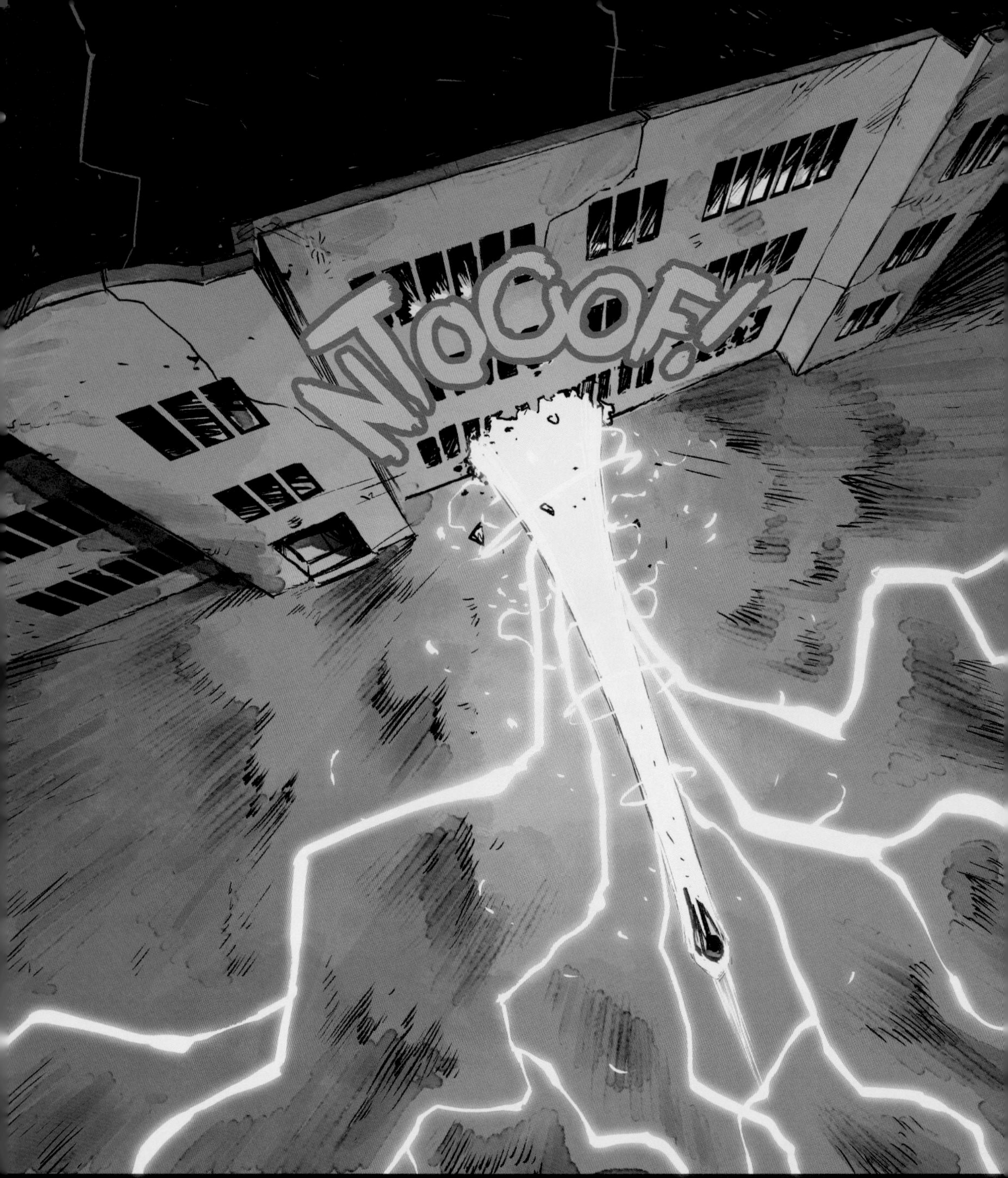
WOOOF!

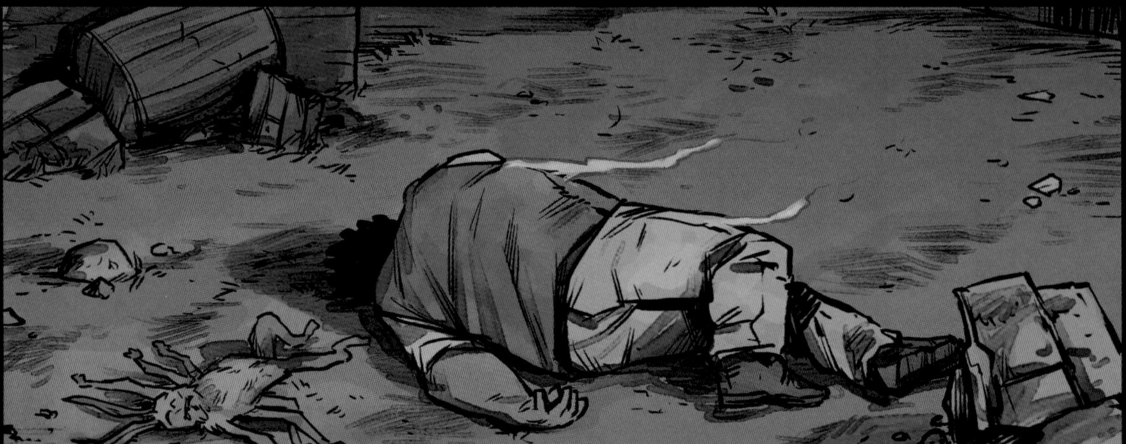

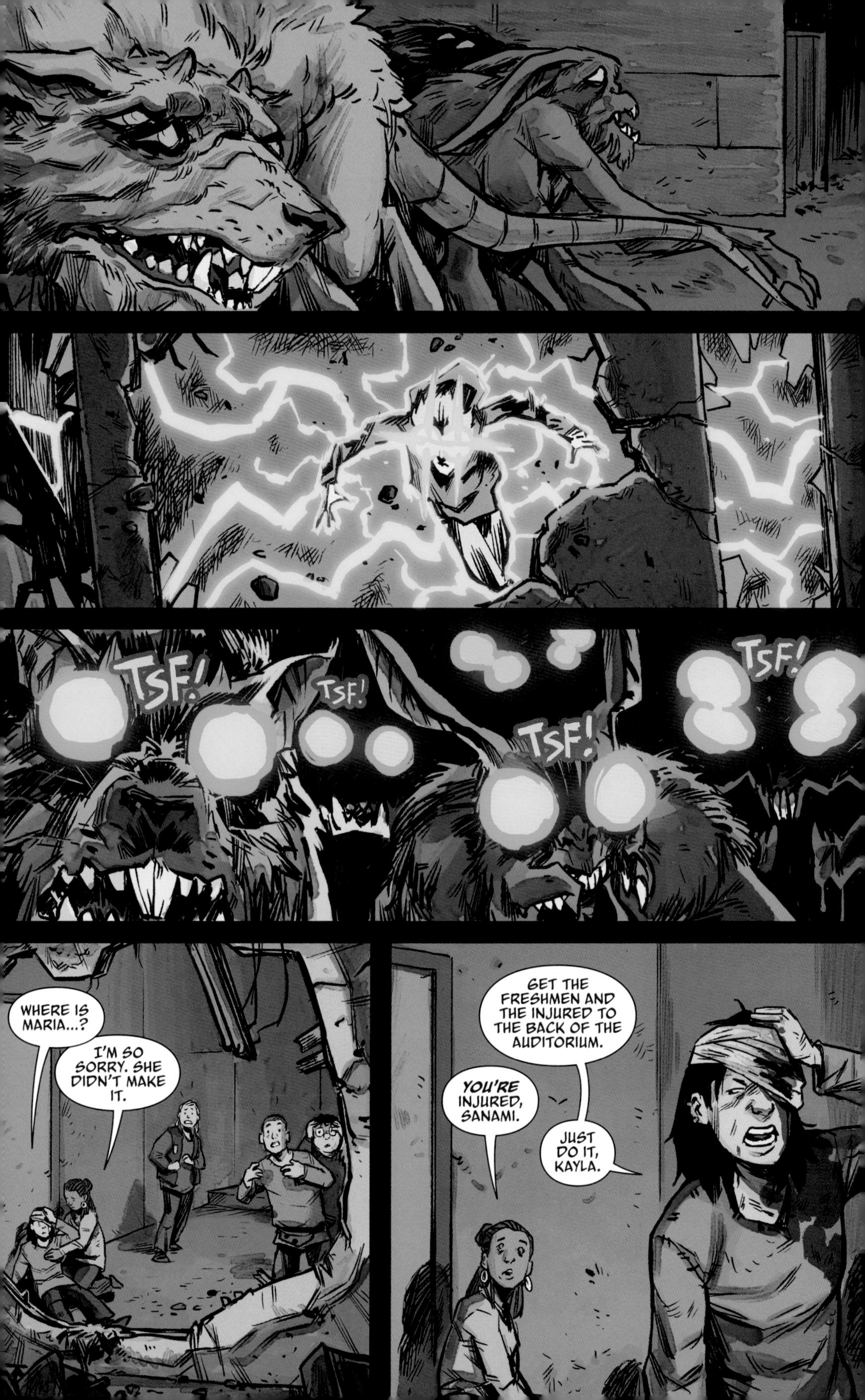
TSF!
TSF!
TSF!
TSF!
WHERE IS MARIA...?
I'M SO SORRY. SHE DIDN'T MAKE IT.
GET THE FRESHMEN AND THE INJURED TO THE BACK OF THE AUDITORIUM.
YOU'RE INJURED, SANAMI.
JUST DO IT, KAYLA.

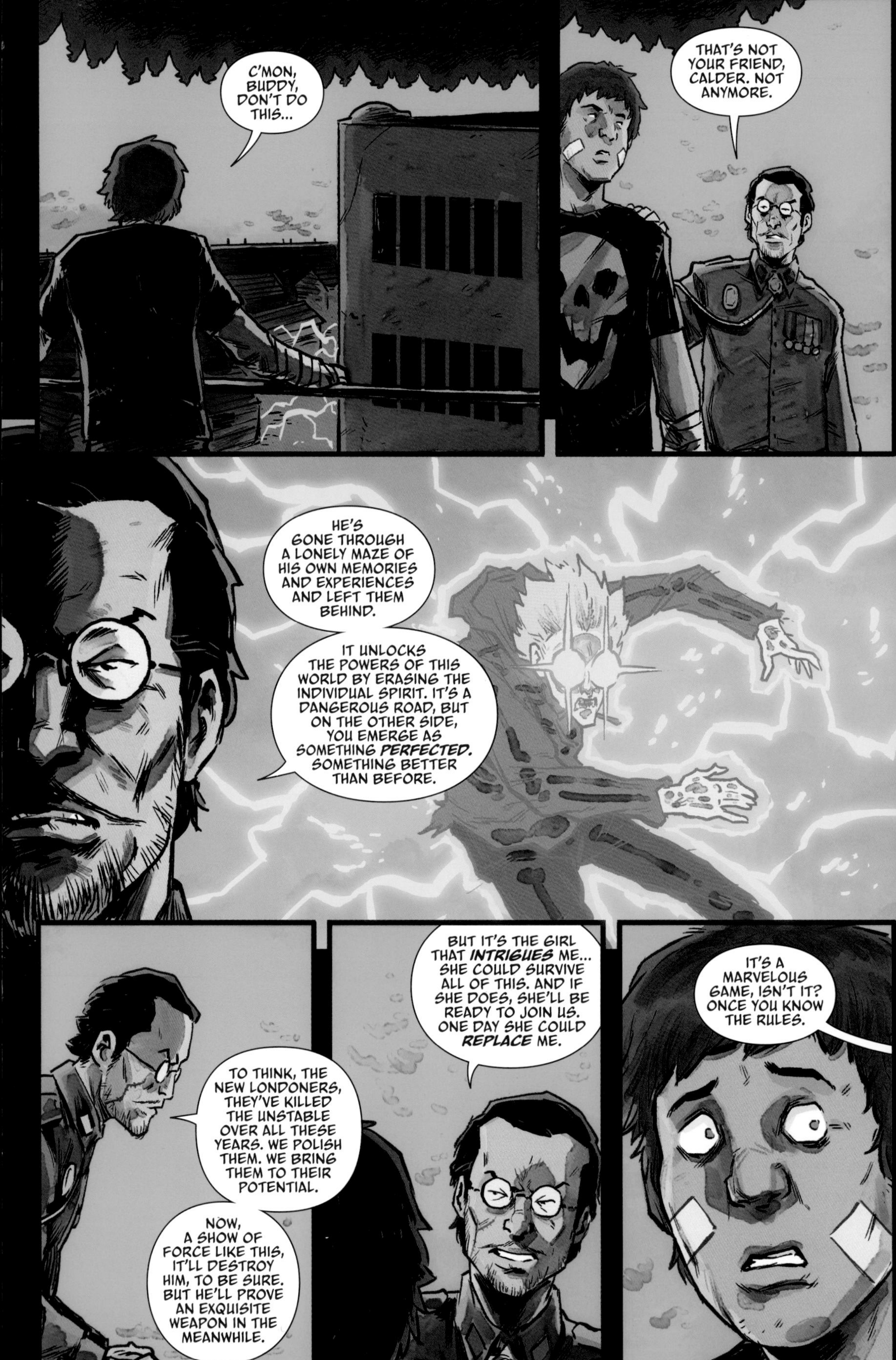
C'MON, BUDDY, DON'T DO THIS...
THAT'S NOT YOUR FRIEND, CALDER. NOT ANYMORE.
HE'S GONE THROUGH A LONELY MAZE OF HIS OWN MEMORIES AND EXPERIENCES AND LEFT THEM BEHIND.
IT UNLOCKS THE POWERS OF THIS WORLD BY ERASING THE INDIVIDUAL SPIRIT. IT'S A DANGEROUS ROAD, BUT ON THE OTHER SIDE, YOU EMERGE AS SOMETHING *PERFECTED.* SOMETHING BETTER THAN BEFORE.
TO THINK, THE NEW LONDONERS, THEY'VE KILLED THE UNSTABLE OVER ALL THESE YEARS. WE POLISH THEM. WE BRING THEM TO THEIR POTENTIAL.
NOW, A SHOW OF FORCE LIKE THIS, IT'LL DESTROY HIM, TO BE SURE. BUT HE'LL PROVE AN EXQUISITE WEAPON IN THE MEANWHILE.
BUT IT'S THE GIRL THAT *INTRIGUES* ME... SHE COULD SURVIVE ALL OF THIS. AND IF SHE DOES, SHE'LL BE READY TO JOIN US. ONE DAY SHE COULD *REPLACE* ME.
IT'S A MARVELOUS GAME, ISN'T IT? ONCE YOU KNOW THE RULES.

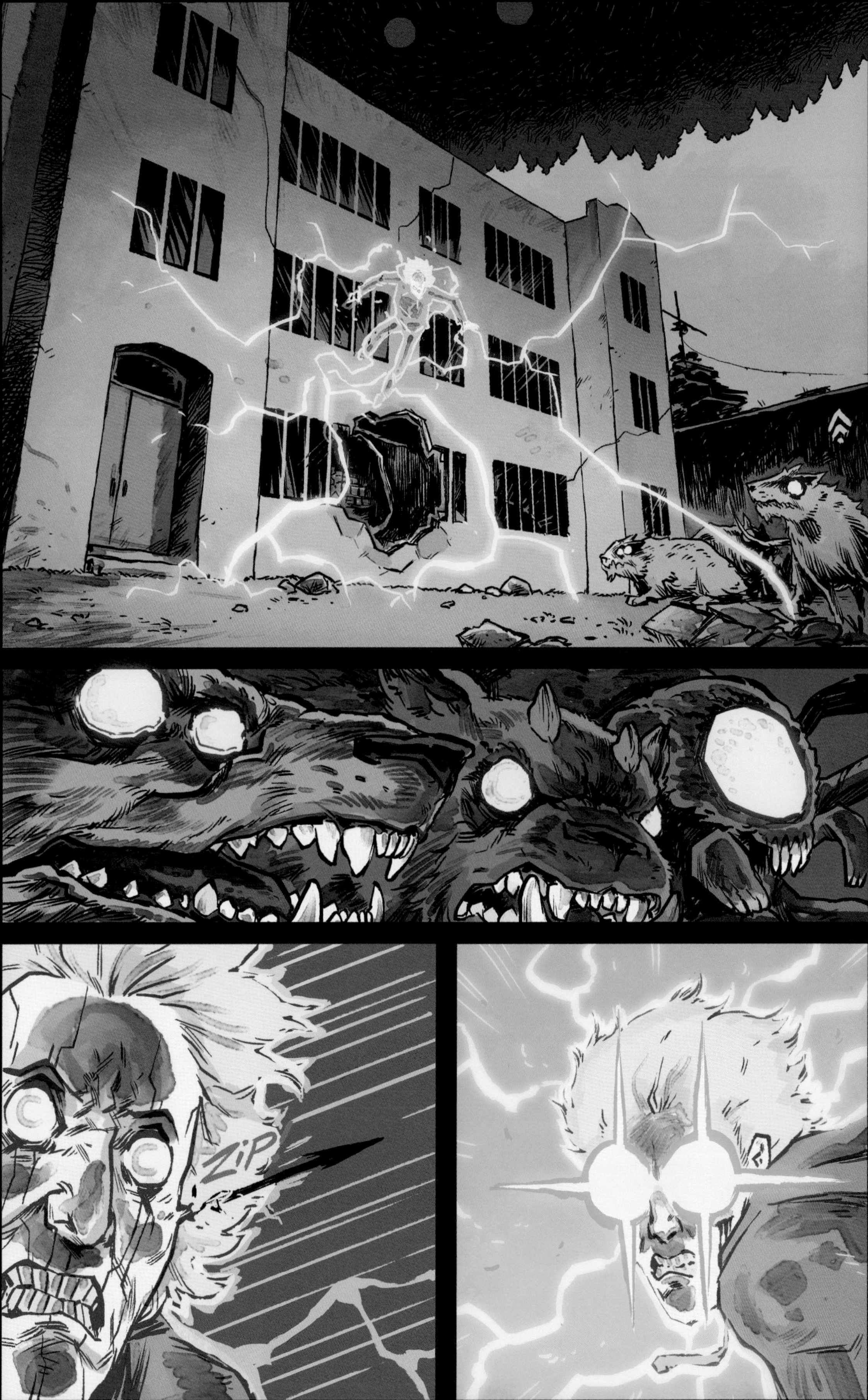
ZIP

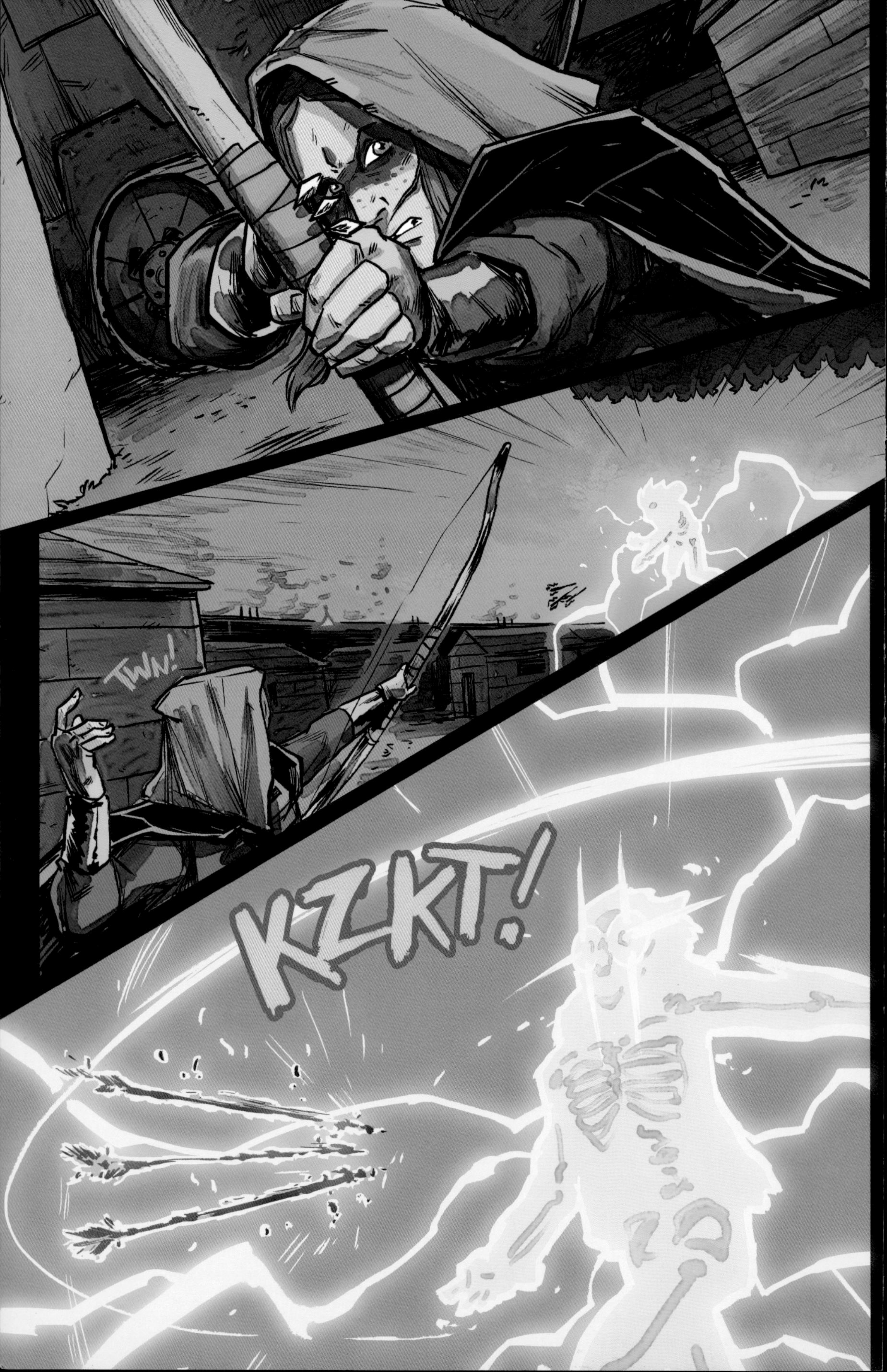
TWN!
KZKT!

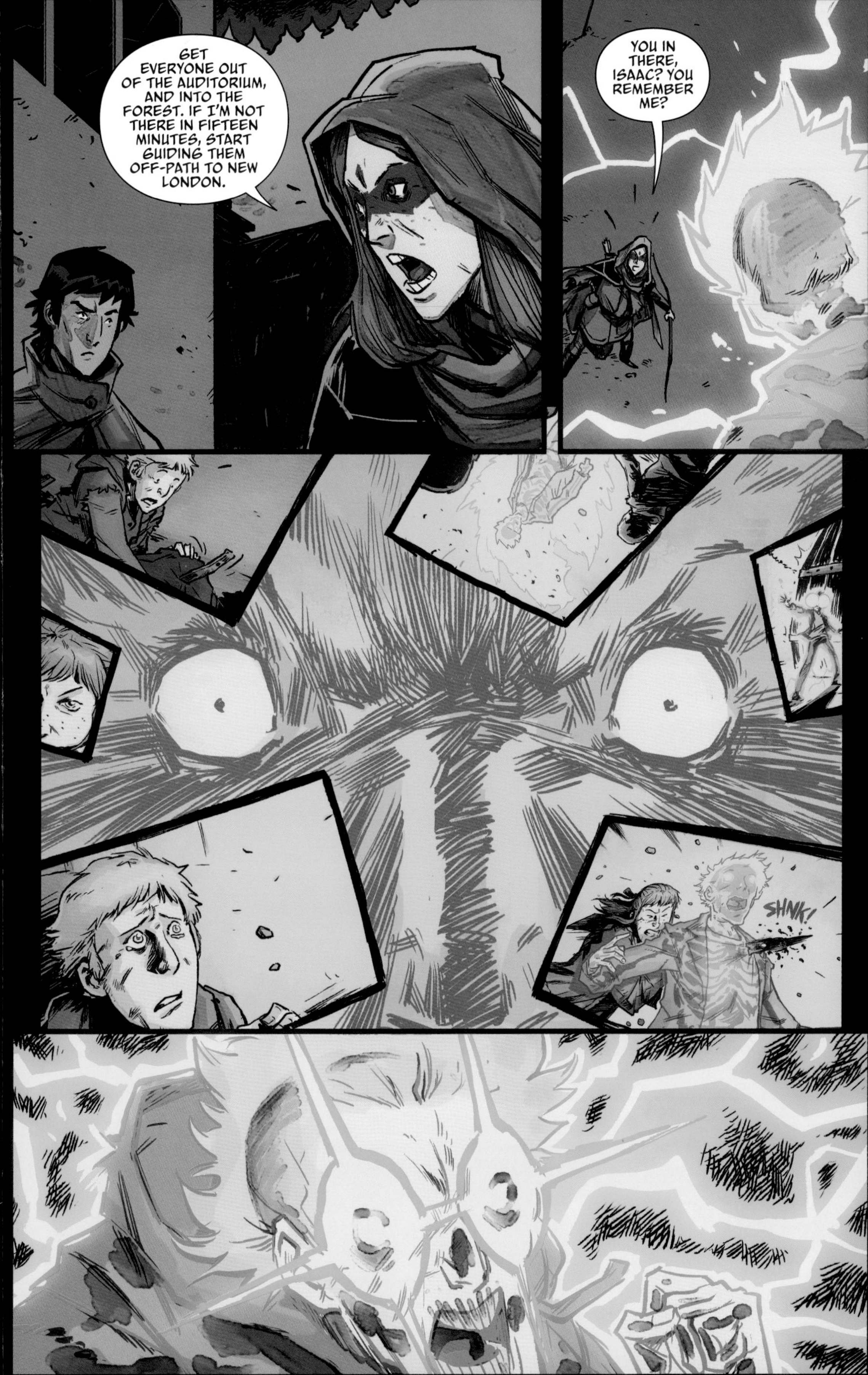
GET EVERYONE OUT OF THE AUDITORIUM, AND INTO THE FOREST. IF I'M NOT THERE IN FIFTEEN MINUTES, START GUIDING THEM OFF-PATH TO NEW LONDON.
YOU IN THERE, ISAAC? YOU REMEMBER ME?
SHNK!

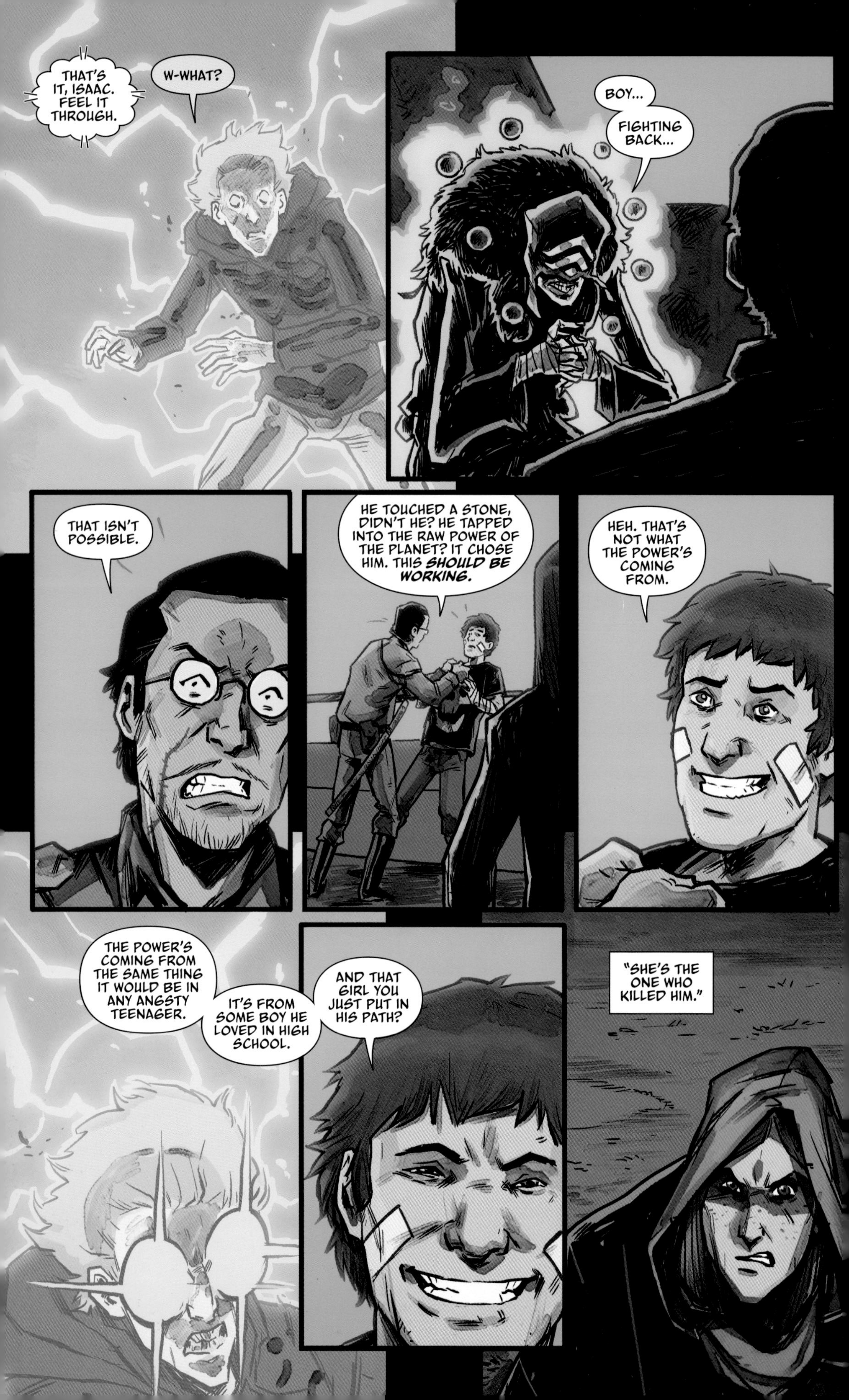

THAT'S IT, ISAAC. FEEL IT THROUGH.
W-WHAT?
BOY...
FIGHTING BACK...
THAT ISN'T POSSIBLE.
HE TOUCHED A STONE, DIDN'T HE? HE TAPPED INTO THE RAW POWER OF THE PLANET? IT CHOSE HIM. THIS SHOULD BE WORKING.
HEH. THAT'S NOT WHAT THE POWER'S COMING FROM.
THE POWER'S COMING FROM THE SAME THING IT WOULD BE IN ANY ANGSTY TEENAGER.
IT'S FROM SOME BOY HE LOVED IN HIGH SCHOOL.
AND THAT GIRL YOU JUST PUT IN HIS PATH?
"SHE'S THE ONE WHO KILLED HIM."

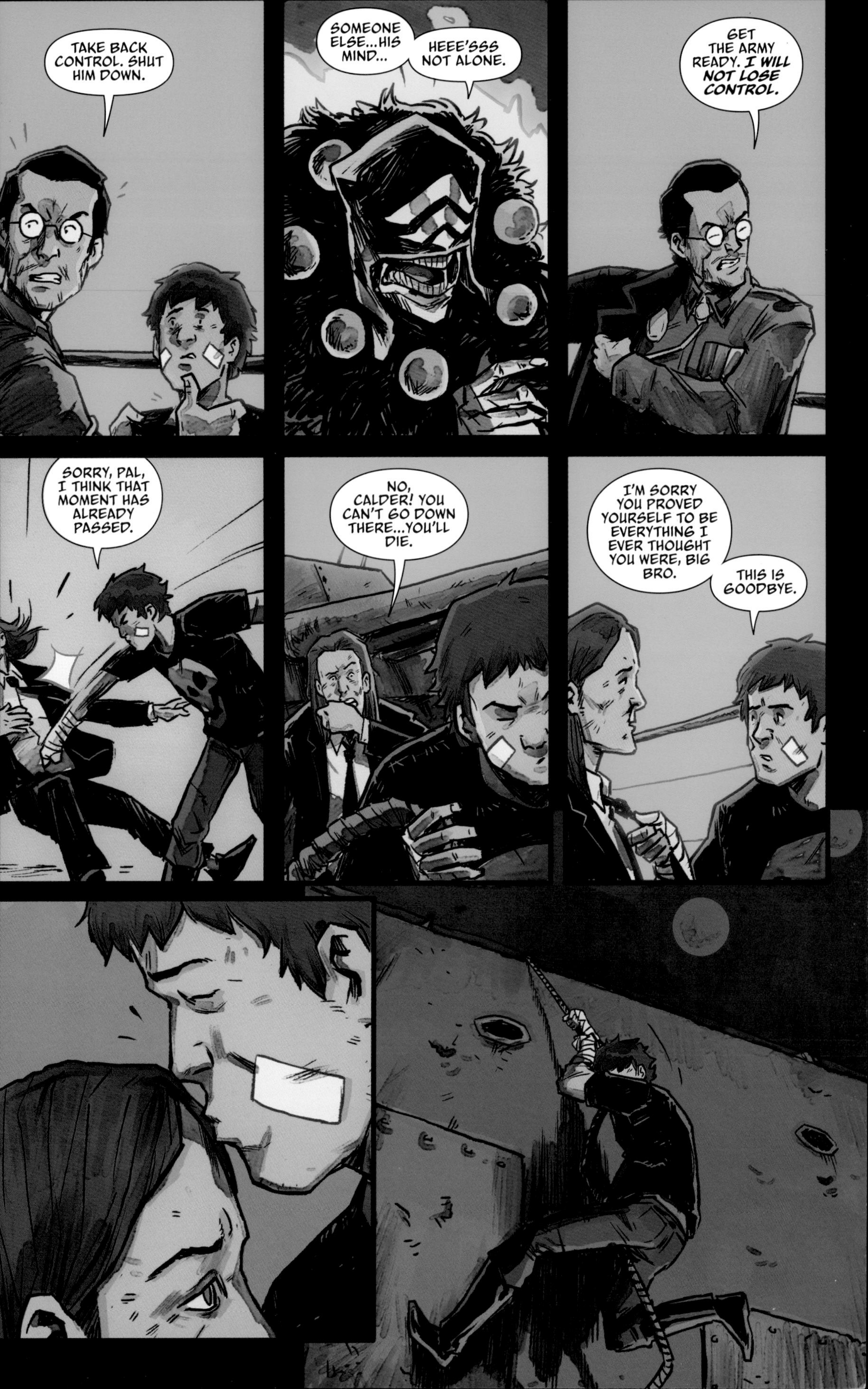
TAKE BACK CONTROL. SHUT HIM DOWN.
SOMEONE ELSE...HIS MIND...
HEEE'SSS NOT ALONE.
GET THE ARMY READY. *I WILL NOT LOSE CONTROL.*
SORRY, PAL, I THINK THAT MOMENT HAS ALREADY PASSED.
NO, CALDER! YOU CAN'T GO DOWN THERE...YOU'LL DIE.
I'M SORRY YOU PROVED YOURSELF TO BE EVERYTHING I EVER THOUGHT YOU WERE, BIG BRO.
THIS IS GOODBYE.

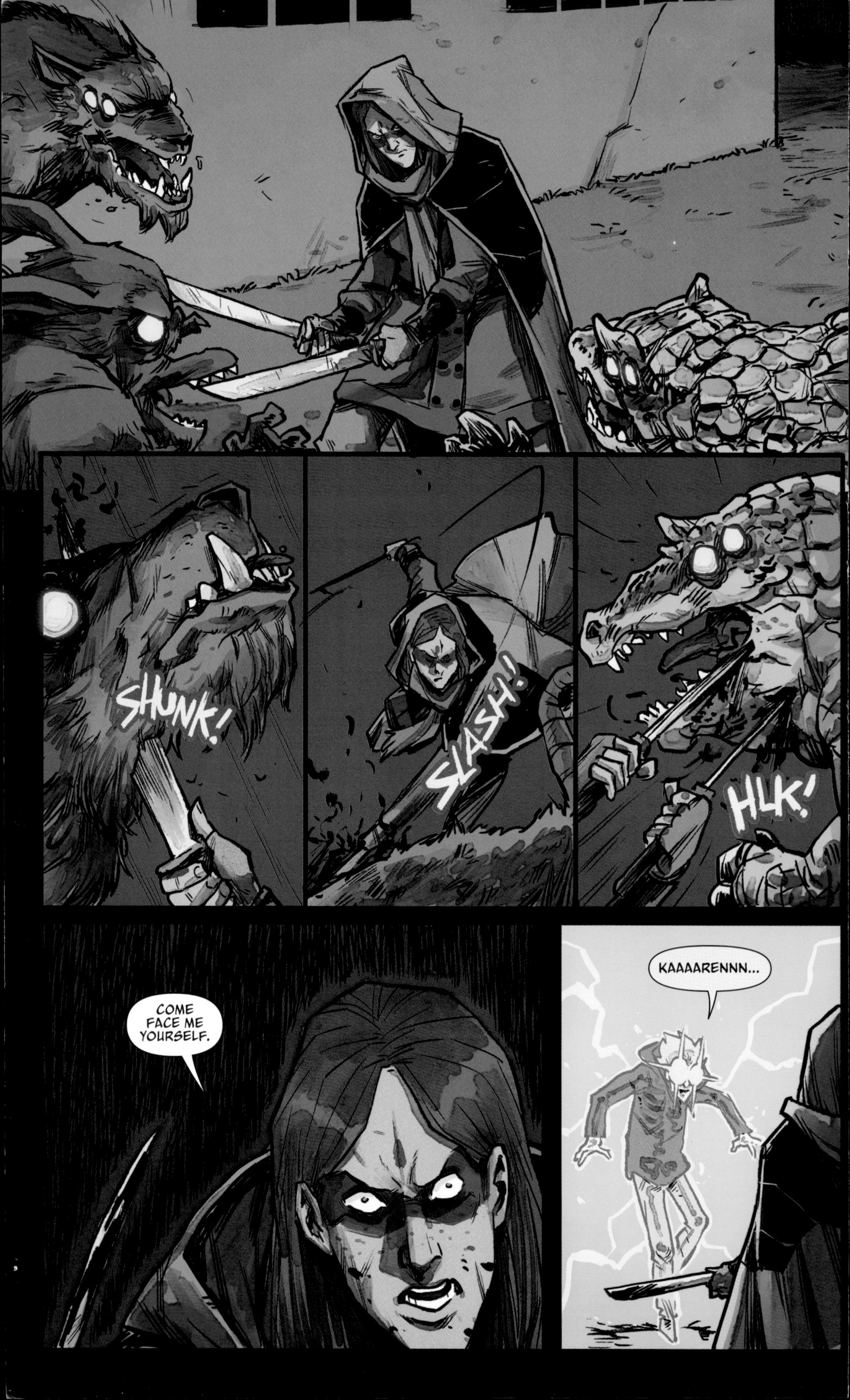
SHUNK!
SLASH!
HLK!
COME FACE ME YOURSELF.
KAAAARENNN...

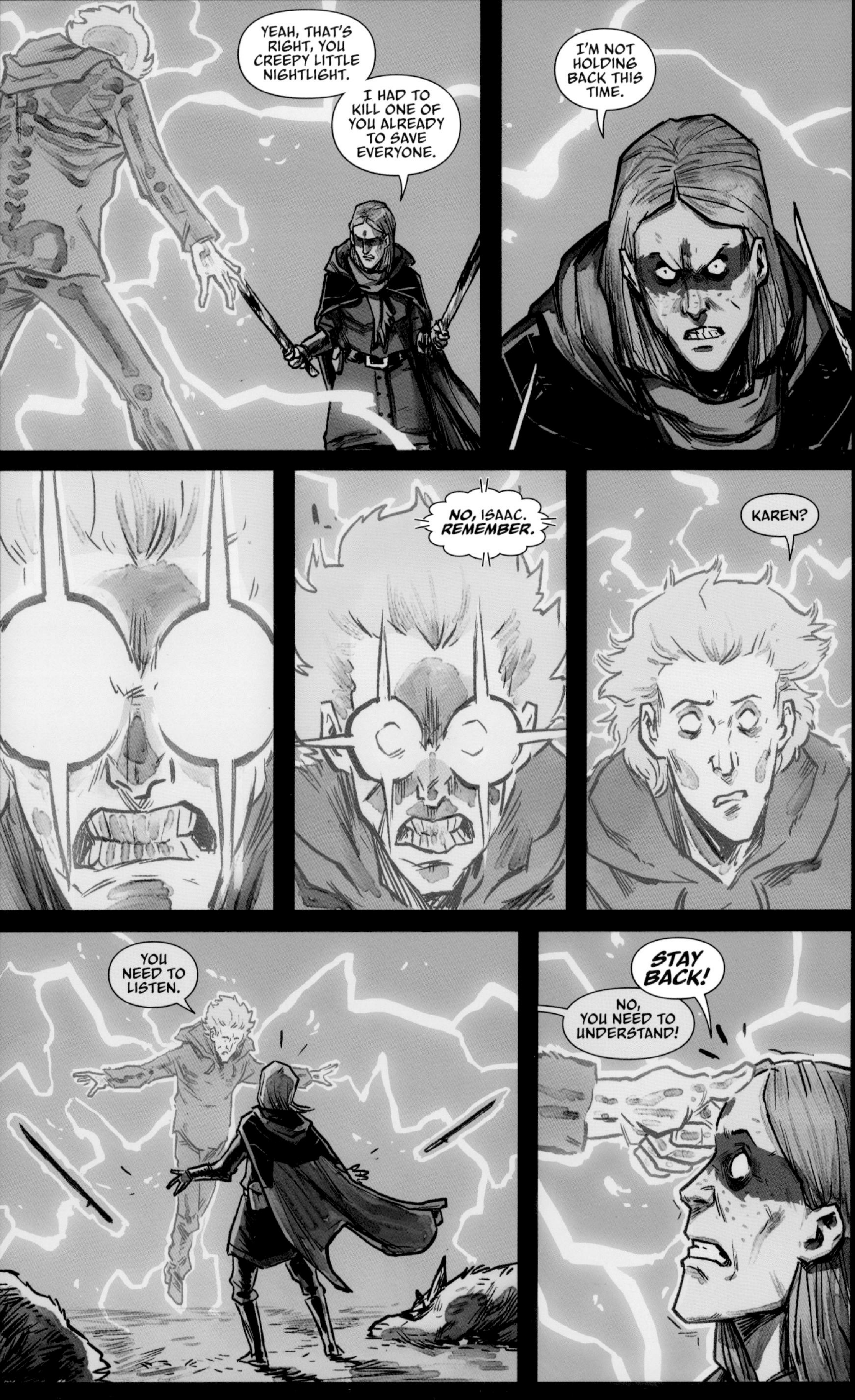
YEAH, THAT'S RIGHT, YOU CREEPY LITTLE NIGHTLIGHT.
I HAD TO KILL ONE OF YOU ALREADY TO SAVE EVERYONE.
I'M NOT HOLDING BACK THIS TIME.
NO, ISAAC. REMEMBER.
KAREN?
YOU NEED TO LISTEN.
STAY BACK!
NO, YOU NEED TO UNDERSTAND!

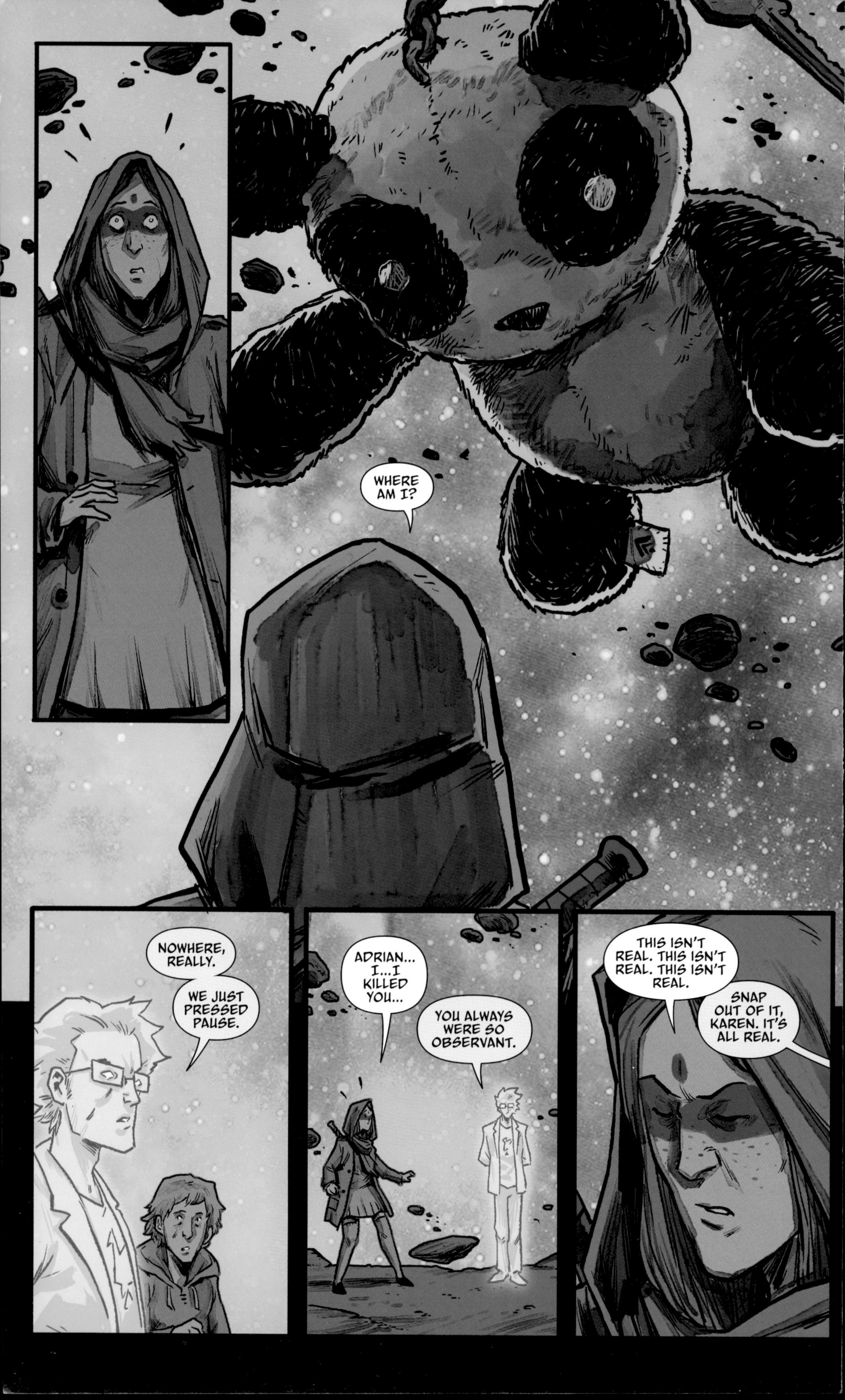
WHERE AM I?
NOWHERE, REALLY.
WE JUST PRESSED PAUSE.
ADRIAN... I...I KILLED YOU...
YOU ALWAYS WERE SO OBSERVANT.
THIS ISN'T REAL. THIS ISN'T REAL. THIS ISN'T REAL.
SNAP OUT OF IT, KAREN. IT'S ALL REAL.

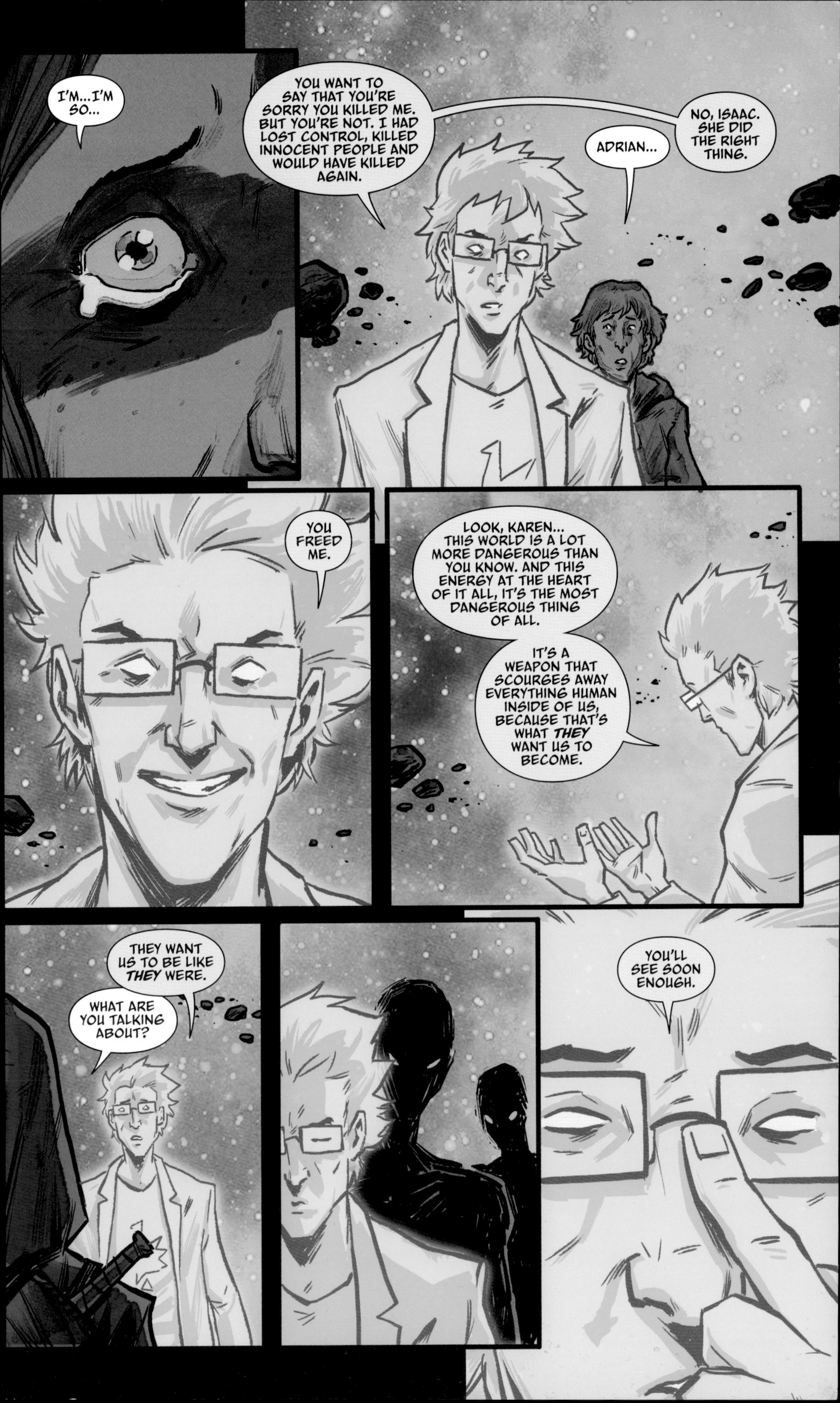
I'M...I'M SO...
YOU WANT TO SAY THAT YOU'RE SORRY YOU KILLED ME. BUT YOU'RE NOT. I HAD LOST CONTROL, KILLED INNOCENT PEOPLE AND WOULD HAVE KILLED AGAIN.
ADRIAN...
NO, ISAAC. SHE DID THE RIGHT THING.
YOU FREED ME.
LOOK, KAREN... THIS WORLD IS A LOT MORE DANGEROUS THAN YOU KNOW. AND THIS ENERGY AT THE HEART OF IT ALL, IT'S THE MOST DANGEROUS THING OF ALL.
IT'S A WEAPON THAT SCOURGES AWAY EVERYTHING HUMAN INSIDE OF US, BECAUSE THAT'S WHAT *THEY* WANT US TO BECOME.
THEY WANT US TO BE LIKE *THEY* WERE.
WHAT ARE YOU TALKING ABOUT?
YOU'LL SEE SOON ENOUGH.

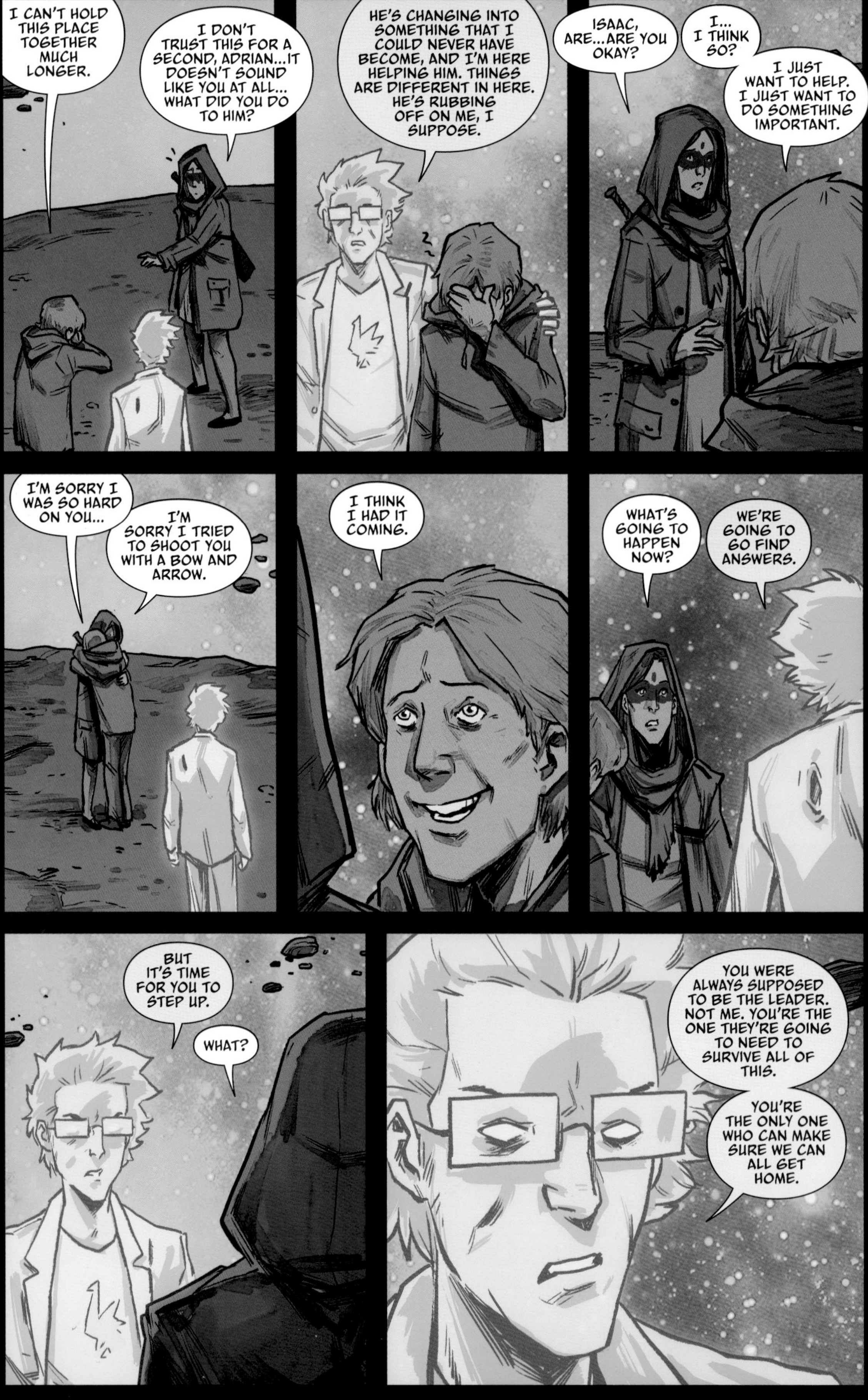
I CAN'T HOLD THIS PLACE TOGETHER MUCH LONGER.
I DON'T TRUST THIS FOR A SECOND, ADRIAN...IT DOESN'T SOUND LIKE YOU AT ALL... WHAT DID YOU DO TO HIM?
HE'S CHANGING INTO SOMETHING THAT I COULD NEVER HAVE BECOME, AND I'M HERE HELPING HIM. THINGS ARE DIFFERENT IN HERE. HE'S RUBBING OFF ON ME, I SUPPOSE.
ISAAC, ARE...ARE YOU OKAY?
I... I THINK SO?
I JUST WANT TO HELP. I JUST WANT TO DO SOMETHING IMPORTANT.
I'M SORRY I WAS SO HARD ON YOU...
I'M SORRY I TRIED TO SHOOT YOU WITH A BOW AND ARROW.
I THINK I HAD IT COMING.
WHAT'S GOING TO HAPPEN NOW?
WE'RE GOING TO GO FIND ANSWERS.
BUT IT'S TIME FOR YOU TO STEP UP.
WHAT?
YOU WERE ALWAYS SUPPOSED TO BE THE LEADER. NOT ME. YOU'RE THE ONE THEY'RE GOING TO NEED TO SURVIVE ALL OF THIS.
YOU'RE THE ONLY ONE WHO CAN MAKE SURE WE CAN ALL GET HOME.

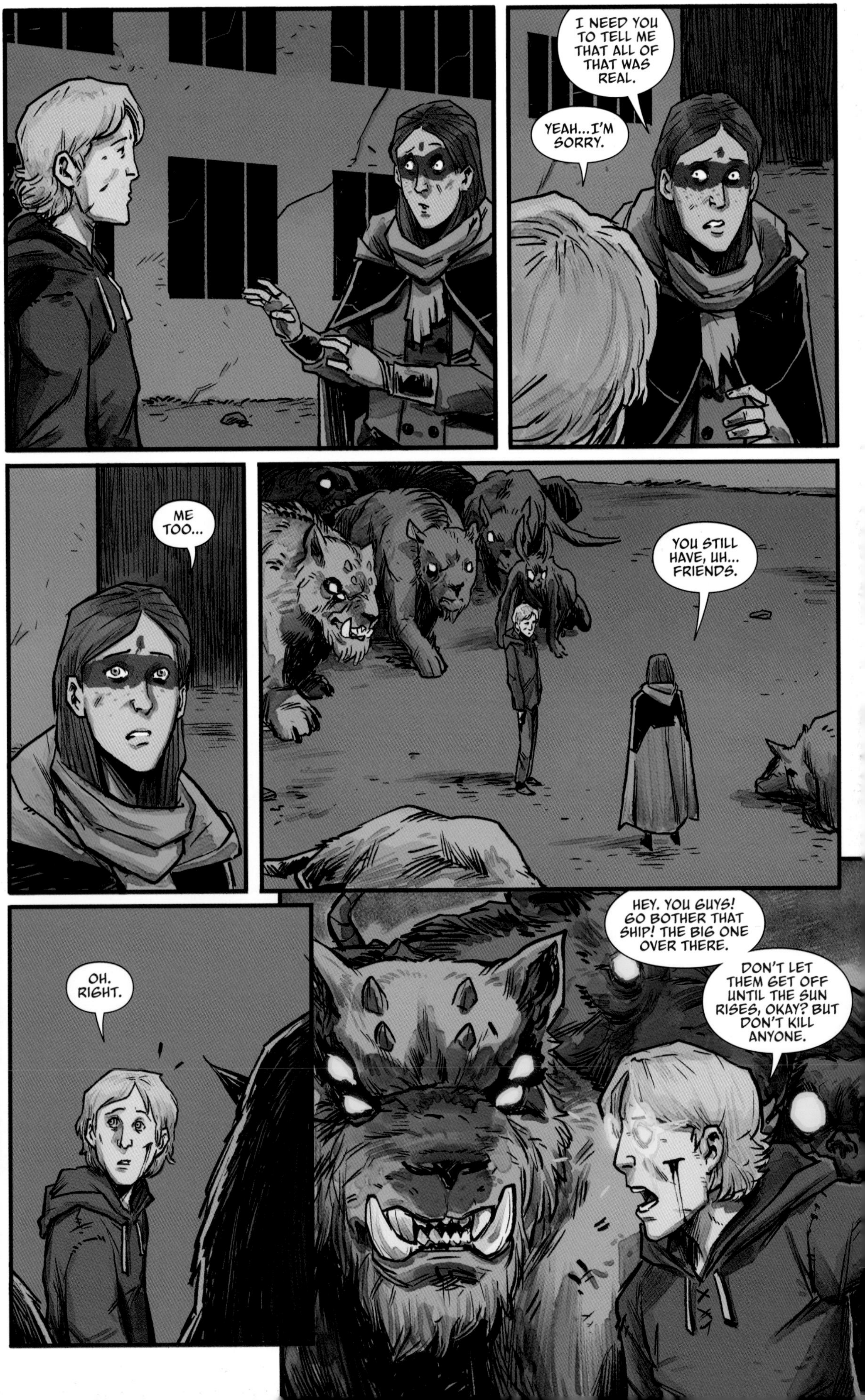
I NEED YOU TO TELL ME THAT ALL OF THAT WAS REAL.
YEAH...I'M SORRY.
ME TOO...
YOU STILL HAVE, UH... FRIENDS.
OH. RIGHT.
HEY. YOU GUYS! GO BOTHER THAT SHIP! THE BIG ONE OVER THERE.
DON'T LET THEM GET OFF UNTIL THE SUN RISES, OKAY? BUT DON'T KILL ANYONE.

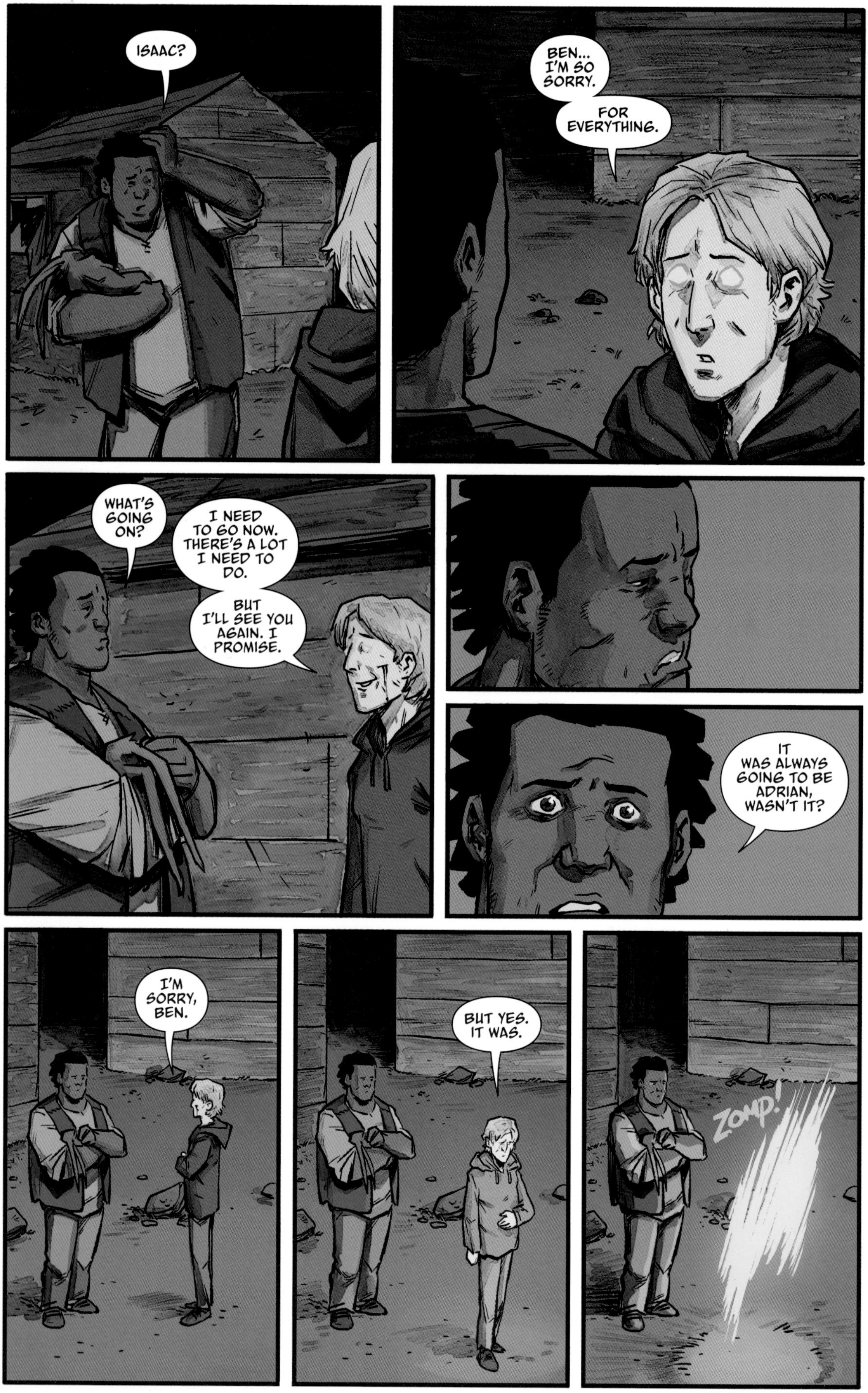
ISAAC?
BEN... I'M SO SORRY.
FOR EVERYTHING.
WHAT'S GOING ON?
I NEED TO GO NOW. THERE'S A LOT I NEED TO DO.
BUT I'LL SEE YOU AGAIN. I PROMISE.
IT WAS ALWAYS GOING TO BE ADRIAN, WASN'T IT?
I'M SORRY, BEN.
BUT YES. IT WAS.
ZOMP!

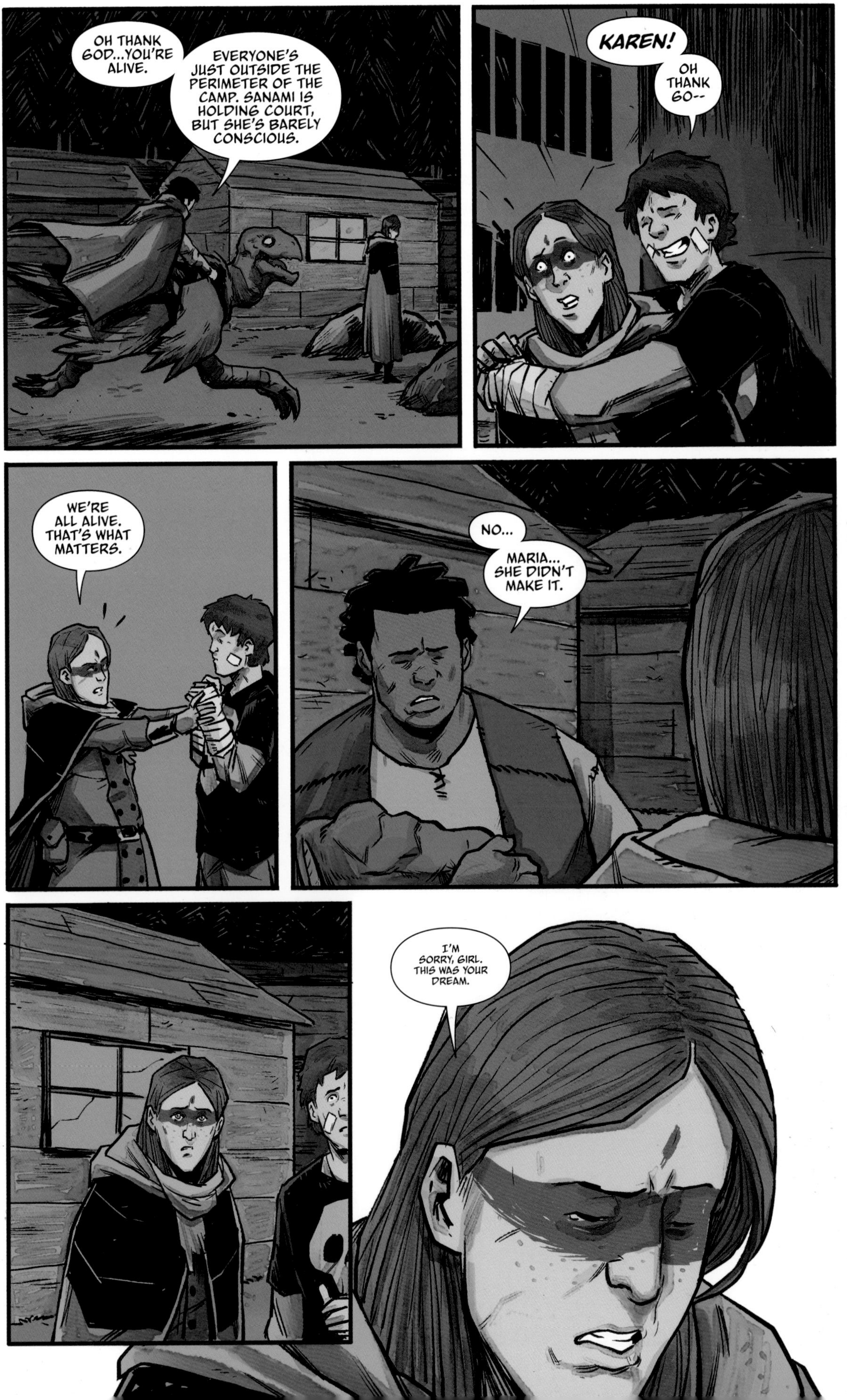
OH THANK GOD...YOU'RE ALIVE.
EVERYONE'S JUST OUTSIDE THE PERIMETER OF THE CAMP. SANAMI IS HOLDING COURT, BUT SHE'S BARELY CONSCIOUS.
KAREN!
OH THANK GO--
WE'RE ALL ALIVE. THAT'S WHAT MATTERS.
NO...
MARIA... SHE DIDN'T MAKE IT.
I'M SORRY, GIRL. THIS WAS YOUR DREAM.

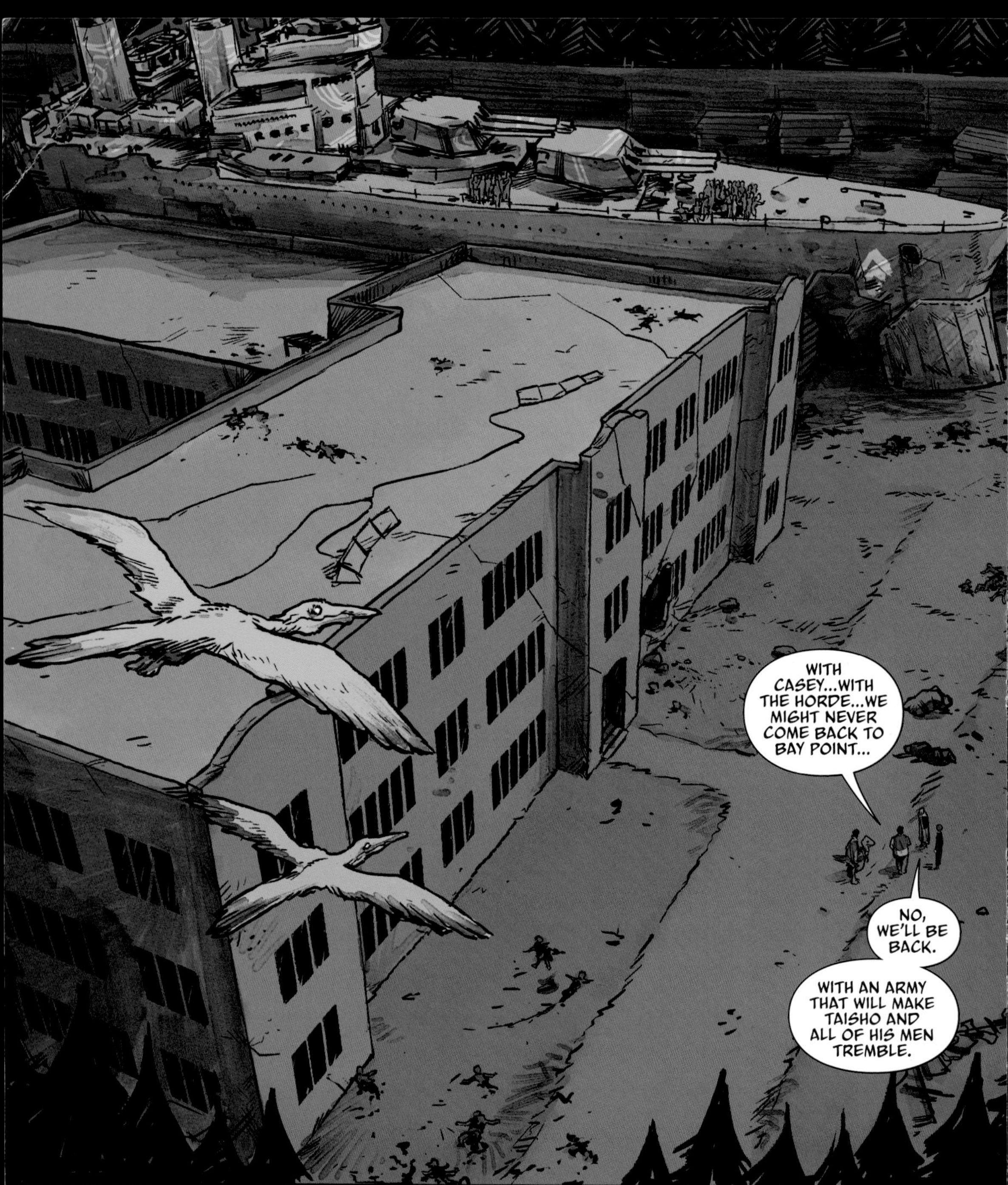
WITH CASEY...WITH THE HORDE...WE MIGHT NEVER COME BACK TO BAY POINT...
NO, WE'LL BE BACK.
WITH AN ARMY THAT WILL MAKE TAISHO AND ALL OF HIS MEN TREMBLE.

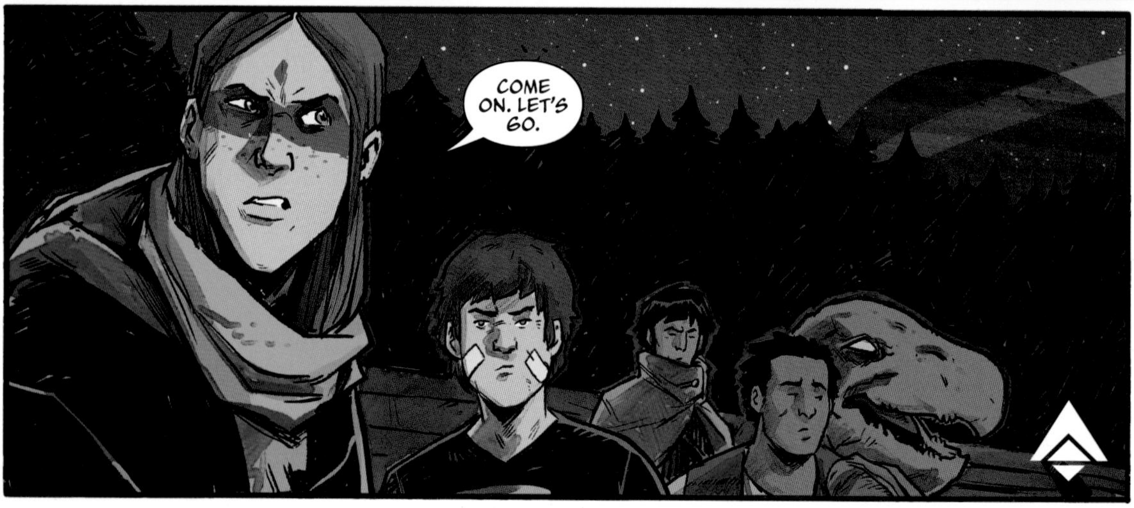
COME ON. LET'S GO.

COVER
GALLERY

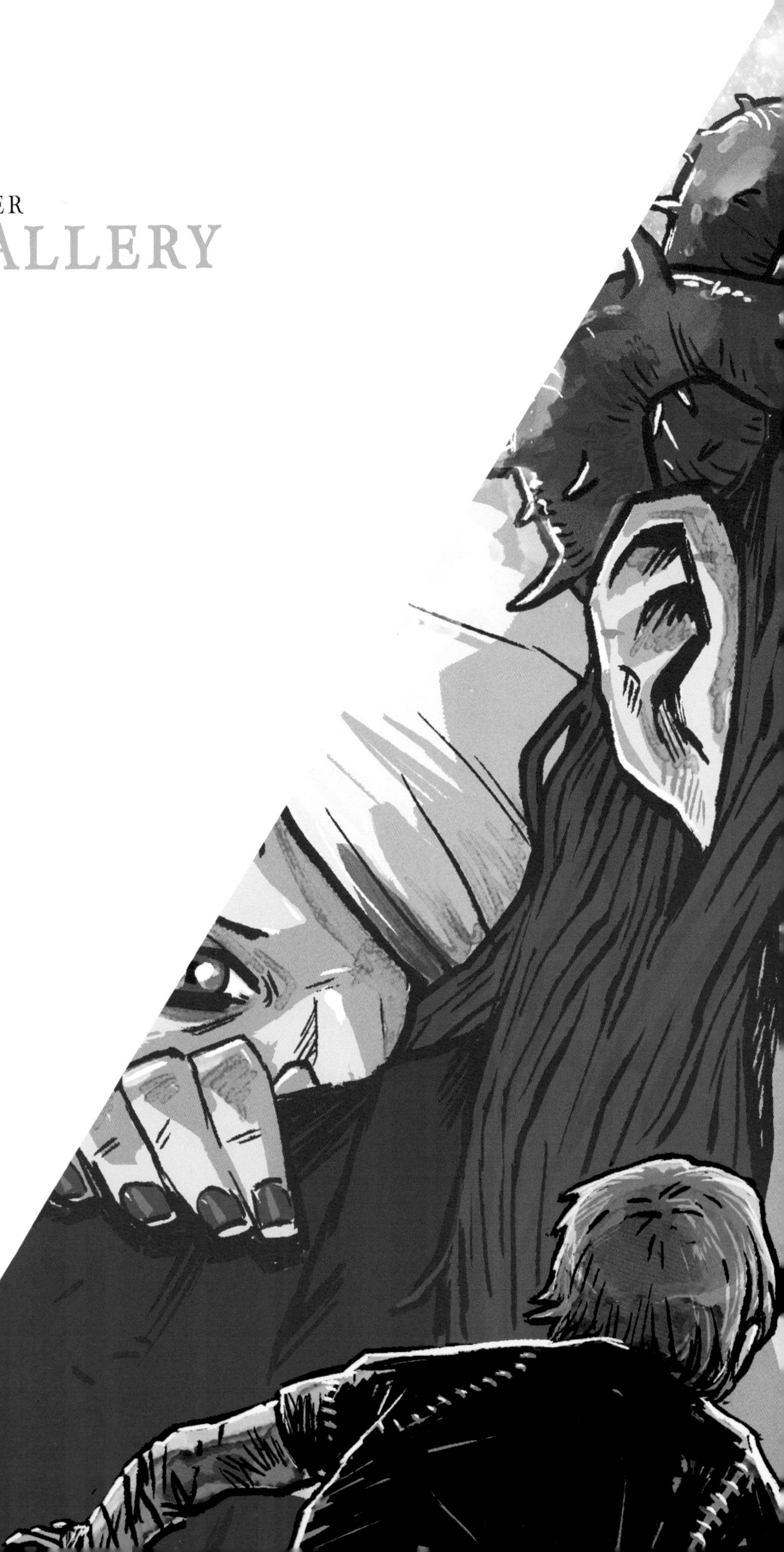

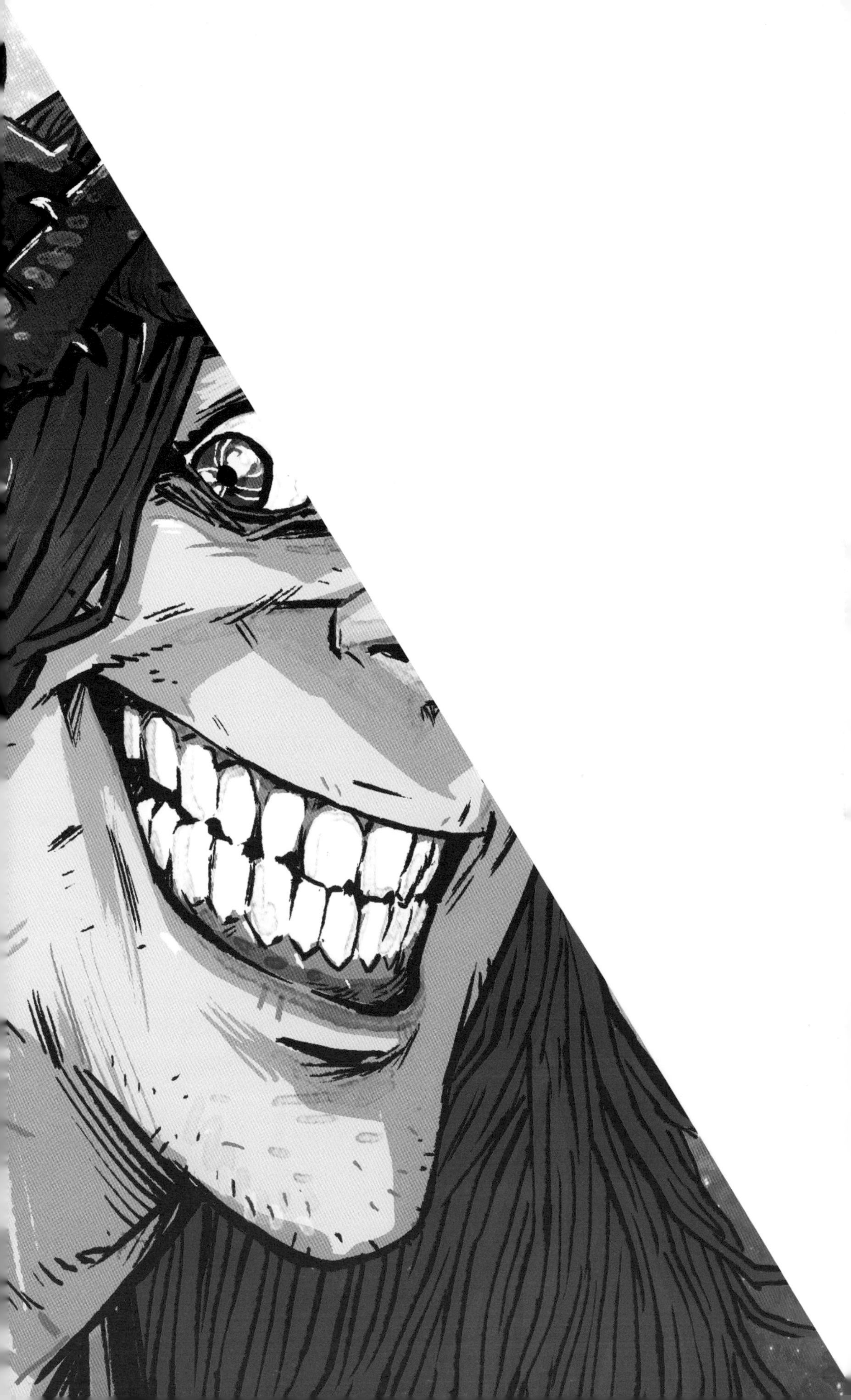

ISSUE SEVENTEEN COVER **MICHAEL DIALYNAS**

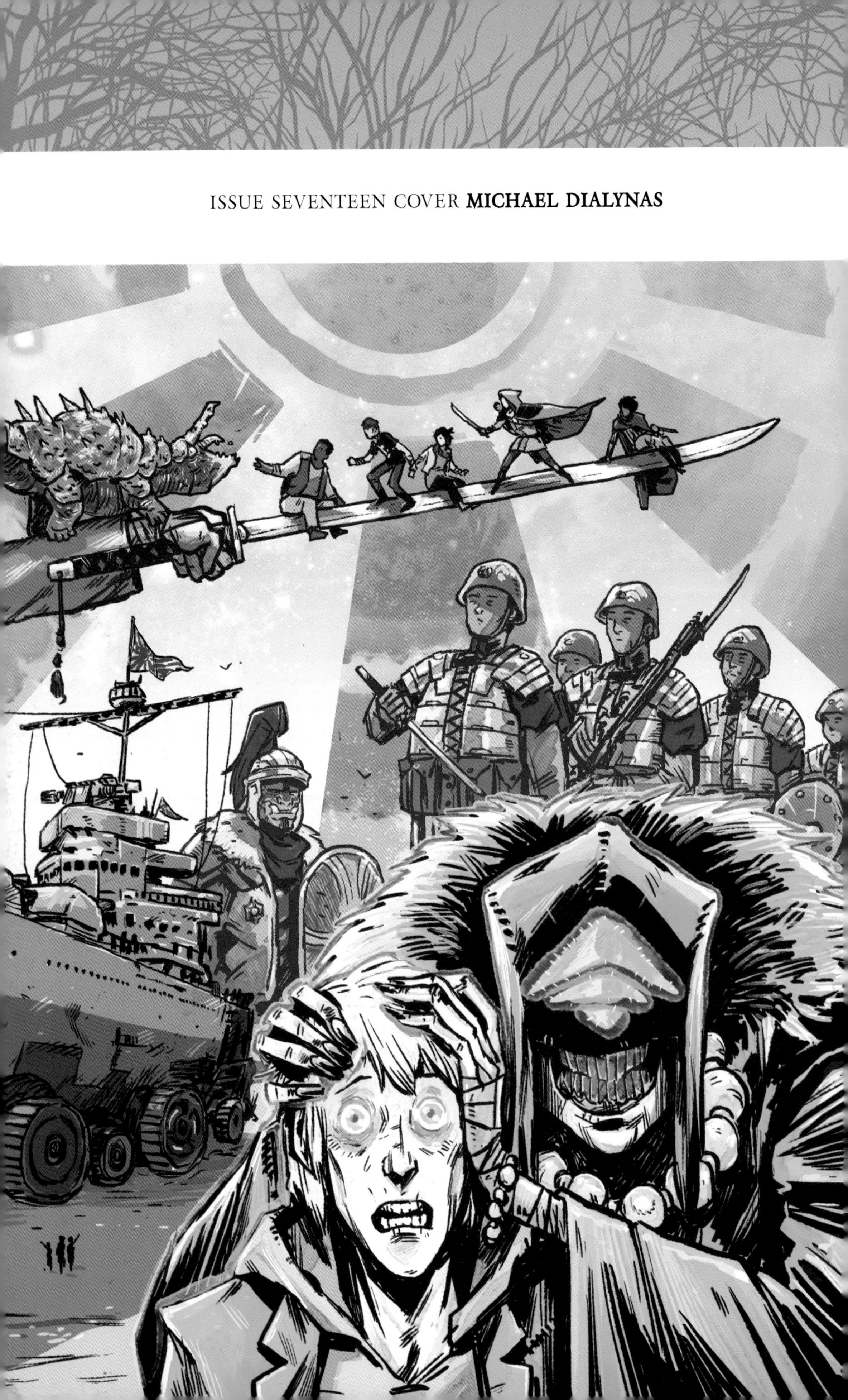

ISSUE EIGHTEEN COVER **MICHAEL DIALYNAS**

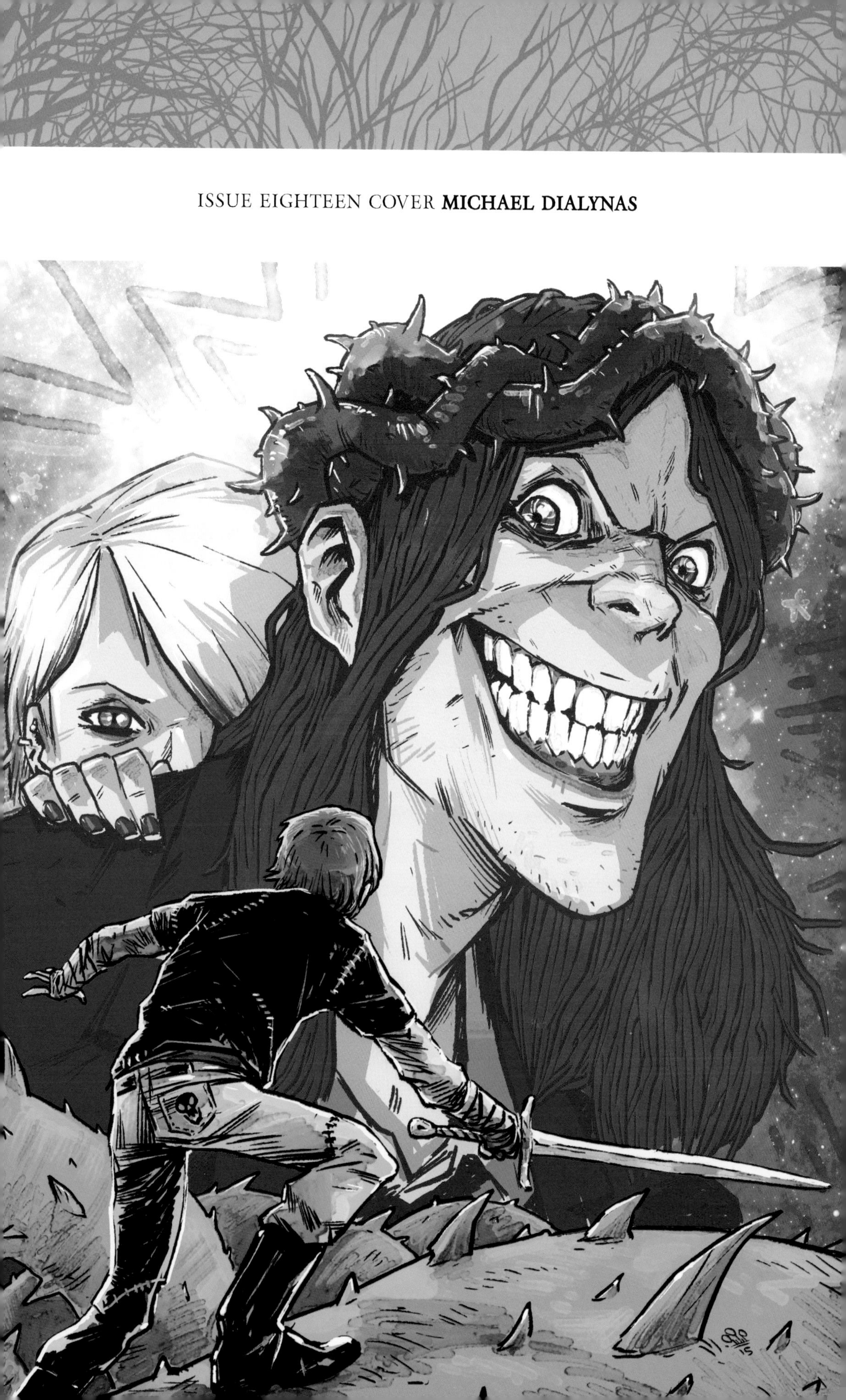

ISSUE NINETEEN COVER **MICHAEL DIALYNAS**

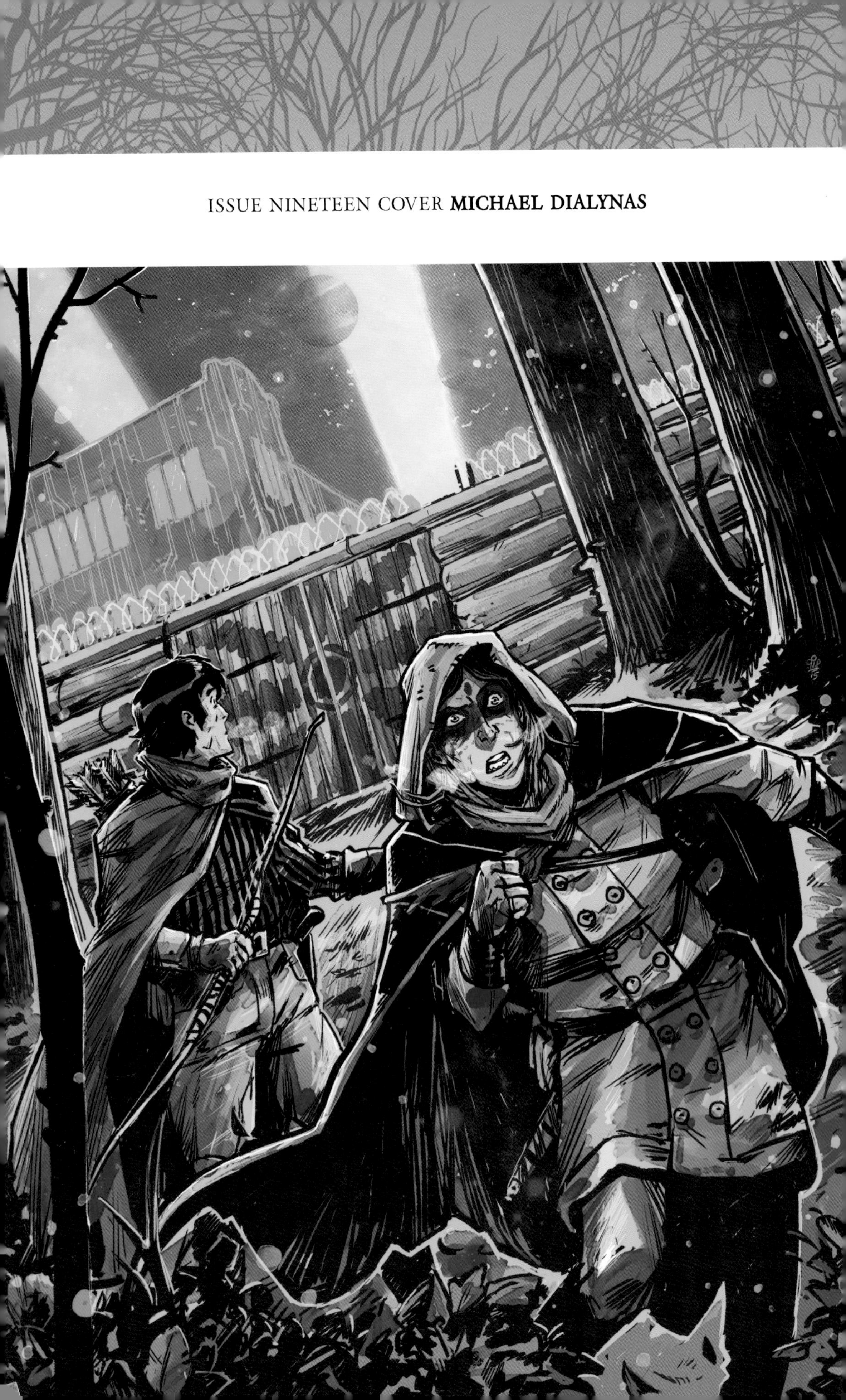

ISSUE TWENTY COVER **MICHAEL DIALYNAS**

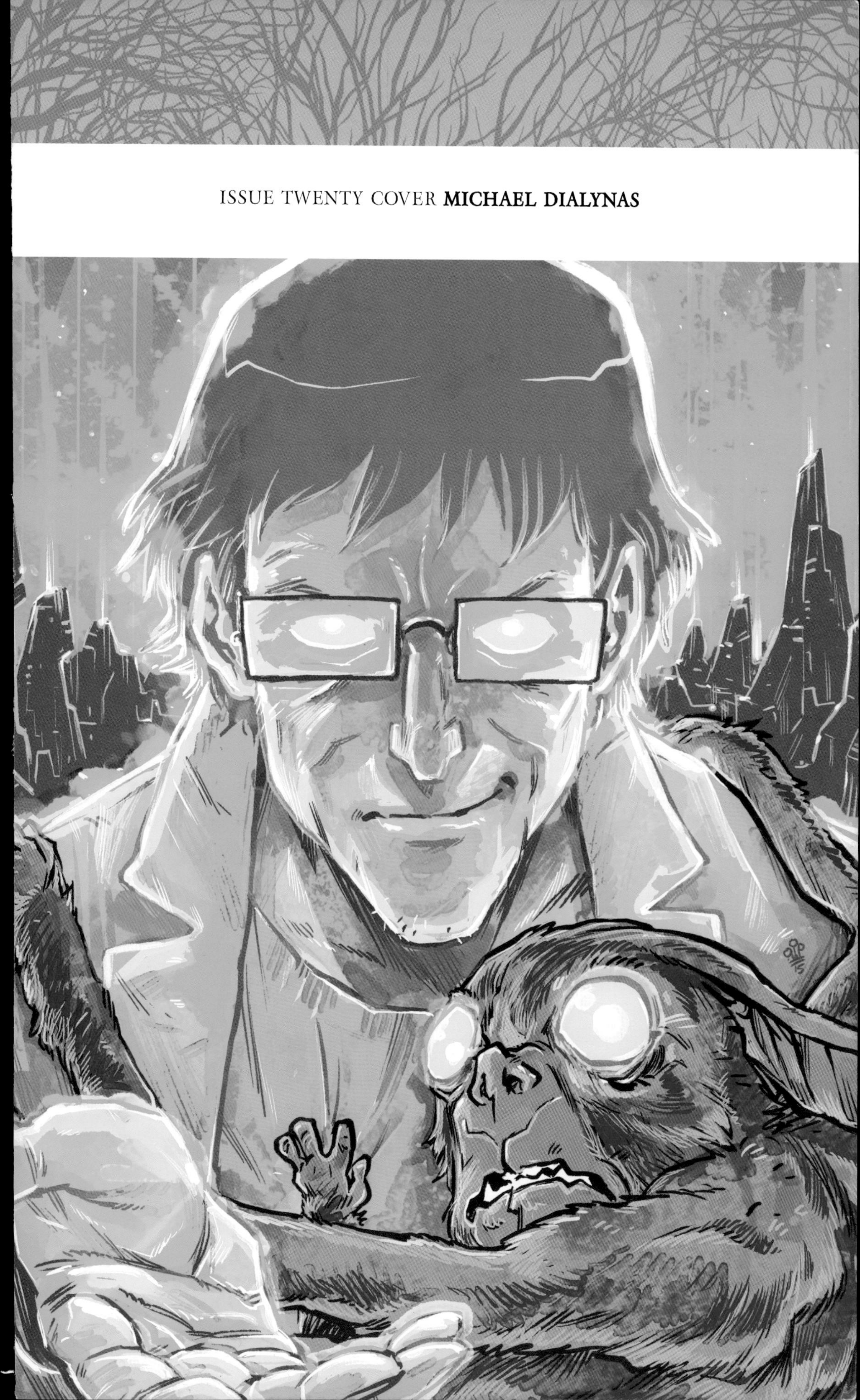

MICHAEL DIALYNAS
SKETCHBOOK

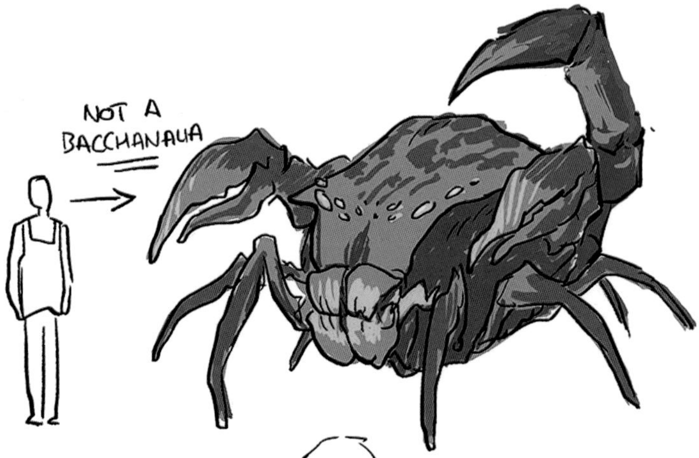
NOT A
BACCHANALIA

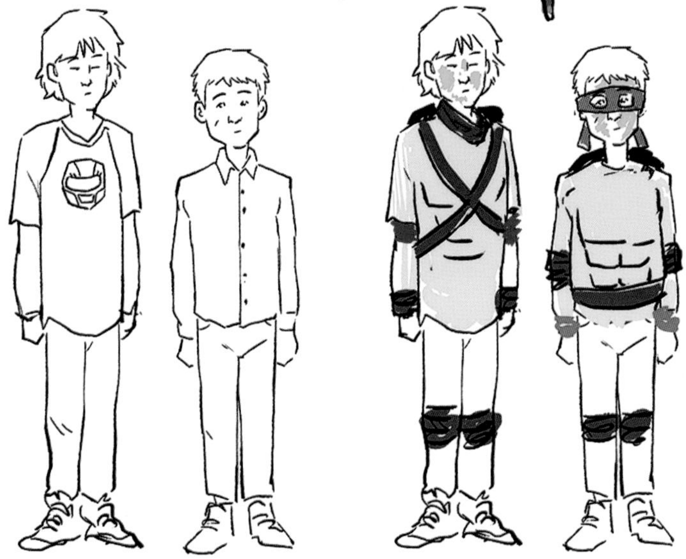

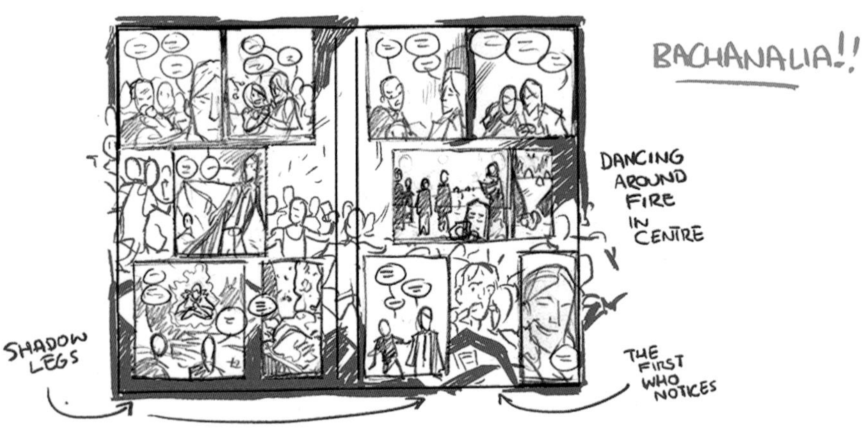
BACHANALIA!!
DANCING
AROUND
FIRE
IN
CENTRE
SHADOW
LEGS
THE
FIRST
WHO
NOTICES

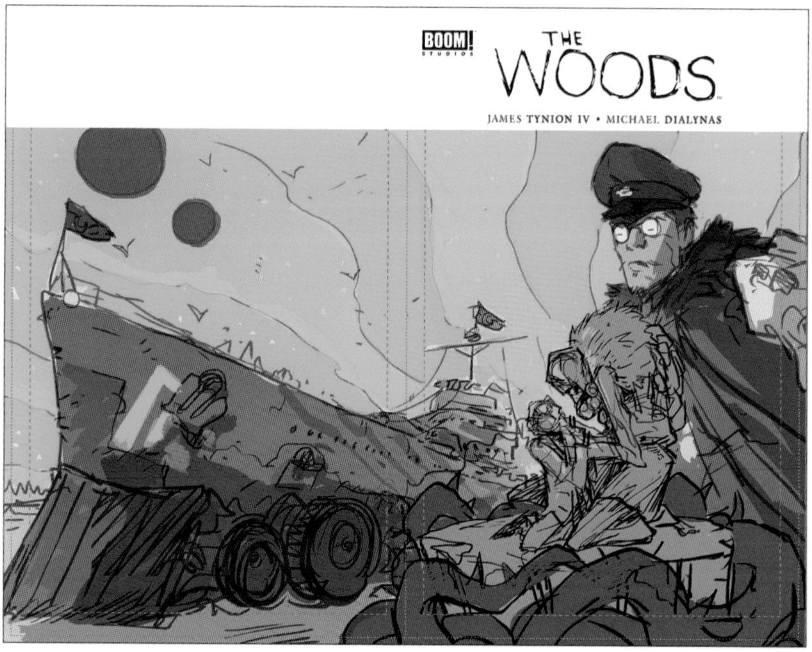
BOOM! STUDIOS
THE WOODS
JAMES TYNION IV • MICHAEL DIALYNAS

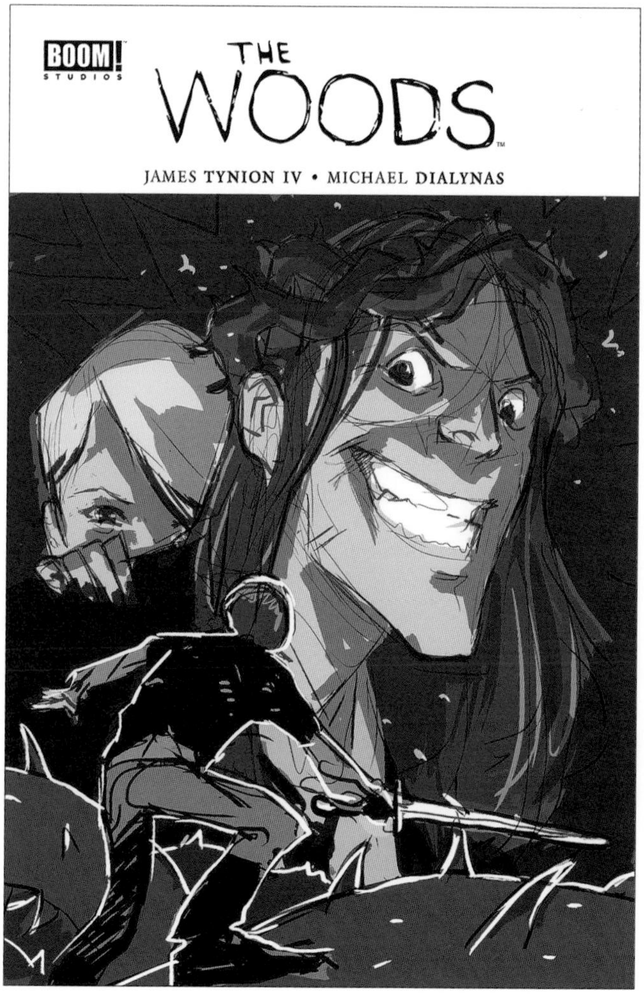
BOOM! STUDIOS
THE WOODS
JAMES TYNION IV • MICHAEL DIALYNAS

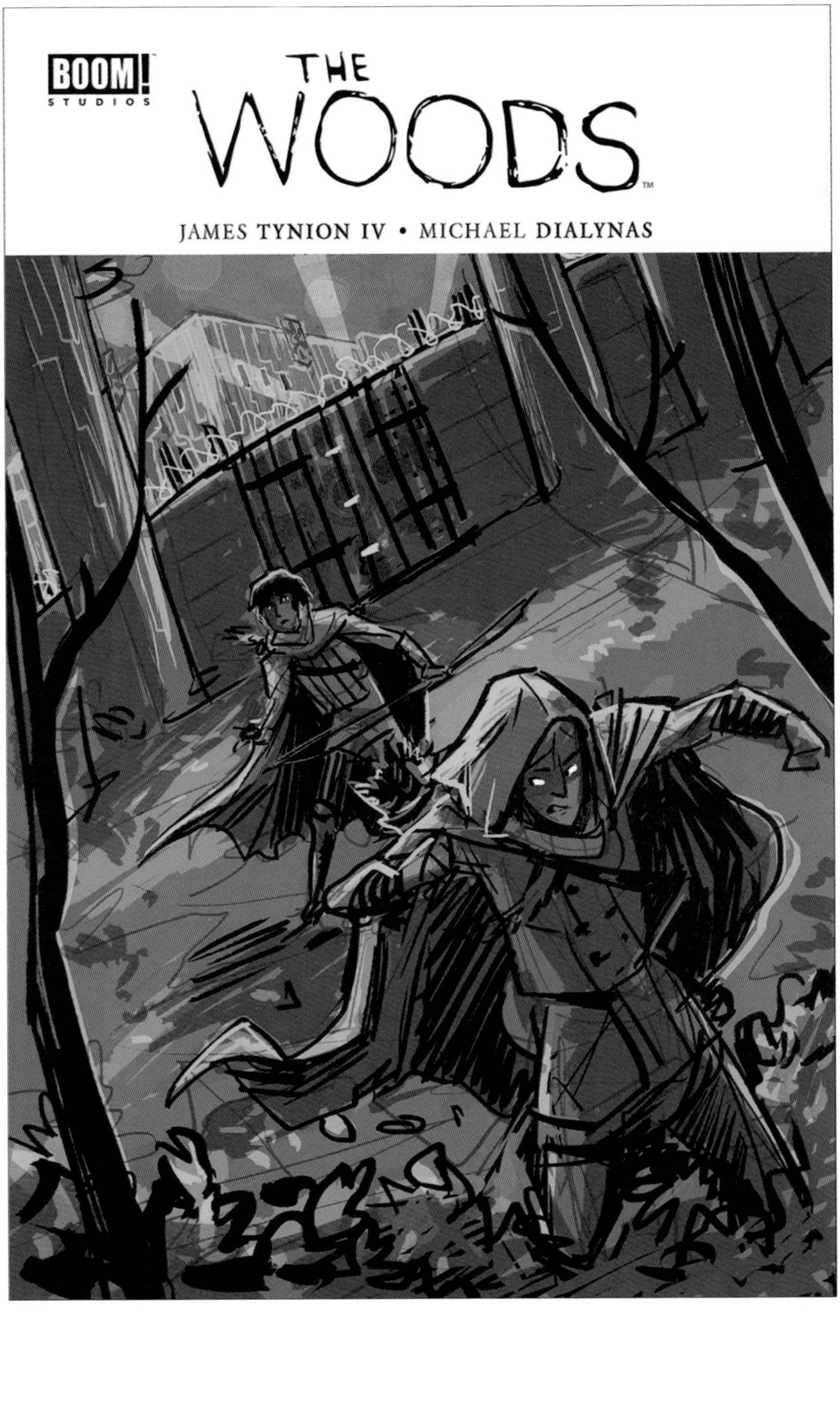
BOOM! STUDIOS
THE WOODS
JAMES TYNION IV • MICHAEL DIALYNAS

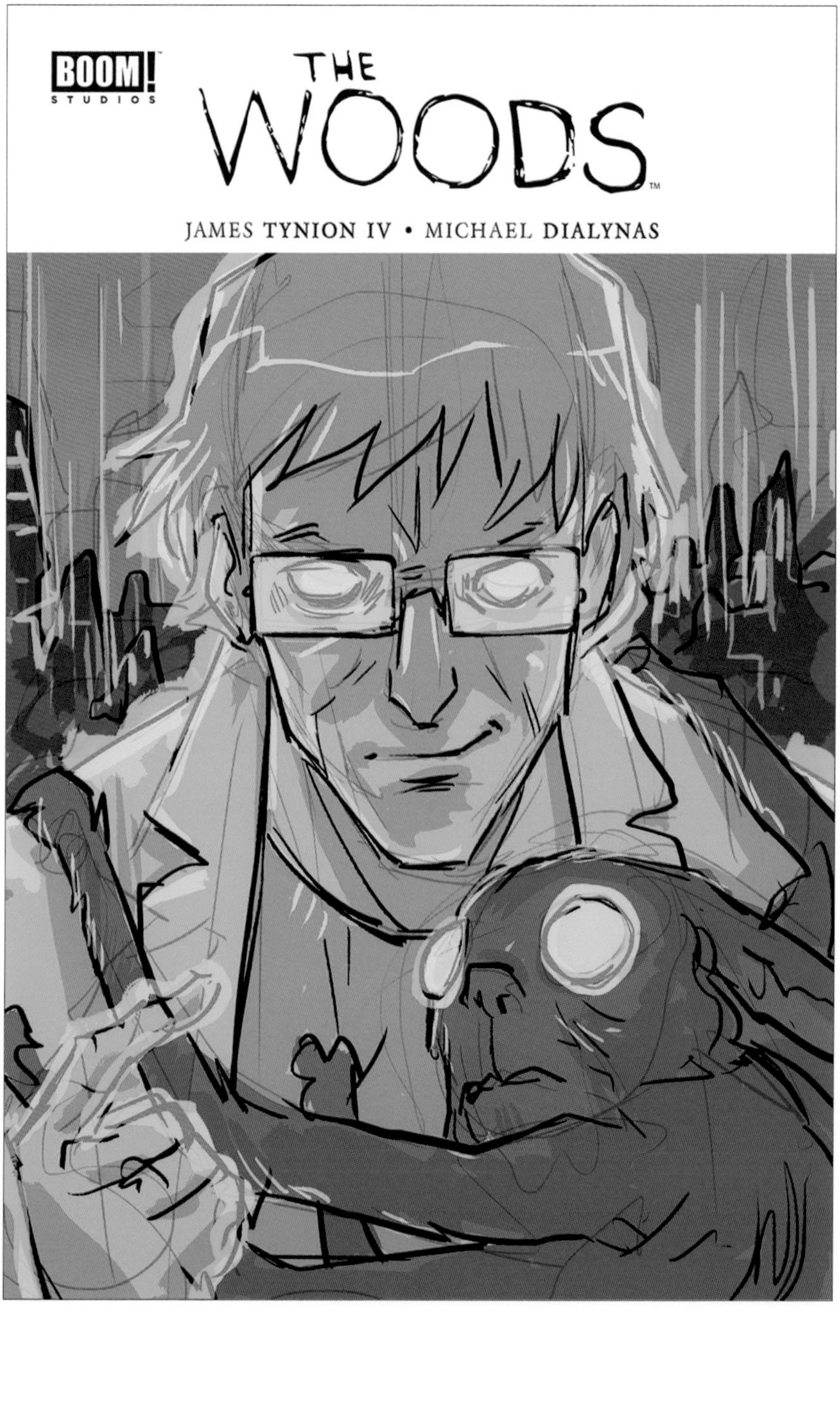
BOOM! STUDIOS
THE WOODS™
JAMES TYNION IV • MICHAEL DIALYNAS

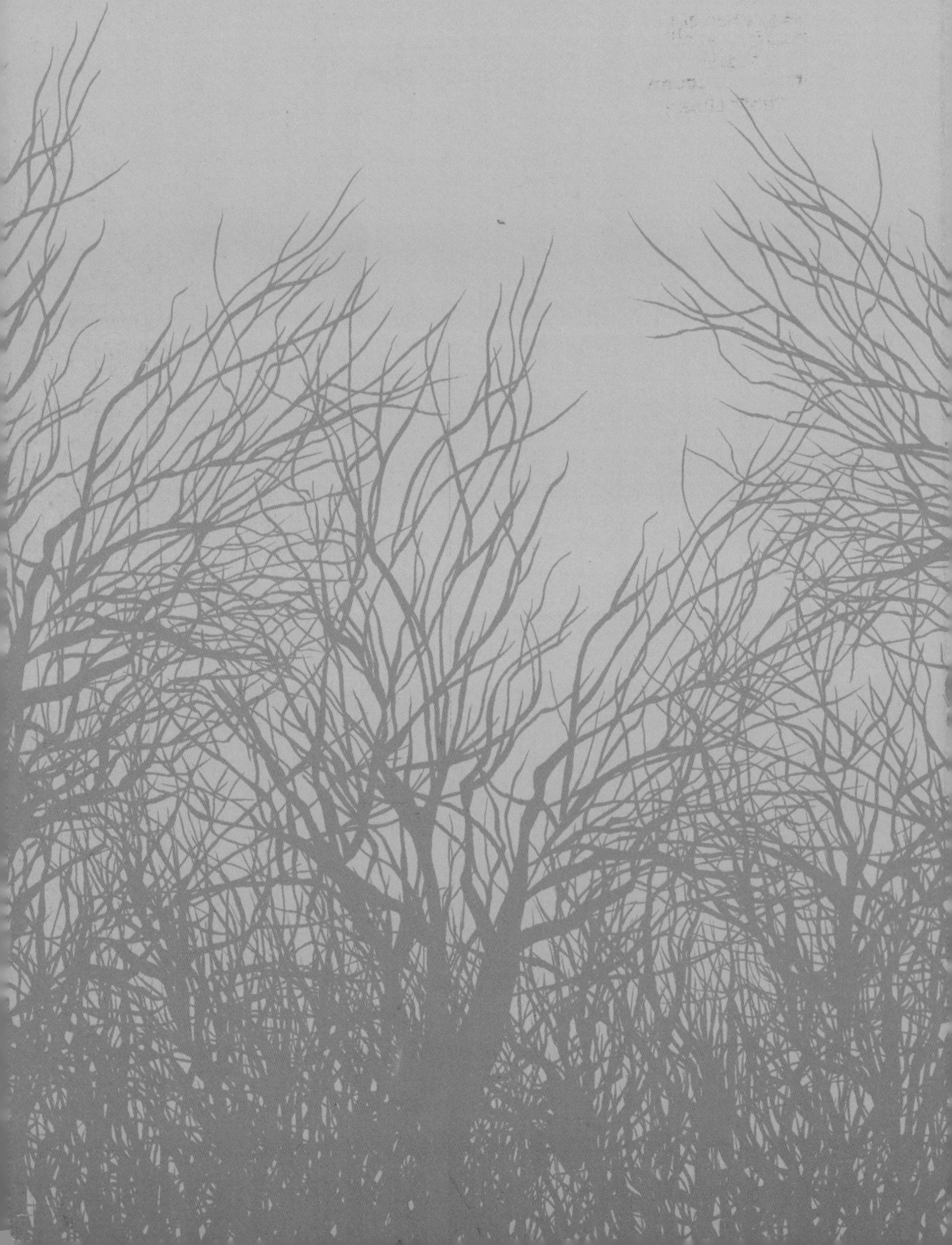